THE NEW FRANCE

THE
NEW
FRANCE

BY EDWARD R. TANNENBAUM

THE UNIVERSITY OF CHICAGO PRESS

Library of Congress Catalog Number: 61-8076

The University of Chicago Press, Chicago 37
The University of Toronto Press, Toronto 5, Canada

© *1961 by The University of Chicago*
Published 1961. Composed and printed by
The University of Chicago Press
Chicago, Illinois, U.S.A.

Designed by Adrian Wilson

To Louis Gottschalk

Preface

This book is designed to give the general reader a broad, inclusive report on the dynamic changes that have taken place in France in recent years. It does not attempt to review the history of French governments and their policies. Only when these are related to the way Frenchmen behave are they mentioned at all. The new France I am concerned with is not De Gaulle's Republic; it is a national community in the process of changing its whole way of life.

I do not pretend to be an expert in the many fields I discuss, and the real experts will undoubtedly object to some of my observations. My purpose was to write a work of synthesis. This undertaking required the examination and sifting of a wide variety of evidence, both first- and secondhand. Perhaps mistakenly, I felt that what I finally had to say would be more readable without the usual footnotes. I have therefore limited my documentation to the text itself and to the "Notes on Sources" at the end of the volume.

While I alone am responsible for any errors of fact or interpretation that may have crept into this book, I wish to acknowledge my heavy debt to those colleagues and friends who generously gave me their time, advice, and encouragement. Louis Gottschalk was both my severest critic and my most steadfast booster at all stages in the preparation of this work for publication. Denis W. Brogan, Shepard B. Clough, Laurence Wylie, Robert R. Palmer, Henry W. Ehrmann, and Sidney Ratner read various drafts of the manuscript and made many valuable suggestions. Jacques Barzun, Jean Fourastié, and Jean Gottmann helped me to reformulate a number of my ideas on specific aspects of French life in the course of several long conversations.

I also want to thank the Rutgers Research Council for a grant that enabled me to study the mass media of communication in France. Finally, I should like to express my gratitude to Mrs. Sabra Meservey for her assistance in reading the proof and preparing the Index.

Contents

France 1960

Until only yesterday France seemed to be in a rut of changing governments and old-fashioned ways of doing things. This stereotyped image is itself old-fashioned now. For better or for worse, President de Gaulle has made his countrymen accept a stable political regime and a liberal approach toward their remaining colonial problems. But more important than his leadership is the cultural transformation that has been forced upon the French people by economic and technological progress and by the bureaucratization of political life. Although all modern nations have had to cope with these developments, France has done so in its own special way.

The French may be stragglers, but they are not "the worst stragglers of all"—as the *New York Times* called them in 1953. After lagging behind the British and the Germans until the late 1930's, they finally produced a comprehensive social security system with the most generous family allowances and unemployment benefits in Western Europe. Their trade-union movement remains weak mainly because of Communist meddling rather than any incor-

1

rigible individualism on the part of the workers or management's resistance to collective bargaining. The average Frenchman's standard of living is slightly higher than that of his Continental neighbors and is rising each year. In fact, now that France has more automobiles per capita than any other European country except Great Britain, her major cities are advancing to the point reached by New York and Los Angeles with regard to parking difficulties, traffic congestion, and air pollution.

Many of the traditional ways in which Frenchmen think and live are scarcely different from those of other Europeans. Social barriers and limitations on opportunities for advanced education have not disappeared completely anywhere in the Old World. Marginal farmers, small shopkeepers, and self-employed artisans are just as "backward" in Germany or Sweden as they are in France—and there are sleepy, run-down villages in these countries too. Like their Parisian colleagues, nostalgic aesthetes in Rome and London also oppose the building of contemporary structures that spoil their familiar skyline.

The face of France could surely use a dusting and a fresh coat of paint, for the French do cling to a certain shabby splendor in their public places. Millions of new dwellings are needed, though effective steps have at last been taken to construct them. Paris itself may impress the casual tourist as a conglomeration of faded monuments and seedy apartment houses guarded by frowzy concierges with their knitting and their dogs. Except on the way to the airport he does not see the complex of modern factories and housing developments that encircle this ancient city. Its ordinary inhabitants strike him as glib, superficial, and cold, yet they are more respectful toward individual privacy and artistic innovation than most people who live in glass skyscrapers or split-level ranch houses.

Like her physical appearance, France's ephemeral governments have hidden more than they have revealed about the way her citizens respond to the modern world. Under the Third and Fourth Republics French politics often resembled a ritual drama in which the performers acted out roles according to a script that sometimes had little to do with the interests and needs of the audience or the world outside the theater. The multi-party system in itself was not the main cause of political disequilibrium. Actually, each party represented only an *abstraction* purged of any compromising connection with a social class, an economic group, or a religious creed. Even when the workers voted for the Communists—who claimed to represent them—they were often the victims of a kind of mysticism that confused doctrine with action.

France's political parties have rarely had any relation to the realities that make up the daily lives of her people. A Frenchman is a wage-earner, a farmer, or a shopkeeper; he is from Limoges, Juan-les-Pins, or Lorraine. He is not "Democratic Alliance," "Rally of the Left Republicans," "Radical and Radical Socialist," or "Union for the New Republic." These are pure abstractions—almost mystic symbols. In the United States the names of the Democratic and Republican parties are also abstractions, but political action has been more meaningful here because of two corrective factors. First,

4

pressure groups representing economic classes and special interests—publicly as well as secretly—counterbalance each other fairly effectively without immobilizing our national politics. Second, the American federal structure, which is reflected in a considerable degree of decentralization in party leadership, allows the parties to represent different local interests in various parts of the country.

Not only have Frenchmen had few opportunities to take part in political decision-making on the local level, they have seemed to avoid active participation in any kind of voluntary organization. In politics their unwillingness to co-operate and compromise dates back to the Old Regime. Under Louis XVI each traditional "estate" and privileged order stubbornly defended its own interests and made reform from above impossible. The Revolution generated a passionate civic spirit for a few years, but Napoleon killed this by trying to substitute glory for liberty as its reward. Then the alternation between democratic and authoritarian regimes in the nineteenth century made people in France view the merits of both more critically than citizens of countries where one or the other predominated until it was gradually changed. A similar lack of agreement about community values was apparent in social and economic relations.

Beyond the family circle, the French became increasingly unwilling to submit to decisions made by a leader or a majority vote. They shared certain basic norms for personal behavior, but these did not work well for large groups. Call it individualism, self-reliance, nonconformism, or suspicion of outsiders—the fact remains that Frenchmen were not "joiners" like Britishers, Swiss, Scandinavians, and Americans. Until the late 1940's there were relatively few fraternal organizations, church auxiliaries, amateur theatrical and choral societies, or non-professional sports teams in France. Even socialites who consciously aped English manners were only partially successful in adapting themselves to club life.

Apparently, then, most Frenchmen have not worked well together in organizations that were supposed to serve their needs. In both their national and local affairs they have had little practical experience in co-operating with people from different backgrounds and in handling problems of planning, administration, and public

5

relations. Since the political parties themselves do not correspond to any clearly determined economic and social realities, France's citizens have tended to think of each of them as "a state of mind," rather than as an instrument for effective group action. The politicians, in turn, have treated politics as a game, which they monopolized and which they played according to their own rules (except during the two world wars) until the end of the Fourth Republic.

But behind the façade of parliamentary democracy there were stabilizing agencies whose powers were not derived from the individual voters. The permanent bureaucracy carried on the work of government at all times and was virtually unaffected by periodic cabinet crises or even changes in regime. Frenchmen were certainly aware of the power of the civil administration. They felt this in their everyday dealings with the law courts, the police, the various ministries, and the government-operated public services and utilities. Long before the twentieth century they had become accustomed to viewing the state as a transcendent power embodied in a bureaucratic, almost military, structure. It had been founded by the Bourbon kings and given its permanent form by the two Napoleons. During the Vichy period it maintained some semblance of order even toward the end, when Pétain's puppet regime was virtually powerless.

Despite all the rites and symbols that have identified the Republic with the Nation since the Revolution, most Frenchmen have continued to view it as if it were still the private patrimony of Louis XIV. They have criticized it, cheated it, and complained about its taxes and red tape. At the same time, they have placated it and revered it as an omnipresent power. For them *La France* is not the French people; it is, on the one hand, a glorious myth of which they want to feel proud and, on the other hand, a group of politicians, generals, and administrators who dispense progress, security, and justice. Its citizens have expected all these benefits, believing that, in return, their main duty was to risk their lives for it in time of war.

Indeed, the behavior of many Frenchmen toward the state has often resembled that of draftees in a modern army, where the goals are to preserve one's individuality, evade the regulations whenever possible, and obtain special privileges, preferably on a permanent basis. Unlike soldiers, the French people have had the illusion of control over the central decision-making bodies through their elected representatives, though they have usually treated their deputies as "influence peddlers" rather than lawmakers. The contrast between belief and reality has been evident even in the symbol of the Republic, Marianne. She wears a Phrygian bonnet; she should be wearing a military cap.

For over a century the Council of State has served as a superior tribunal over the administrative agencies of public power and has approved or disapproved the appointment, retirement, and promotion of every official by a government or cabinet minister. Parliamentary deputies rarely "investigated" the activities of the bureaucracy under the Third and Fourth Republics, and when they did they failed to weaken its authority. Few people knew of the arbitrary way in which the Council of State interpreted the laws enacted by the legislature and sometimes quietly buried them. Fewer still understood to what extent the financial administration modified and interpreted the budget—how it sometimes determined the life or death of a government through its control over state revenue and expenditure. Hadn't the constitution given parliament the legislative power that had been achieved historically in all democracies through the control over the nation's purse strings exercised by the representatives of the people?

Their habit of confusing theory with practice prevented most Frenchmen from understanding the true organization of power in their own country. Their growing cynicism toward the government and toward politics in general was therefore naïve. It resembled the unsophisticated mistrust of a small shopkeeper or farmer toward anything big or new. These people explained the motives of others, great and small, as examples of petty self-aggrandizement without being aware of the kinds of stakes involved. Many Americans attached a similarly limited interpretation to the gifts of mink coats presented to certain Washington secretaries by businessmen seeking government contracts immediately after the Second World War. Herblock, the well-known newspaper cartoonist, portrayed the situation more accurately in the form of two giant financiers

7

leaning possessively on a dwarf-sized Capitol. One of them is saying to the other: "Mink is for peasants."

Another extra-constitutional development in France during the first half of the twentieth century was the growing importance of powerful parliamentary committees—especially the one in charge of public finance. These practically monopolized the initiation of many laws and sometimes influenced the fall and formation of cabinets. At their closed hearings the representatives of special interest groups could press for alterations in pending legislation with virtually no interference from the majority of the deputies or the public. The ministries affected by these discussions defended their own interests by appointing special agents to supervise the committee chairmen in preparing their reports to parliament. Hence, a structural change was taking place whereby organized pressure on relatively permanent and irresponsible standing committees was supplanting open debate on the floor of the national assembly as the real lawmaking procedure.

The practice of trying to influence the rulers of states for private ends is as old as civilized society itself. All governments make and enforce political decisions, and most of the time they have complete control over the agencies that serve these functions. Any individual or group that wants these decisions—and their enforcement or lack of enforcement—to benefit them must either put pressure on those people who hold power or else seize it themselves. In ancient Rome armies stationed in the provinces made and broke consuls and emperors. The medieval popes and the prelates of the national churches forced kings to do their bidding in a variety of ways. And court favorites from Madame de Pompadour to Sherman Adams have always been able to help their friends.

As various countries became industrialized in the nineteenth century, the role of governments in economic affairs increased, and pressure groups began to influence them. The most consistent issue was tariffs—for example, the British Anti–Corn Law League and the conflict between Northern industrialists and Southern planters in the United States—but ideological motives also produced movements like the American Abolitionists, French Republicans, Pan-Germanists, and Pan-Slavists. Organizations of both types became active in autocratic as well as in liberal political systems. French bankers and manufacturers succeeded in persuading King Louis Philippe in the 1840's and the republican premier in the 1890's to safeguard their interests against unfavorable fiscal measures and foreign competition.

In the twentieth century the trend toward group action in politics has grown in France as elsewhere. The Bank of France, the army, the high civil service, and certain business trusts have periodically used their power and influence on the government for their own purposes. Freemasons, lay Catholic associations, veterans' leagues, and the trade unions expanded their membership during the interwar years and tried increasingly to determine public policy. Since the Second World War the most striking change in French political behavior has been the participation in organizations for collective defense by traditionally individualistic small producers and merchants, professional men, writers, and even students.

Thus, pressure groups seemed to be eliminating the importance of the individual in French politics. For a long time most Frenchmen hardly understood what was happening, but by the 1950's the change was apparent to everyone. Sugar-beet growers, antitax leagues, colonial lobbies, and, finally, the army itself, came out into the open to defend their vested interests against those of their rivals. Although their professional organizers still tried to bully the elected representatives of the people, they directed their main persuasive efforts at the appointed officials of the Fourth Republic. Some of the leaders of the trade associations representing big business had been lured away from the civil service by high salaries and were especially adept at utilizing their personal contacts with their former colleagues for the benefit of their new employers.

It should be noted that many top-ranking French civil servants are no longer old-style bureaucrats but brilliant young technical experts. Despite the subtle attempts to influence them, they have maintained their high principles and their determination to make France an efficient, modern nation. They were already accomplishing this (the work of the Monnet Plan for Modernization and Reequipment is only one outstanding example) while the rival political parties and pressure groups were approaching a stalemate in the early 1950's. Yet they too fell into a certain inertia for want of galvanizing leadership.

As the Fourth Republic practically ceased to function effectively, power passed unobtrusively into the hands of non-elected officials. The majority of France's citizens knew that constitutional reforms were necessary in order to make their democracy work, but, as in the case of so many other issues, they could not agree on any positive program of action. By the mid-1950's they began to lose interest in politics altogether—they were becoming "depolitized." Liberal-minded Frenchmen have decried these developments and have said that the Fifth Republic—despite its preservation of parliament and the multi-party system—is basically authoritarian. Although the long-term effects of the new constitution and electoral law are difficult to foresee, it is clear that President de Gaulle now relies heavily on the experts who advise him. He has brought about the *de jure* transfer of power to the technocratic bureaucracy.

It is unlikely that France or any other country will ever become a pure technocracy à la Saint-Simon or Aldous Huxley. This kind of Brave New World is almost as utopian as the stateless, classless society forecast by Marx. Wherever there is power there will be politics. The "Big Daddy" type of politician, whether war hero or party boss, may go down in the struggle for control of the state between new technical elites in administration, industry, "human engineering," and the military; or he may survive as a front-man to win over the masses. But as long as there are "summits" to be climbed and conflicting interests to be reconciled, there will be a need for statesmen as well as technicians.

There has been no "thirteenth of May" to dramatize the silent revolution in France's economic life, which has met with a more sustained resistance than its political counterpart. The fact is, however, that the gross output of all goods and services at market prices has increased at an average annual rate of 5 per cent since 1953. Not all Frenchmen have experienced an equal rise in their standard of living, and various sectors of the economy have expanded at different rates. (In industry alone the annual rate of increase was close to 10 per cent between 1953 and 1957 and again in 1959.) But the pattern of growth has established itself and has begun to color most people's expectations about the future. (The main reason for the rising standard of living among most wage-earners was that, by 1957, wages had risen to 132 of the 1952 base of 100, while the cost of living had remained virtually unchanged during those five years.) After over two decades of living off their capital the French have been increasing their production of everything, including children.

In the early fifties the utilization of previously unused productive capacity was a major cause for the increase in national production and in the general wage level. Many steel mills, coal and iron mines, vineyards, and shoe factories raised their output simply by using more existing equipment and resources. The labor force was also utilized more fully by the elimination of unemployment and the lengthening of the average workweek to forty-six hours. Workers were thus able to produce more goods and to make more money without necessarily improving their efficiency. In the long run, though, greater productivity based on technological progress has been the main factor in economic growth and in the higher standard of living that has resulted from it.

France did not really move into the steam age until the second half of the nineteenth century. Like other Western countries she began the process of industrialization by improving manufacturing and organizational techniques, by exploiting hitherto unused or partially used resources, and by transferring labor from less productive to more productive forms of employment. The steam engine gave her a modern transportation system and a nascent heavy industry. During the period of the Second Empire new credit institutions stimulated expansion, which was also aided by railroad-building and municipal works programs. The government of Napoleon III guaranteed the interest on investments in corporations set up to finance these projects, and in 1867 it passed a law facilitating the formation of private companies with limited liability. Despite France's relatively late start, the real value of her industrial production per man-hour (her productivity) increased at a higher rate than in Germany, the United States, or Great Britain from the 1850's until 1900. After that it fell into last place.

Although less pronounced than in Great Britain or Germany, the migration of people from rural to urban areas continued slowly but steadily in France. Between 1856 and 1956 the proportion of Frenchmen living in cities increased from 28 per cent to 55 per cent of the total population. This trend toward urbanization has been accompanied by a movement from agriculture into industry or into commerce, administration, and other services—a universal sign of economic development. In 1960 less than 25 per cent of all economically active Frenchmen were engaged in agricultural pursuits (the figures were 44 per cent in 1906 and 35 per cent in 1936), while around 35 per cent were in industry and 40 per cent in the other sectors of the economy.

These changes in population distribution were a part of France's second industrial revolution. Despite the inferiority of her coal for coking purposes, she was producing respectable quantities of steel before 1914. She also began using water power and petroleum as new fuels for the production of electricity and the operation of internal combustion engines. Although the temporary loss of the factories and mines in the Northeast reduced the country's total output during the First World War, defense needs stimulated the use of assembly-line techniques in the manufacture of munitions, motor vehicles, and airplanes. In the 1920's both total production and productivity increased, but after 1930 they stagnated for almost two decades. The continual improvement of the standard of living until 1939, especially in the cities, was at the expense of capital investments in new productive capacity.

France fell far behind the other industrial powers during the thirties and forties. Some of the psychological and cultural reasons for this lag will be discussed in chapter 3. The important point here is that the French did not improve their level of productivity by the widespread application of technological innovations, and they did not launch big public works projects to stimulate business activity. They were just beginning to recuperate from the depression when the Second World War began. Then four years of occupation and Nazi exploitation caused a further economic regression. The late forties were devoted to reconstruction and the restoration of prewar levels of output, as in all the former belligerent countries of Europe.

By the early fifties, however, the efforts of the Monnet Plan for Modernization and Re-equipment had helped the French economy to overcome the stagnation of the preceding decades. This government agency is unique in the history of France—and of all "capitalist" countries—in its emphasis on long-term planning and in the spirit of its members. For these men productivity has become a new gospel. They supervised the allocation of 40 per cent of all the capital invested in the French economy between 1947 and 1957 in such a way that industrially France forged ahead of the United States and Great Britain (but not West Germany and Italy) in her annual rate of growth after 1953. Except in agriculture and small-scale commerce France's present economic plant is as well equipped physically—including oil and natural gas reserves, atomic energy, modern transportation and communication facilities, and electronically controlled equipment in factories and offices—as that of most European countries. The main changes that are now needed are in risk-taking, organization, and management, rather than in machines.

The efficiency expert, the personnel director, and the technical executive are new types of Frenchmen. (They are so new that French social scientists still do not have names for them and call them collectively "le management.") Owing to their efforts, the French can produce automobiles, airplanes, locomotives, chemical products, coal, steel, and aluminum as cheaply and efficiently as the most advanced nations. There are many examples of how new methods and new incentives have affected the productivity of French workers; the following one is typical. In 1951 a French company contracted to build a pipeline between Rouen and Paris. Using equipment identical with that of similar American firms, it advanced at a rate of 700–800 meters a day, while the American average for such a job was twice this distance. The same company later began building a pipeline in Morocco, this time with the help of a few American engineers. These men introduced no technical changes; their only innovations were in planning and in the distribution of bonuses on a piecework basis. Within a few weeks the

French workers not only speeded up their daily average to 1,500 meters, they raised it to 2 kilometers. As their wages began to equal those of American workers, so did their standard of living.

Not all branches of France's economy and all regions of the country have increased their productivity at the same rate. The greatest advances have been made in heavy industry, transportation, and communication. Administration and commerce lag somewhat behind, and agriculture remains, for the most part, notoriously archaic. Furthermore, much of the southern and western half of France is underdeveloped, despite the pockets of manufacturing around the larger cities. Beginning in 1955 the government tried to encourage the movement of industries from metropolitan Paris to these depressed regions. So far its inducements—bonuses, moving expenses, and tax benefits—have hardly been used. The relocation of factories that has taken place has been on a voluntary basis and has mainly benefited the already industrialized North and Northeast.

Millions of farmers, shopkeepers, and artisans—especially in the South and West—continue to eke out a meager living in their small, inefficient enterprises, but the age of this type of economic unit—except possibly in agriculture—is over in France. Although only 1.3 per cent of the nation's private enterprises have more than one hundred people on their payrolls, they employ over half of France's workers. (The public utilities and nationalized industries are the biggest mass employers of all.) The degree of concentration is greater in industry than in commerce (except in food distribution, where the chain store is gradually replacing the self-employed shopkeeper). While businesses with zero to five employees continue to flourish in retail trade and services, those engaged in manufacturing are becoming increasingly dependent upon the big corporations, which they often serve on a subcontract basis. In any case, all of them together employ only 12 per cent of the total labor force (this figure is the same in West Germany). France is becoming less and less a country of small enterprises.

There have been fewer changes in the way goods are distributed in France than in their production, but certain innovations reflect a mass desire for a higher standard of living. Everything from men's suits to vacuum cleaners can now be bought on the instalment plan (*vente à tempérament*), though many Frenchmen, like other Europeans, still hesitate to jeopardize their financial security in this way. Another novelty in France is the supermarket. It too has gained popularity slowly because of conservative buying habits. Even so, the French are confronted every day with new marketing techniques, and these are bound to attract more and more customers. "Le self-service" is not restricted to cafeterias any more; it is offered in department stores and even in a few flower shops! Parisian merchants have become so accustomed to having clearance sales that they hold these in July rather than August, in order to allow more people to take advantage of them before vacation time.

In France the total amount of money spent on advertising is smaller than in other countries with a comparable economic structure. Its effect on stimulating growth is sometimes debated, but the two factors are probably related, since those nations with the highest per capita expenditure on this type of sales promotion also have the highest income per capita. Besides, by creating mass markets and, hence, mass production, advertising can ultimately lower retail prices, in spite of its own cost. French advertising has been big business only since the early 1950's, but many second-rate writers, designers, and artists are already "going commercial." Their problem is to find the most effective ways of reaching buyers who are not used to this kind of huckstering. So far they have maintained a strikingly high level of quality, originality, and wit in their copy and artwork, and few Frenchmen seem to object to the results.

What French consumers do object to is standardization. They are reluctant to abandon the centuries-old habit of having the goods and services they use tailored to their individual tastes. In the early 1950's the number of self-employed artisans catering to them actually increased. Even mass-produced articles like shirts, refrigerators, and automobiles—the Simca Company alone offered twenty-three basic models in 1960, with various possibilities for changes in exterior and interior décor—come in an amazing diversity of shapes and styles. Nevertheless, there is a perceptible trend toward simplification and uniformity in all but the most expensive luxury items.

The example of women's clothing illustrates this point. Until recently the rich had their dresses made by the world-famous houses of high fashion, the poor bought them off the hanger at the cheaper department stores, and the middle classes patronized obscure little dressmakers. Today the whole pattern is changing. Dior and Balmain make more money selling their designs to manufacturers— especially in the United States—than in creating gowns for individual clients. At the same time millions of French women are becoming dissatisfied with the slowness and capriciousness of the little dressmakers and the shoddiness of the cheap ready-to-wear merchandise. They are now shopping at a new type of establishment, called *prêt-à-porter*, which sells good quality clothes and either alters the customer's selection to suit her needs or has it made from a pattern in a workshop to fit her individual measurements. These frocks are too high-priced to challenge the off-the-hanger market, but they are driving one more type of small operator, the *petite couturière*, out of business.

In the twentieth century everyone wants more of everything: material comfort, the latest fashions, education, political power, and social standing. These things were formerly the birthright of a privileged elite. Now young men and women everywhere are demanding an increasing share in the benefits of industrial civilization, once they learn what these can mean for them. Their level of aspiration is far higher than that of their parents, and it is rising steadily. Thirty years ago Ortega y Gasset called this trend "The Revolt of the Masses."

The *sans-culottes* of Paris first asserted themselves on July 14, 1789, but their revolt did not raise their standard of living or eliminate the class system. Bourgeois lawyers gave them the Rights of Man and told them to keep their proper place in society. Meanwhile, the bulk of the population clung to a traditional cultural pattern for over a century. Today this way of life is not only impossible, it is not enough.

Beginning in the 1930's millions of ordinary Frenchmen were

finding it increasingly difficult to live in their closed little worlds. The welfare program of the Popular Front showed the workers the possibility of social justice and integration into the rest of the nation. Then, the defeat of 1940 and the German occupation destroyed the myth of the country's impregnability to outside forces. After 1945 America's presence was felt, not only in the form of money and soldiers, but also through cultural products like Coca-Cola, chewing gum, bebop, and blue jeans. But the main challenge to traditional ways of doing things has been the transformation of France's economy and technology. These changes have been made apparent to everyone through what they see and hear in the street, on billboards, in movies, newsreels, and press, over radio and television.

The political immobilism of the early fifties masked the fact that millions of Frenchmen were gradually adopting new forms of economic and social behavior. Regrets about the past and fear of the future were still strong among many intellectuals and the non-productive members of society, but they no longer immobilized the whole country, as they had done in the preceding decades. Peasant girls in shorts, middle-aged ladies on motor-scooters, coal-miners on television shows, and office clerks in the casino at Cannes—these are the signs of the new world of mid-century France.

Economic development and Revolt of the Masses have not yet broken down the barriers in French society, but they have transformed the existing system in many ways. Especially significant is the disintegration of the older peasant class and the gradual disappearance of differences between the rural and urban social structures. Although there are still almost five million agriculturalists in France, the size of their holdings and the techniques they use vary considerably, even within the same section of the country. One farmer will cultivate several hundred acres of marketable crops with machines and hired hands, while another will try to subsist on a small plot by putting his whole family to work. Each of these proprietors leads a different style of life. The agricultural workers too are no longer simply poorer members of one big rural "class," but have come to resemble the urban proletariat in their social attitudes and standard of living. Finally, the distinction between town and country is breaking down in what used to be the outlying areas of industrial communities. In the same household, one brother will work in the fields and another in a nearby factory. The younger women also copy the fashions and tastes of their city cousins, which railroads, magazines, movies, and television bring to all but the most remote regions.

In the villages that serve the rural population the old equilibrium between artisans and farmers is being destroyed by depopulation and the mechanization of agriculture. As the more ambitious and intelligent children of subsistence farmers go away to the city, the local shopkeepers have fewer customers and a number of them are forced out of business. The old father on the farm will do nothing to improve its operation if his only heir has become a railroad workman or a policeman, so his standard of living goes down. Those proprietors who have switched to tractors and factory-made tools no longer need the services of harness-makers, blacksmiths, and coopers. These craftsmen thus lose their source of livelihood and are forced to take odd jobs in the larger towns, since they have no vocational training suitable for industry.

Many rural and small-town people seem to have a lower standard of living than their means would permit. They still preserve the ancient habit of keeping up a shabby appearance in order to fool the tax-assessor (even though this ruse no longer really works). Their housing and sanitary facilities are considerably below the standard in urban centers, but as long as their health is good they see no reason to change. They are even more hesitant to buy things on credit than city-dwellers, but, unless they are on the verge of bankruptcy, the younger farmers and shopkeepers want more comforts than their parents would have considered necessary.

Perhaps the most novel change in the behavior of rural people is their participation in various co-operative enterprises. In most cases these serve a purely economic function, and their educational and recreational aspects are insignificant. There are now over seven thousand consumers' co-ops in provincial France, and they sell between a quarter and a half billion dollars' worth of goods to their members each year. Since 1950 many farmers have also formed vocational training groups (*centres d'études des techniques agricoles*) in which they pool their own experiences and seek guidance in new methods from visiting experts. Another organization that has recently spread in urban as well as rural areas is the Union des Castors, whose goal is the building of apartment dwellings by the people who will live in them. These kinds of co-operation may eventually stimulate habits of working together for other purposes as well.

The more highly industrialized a country becomes, the more people are rewarded with income and status according to their specialized qualifications. Today about 65 per cent of France's twenty million breadwinners earn their living in wages or salaries. (In the United States the figure is 81 per cent, in Great Britain 89 per cent, in Sweden 80 per cent, and in Belgium 71 per cent.) There is still a great difference between the income of a high executive and an unskilled laborer, but a perceptible leveling has occurred since the beginning of the century. Its general causes have been a pronounced rise in the wages of rural and female workers and in social and family allowances.

Since 1912 the range between the highest and lowest salaries has narrowed most among government functionaries. These include teachers, professors, military personnel, judges, and over a million other civil servants. Until 1951 the lower ranks received greater increases than the average worker; the middle group retained about the same purchasing power; and the real income of high officials declined from 10 to 40 per cent. A director-general who earned thirteen times as much as a postman fifty years ago now earns only six and a half times as much.

Except for top government administrators, this general trend toward the equalization of earnings has come about largely through a rise in the income of the masses; but not all wage-earners feel that they have benefited sufficiently. According to a 1956 opinion survey, 52 per cent of French workers saw no improvement in their standard of living. Many also believed that their comrades in other branches of industry had an advantage over them. Despite the fact that their purchasing power had been rising statistically for over five years, they did not think that they had a real share in the national prosperity or that their situation would improve in the near future.

Frenchmen's views on the country's economic improvement are a direct function of their own standard of living. Business executives, white-collar employees, and better-paid workers have the greatest purchasing power and are also the most optimistic. At the rate of 4.9 new francs to the dollar, the straight salary of a stenographer in 1959 was $110–$140 a month; a garage mechanic earned $100, a tool-and-dye adjuster $150, and a television producer up to $800. These sums are considerably augmented when the wife works—which is the case with one-third of the workers and employees and one-fifth of the supervisory personnel—and when there are two or more children, entitling the parents to generous family allowances. Thus, in 1959 the median "take-home" income of a manual laborer in Paris was $95 a month if he was a bachelor and $143 if he had five children. For a single skilled worker the median figure was $111, and for one with five children it was $221; for an unmarried clerk it was $120 and for an unmarried supervisor $131.

If they had a choice, most workers would want their children to improve their standard of living by acquiring specialized skills and going into other occupations. This response contradicts their traditional class solidarity and is a more modern form of the Revolt of the Masses. Twenty-seven per cent would choose skilled jobs like mechanic or electrician; 15 per cent, engineer or technician; 10 per cent each, government functionary or schoolteacher; 12 per cent, liberal professions; 7 per cent, public transportation or the military and police force. Only 11 per cent would select the career of shopkeeper or artisan, and only 4 per cent would want a white-collar position. Given the present capacity of France's educational institutions and the surviving prejudices of the upper classes, these aspirations are merely pipe dreams. Most workers know this, so, in practice, they do not urge their children to try to rise socially. But an increasing number of them want washing machines, television sets, automobiles, and their own homes, while, at the same time, doubting that they will ever have them. Their frustration and discontent in this regard thus accentuate their feeling of being socially underprivileged.

While the workers want more physical comforts, the white-collar employees are concerned with climbing the social ladder. They are in a particularly ambiguous position, for they have the same demands and feelings of exploitation as the working class, yet they try to be respectable and conformist petit-bourgeois. Their office surroundings and their daily contact with the managerial elite has made them constantly aware of their employers' outlook and style of life. They are either more loyal to or more critical of these than the ordinary laborers, who are usually indifferent to such matters. Many ambitious employees consciously copy the reading habits, tastes in amusement, dress, manners, and even the political attitudes of the middle classes. They are especially manipulable by the mass media of communication, which disseminate these norms.

In modern society a person's social rank is determined primarily by his function rather than by his own image of himself. Not only in the Soviet Union and the United States, but in Old Europe as well, the traditional symbols of class distinctions are becoming less meaningful. Any American with enough money for the down payment can have wall-to-wall carpeting, and any urban Russian with the price of a ticket can go to the opera. Even in France the better-paid workers—especially in the nationalized enterprises, where they are technically *fonctionnaires*—are becoming petit-bourgeois in their style of life, while office clerks and secretaries are being treated increasingly as appendages of computing machines and dictaphones. The income of the latter is still slightly higher than that of the ordinary laborer, but their relations with their employers are less personal than they were in the recent past. A bookkeeper's wife who owns a fur coat may think she is a lady, but she is not any more likely to be invited to the boss's house than her working-class sister.

In addition to industrial expansion and demands for a higher standard of living, the recent increase in the number of children is hastening the transformation of France's economic and social structure. For over a hundred years there was a reciprocal relationship between Frenchmen's general conservatism and their tendency to limit the size of their families. Until a break came in one, a change in the other was difficult. The break finally came in the early forties, when the birth rate began to rise considerably. Not only has this development increased the population after a century of stability, but it has created a larger group of young people than the country has known for a long time. This crop of youngsters is now overcrowding the schools, and in a few more years it will be economically active.

Why did French women begin to have more babies after 1942? (The main increase has come from the number of second and third births to the same mother.) Some observers attribute this change in their behavior to the family allowances of Pétain and the post-Liberation governments, but the evidence is not conclusive. Others say that it is part of a world pattern since the early forties, though the increase in France has been greater than in most Western countries. Still another view is that the apparent rise in the birth rate may be in fact a decline in the prewar abortion rate. There is no completely scientific explanation of the choices people make, especially when they live under crisis conditions. The war and the German occupation may have strengthened the values of family life and given Frenchmen an urge to survive as a nation. In any case, the growth in the size of the French family indicates a new vitality in what was previously considered a "decadent" country.

This trend toward a growing population seems to be a permanent one. The maximum rate was reached in 1947, with 213 live births per 10,000 people, after which it declined and leveled off at about 200. For the past decade the average yearly excess of births over deaths has been around 300,000, compared to an annual excess of deaths over births of 20,000 in the 1930's. The low birth rate at that time is having its effect today in the form of fewer married couples. Even so, these people are producing more children (800,000 in 1957) than their more numerous parents (who produced 620,000 children in 1931).

The versatility and resourcefulness of French women have made it possible for them to have larger families and, at the same time, to increase their contribution to the nation's economic life. Over 40 per cent of all females between the ages of fifteen and sixty-four are gainfully employed. This figure has varied little in fifty years, but the proportion of wives who work has increased markedly. Economic need and wider choice of careers are the major factors that have brought about this change. Women have shifted away from independent and home activities toward wage work, and from factories to offices and the professions. The men have not only allowed them to hold high positions that were formerly reserved for males, but they have given them equal wages in all jobs. They have also "emancipated" them from their age-old legal inferiority, and the expression "the wife owes obedience to the husband" no longer appears in the Civil Code. Furthermore, wives now have the same rights as single women with regard to their own property, unless their marriage contracts (whose number continues to decline) make specific provisions to the contrary.

The average French housewife now has more time and a greater inclination to modify her traditional prejudices than her husband. Labor-saving devices, new food and textile products, and the latest medical wonders are convincing her that the old ways of doing things are no longer the best ways. Permanent waves and hair-dyes have given her faith in modern science and technology. She is also changing her conception of child-care. If she works, she readily sends her children to a nursery, and if she wants to go out at night, she may even hire a baby-sitter. This practice is completely new. So far, the few available "sitters" are not old ladies or high-school girls, but male medical students! When the French "go modern" they go all out.

Children of the Past

The French have been reluctant to abandon their earlier way of life because this seemed to have "worked" so well for so long. Not only have they resisted cultural change at home; fewer of them have been willing to pull up stakes and move to strange new lands than the inhabitants of any other major nation. Though their traditional culture was never as idyllic as some of its literary admirers have liked to believe, virtually all Frenchmen have tried to remain loyal to it. They claim that it was able to endure because of the way in which it combined variety and stability. According to them it allowed each individual to contribute creatively to its renewal without altering its basic configurations. This assumption has been the basis for and the reflection of child-training, formal education, and a striking diversity of attitudes toward religion within an essentially Catholic setting.

Every culture has its own conception of personal happiness; in France it is a delicate balance called *le bonheur*. French parents

24

2

teach their children that they can achieve this as adults by learning skill, foresight, and the exercise of enlightened control. It is something that comes only with maturity and with the human dignity and privacy that a full-grown person alone can possess. Even the pleasures of the table and the bed cannot be appreciated adequately without a long apprenticeship in assimilating the proper refinements. Many of today's emancipated youths are skipping these for snack-bars and "dates" with partners from their own class, but the earlier view persists. Traditionally, boys sleep with older women (usually from outside their normal social circle), and in later life teach younger and inexperienced women. Millions of Frenchmen believe that this is the way sexual knowledge should be transmitted (and that the trouble with Americans is that they always sleep with women their own age and never learn anything).

French children are still taught that, with self-discipline and rational planning, they stand a good chance of achieving personal satisfactions; they also learn that rewards and deprivations may be equally undeserved. For French adults like to think of themselves as realists. They teach their offspring that, if one cannot have what he wants, then he must make the best of what he has—that the world is not organized to satisfy human wishes and that those people who try to change it will surely fail. France has produced her share of utopian idealists, including men like Calvin and Robespierre, but most Frenchmen seem to agree with the closing sentiments of Voltaire's *Candide*. They believe that, like this hero, they have done everything and had everything done to them and that in the end everyone must be satisfied with cultivating his own garden. There is no Eldorado, no Heavenly City on earth, no Republic of Virtue, and no supernatural or natural justice which one can rely on here and now. All that we are capable of understanding and controlling are human behavior and the physical objects around us.

For the French people human values and relationships are both universal and comprehensible when clearly expressed. The language of the educated classes is itself the product of a striving for precision and clarity. Conversational probing and the widespread habit of leaving few things unsaid lead to a frankness that foreigners dismiss as bad manners. In politics this candor has often prevented tacit agreements, customary elsewhere, to be silent about certain awkward questions. But it has given to non-political relations a clearness and definiteness lacking in many other modern cultures.

Even the notorious individualism of the French has been subject to standards of one sort or another. They assume that these exist in the external world and are learned by approximation. When they say "each one to his own taste," they are referring to people who have already assimilated those cultural norms that are the necessary means for and the measure of individual self-expression. A related belief is that the most complex and personally stated idea is communicable if it can be related logically to the traditional and the known. French "logic" consists in assigning things and ideas to their proper categories. If one wants to achieve personal happiness, he must behave in a manner appropriate for each particular compartment of life. Frustration and maladjustment will follow inevitably if behavior suitable to one compartment is manifested in another.

Hence, when Frenchmen define themselves as individualists, they are not using this word as a synonym for eccentrics or rebels. They mean that, as adults, they feel free to make choices and to improvise in ways that will be understood by other persons with the same background of home training and education. Within the broad limits of their old and sophisticated civilization they believe that there are enough alternative forms of behavior to accommodate all tastes and temperaments. In fact, many of them—including prominent anthropologists and philosophers—have said that French values are universal values. At the same time, they agree that only people born into a French family and raised in France can communicate with one another at all levels of experience.

Fashions in child-rearing and formal education are slowly changing in France, but French culture is more oriented toward the satisfaction of adult wants and the repression of childish ones than American culture, which shows a wider tolerance for the fulfilment of juvenile wishes. In the United States, partly through the influence of the mass media of communication (including the schools), untrained and emotionally immature people seek experiences for which they are unprepared. This kind of behavior is especially striking in the case of children who try to ape adult social practices by going on "dates" and having elaborate parties in their early teens. American boys and girls are also allowed to adopt "grown-up" forms of dress and grooming (long pants for boys and makeup for girls) at a younger age than French children. Finally, commercial advertising, the movies, radio, television, and popular music have shown a more marked appeal to adolescents here than in France.

The French make an absolute distinction between the role of the child and the role of the parents. An American mother—especially after having read Dr. Benjamin Spock's *The Pocket Book of Baby and Child Care*—may feel unready and unsure if her baby does not instinctively take to breast-feeding. In contrast to Dr. Spock, the *Guide de la jeune mère* tells the French mother:

"You have milk, it is the baby who doesn't know what to do." From infancy until adulthood the French child is expected to learn through response, rather than through exploration and experimentation, and to accept correction in order to grow into an acceptable individual. Before it has been trained it is regarded as acting mainly on caprices, to which the mother is not supposed to give in. The experiences of childhood are considered as necessary preparations for growing up rather than as pleasant in themselves. Both parents must initiate and stimulate the proper responses. In their role as educators, they must know and decide, protect and initiate, train and correct. In a word, they "form" the child.

By Anglo-Saxon standards most French children are sheltered. Until they are of school age their parents tend to raise them like rare, hothouse plants. The mother protects them from outside influences (both physical and human), makes all decisions regarding their food, clothing, playmates, and games, disciplines them when they go astray, but, at the same time, gives them almost continuous love and affection. The father has traditionally been more distant until his boy or girl reaches adolescence, although his role is now changing. In the long run, the French people consider the character and behavior of both parents as determining the character of their children. Each child has special needs and abilities, which must be protected and succored. But he is given little freedom to "express his personality" until this is formed for him.

The education of French children in the home consists principally in instilling the habits, knowledge, and skills necessary to adult life before there is an occasion to use them. As the child acquires these he becomes increasingly able to exercise the kind of control that will support and regulate his aptitudes effectively and help him to achieve and maintain the precarious and dignified status of full individuality and maturity. Meanwhile, the boy or girl who acts improperly is immediately reprimanded and given a punishment that lasts until he or she has "learned his lesson." (The effect of this type of discipline on the table manners of a two-year-old is positively astonishing to an American observer.) The commonest sanctions are ridicule, shame, and the deprivation of privileges, but the children also expect spankings as a matter of course. Until a few years ago a rod with leather lashes (*martinet*) was prominently displayed as the symbol of this kind of punishment in some homes.

When the child goes to school, he is often disciplined more severely by his teachers than by his parents. He discovers that being polite in the classroom is as important as learning his lessons. Urban "teen-agers" take minor liberties with a timid instructor, but these *potaches* do not brandish switch blades. In general, French pupils are made to show the proper forms of respect toward adults and to *se tenir comme il faut*, which means that they must not speak without permission or slouch when sitting or standing. Neatness in their work and in their personal habits is also rigorously enforced.

For the majority of children the main reward lies in *not* being punished and in *not* being saddled with avoidable responsibilities. Schoolboys take special delight in seeing how far they can go in breaking the rules without getting caught. They get their first taste of regimentation in school and their second in the army. All the while they dream of "liberty" and of "getting even" with their taskmasters when they grow up. But they conform openly, for they know that if their performance is satisfactory they will be left to themselves to enjoy the normal routine of life with a minimum of interference from anyone in a position of authority. They must remember that they can acquire the privileges of adult status only through a prescribed, "logical," process of development.

The principles taught in the home are also reinforced in the classroom. Though individual teachers use some personal discretion in applying it, the educational program formulated by the Ministry of National Education is identical in every primary school in France. Not only the curriculum but the method of instruction is the same almost everywhere. In teaching arithmetic, grammar, science, or civics, the teacher first introduces a principle or rule that each pupil must memorize. Then concrete illustrations or problems are presented or solved until the pupils can recognize the moral or the abstract principle implicit in the related facts. Neither the facts nor the principles are questioned. The children are led to believe that these are real and unalterable. One can only learn to recognize them and accept them.

Thus, training the French child consists primarily in teaching him rules of correct behavior, providing him with appropriate models, and guiding him toward correct observation. He learns by rote and repetition, by absorbing the behavior of others, and by practicing responses to carefully directed stimulation. The good parent and the good teacher will adapt the pace of the child's learning to his abilities and his interests, but he will always initiate and control the process.

Although most French children get essentially the same type of home training, the country's educational system has segregated them into two different cultural classes—those who have gone to a liberal-arts secondary school (*lycée*) and those who have not. (There is also a subdivision between public and parochial schools, but, except for religious instruction in the latter, the formal curriculum is the same in both.) Any child who wants to get into such an institution must take a rigorous entrance examination when he is eleven years old. Here is where the real separation begins. The pupil who passes this examination may remain in elementary school until he is fourteen or he may go into the sixth or fifth form of the *lycée* within the next year or two. But once he enters the "second degree" of the French educational hierarchy, he becomes part of a privileged minority. Henceforth, his "formation" is of a different kind from that of the majority.

The traditional ideals of the *lycée*—and its church-run equivalent, the *collège*—are disinterested general culture, mental gymnastics, and learning how to learn. Over a third of the students with this kind of education usually fail the state examination (all examinations for diplomas and degrees in France are prepared and administered by the Ministry of National Education) for the baccalaureate, but for the rest of their lives all of them look down on their countrymen who have not crossed the frontier separating it from the "primary degree." They even call the behavior of these "less gifted" people "primary" when it seems to show a lack of imagination, originality, or brilliance. Aside

30

from the implied distinction between different levels of intelligence there has been a language barrier as well, since almost all *lycéens* learned Latin until the late 1940's.

This educational system has aggravated class antagonisms by limiting opportunities and by perpetuating the prestige of nineteenth-century bourgeois cultural values. It has virtually prescribed one course of study for the middle and upper classes and another for the rest of the population. Free secondary schooling and university scholarships have not yet altered its undemocratic effects, as they have in Great Britain. They have attracted few sons and daughters of French workers, employees, farmers, and shopkeepers. These children might take supplementary courses in an elementary school until the age of sixteen and become white-collar employees or skilled industrial workers. But the wall between the primary and secondary degrees has remained. Even the vocational and technical high schools, which are closely modeled on those of the second degree, have catered mainly to the lower and lower-middle classes. Furthermore, France has not developed an elaborate adult-education program (like the Scandinavian countries) to raise the cultural level of the masses.

When this system was launched in the early 1880's, it was geared to the needs of a society dominated by capitalists and professional men. At that time the nation's level of industrialization did not require workers whose mental training extended much beyond the "three R's." Whatever skills they needed, they learned in on-the-job apprenticeships, which they sometimes entered at the age of thirteen. All primary-school children were indoctrinated with patriotic and republican slogans, but they were not encouraged to "better themselves" by competing with the sons and daughters of the dominant classes for the limited number of places in secondary and higher education. As adults most Frenchmen saw the social utility of the learning they had received in the *écoles primaires*. They frequently expressed their feeling of dignity for having acquired it by displaying their diplomas prominently in their homes.

French teachers exercised a remarkable moral and intellectual authority over their pupils and in local affairs outside the larger cities. In thousands of rural communes the lay schoolmaster competed successfully with the priest in forming the attitudes of the young people. Like his rival in clerical garb, he often came from a humble background and acquired a new status and *esprit de corps* during his professional training period. Like the Catholic seminaries France's state normal schools inculcated their own special system of values into the country's future pedagogues. These teachers' colleges were so effective in this endeavor that their pious opponents viewed them as hotbeds of atheistic radicalism (and succeeded in abolishing them temporarily under the Vichy regime). Perhaps they were, but they also perpetuated the nation's basic cultural outlook, with its emphasis on reason, self-reliance, and a humanistic suspicion of machines.

While the primary schools made French children literate and patriotic, and their teachers formed a self-conscious elite of the lower-middle classes, the privileged sections of society looked upon the *lycée* as the core of the country's educational system. There they had learned Greek and Latin in order to read with ease the texts that had been mastered by their fathers and that had formed the modes of being, thinking, and feeling of cultivated Frenchmen before the First World War. By the 1930's, however, the stress was more on grammar and composition—on mental gymnastics in languages remote from contemporary life. Courses in science, mathematics, and history retained their traditional content and paid scant attention to recent developments in these fields. Modern languages were gradually substituted for Greek, but Latin retained its strength until the end of the Second World War.

Like the curriculum, the traditional method of instruction in the *lycée* changed slowly. It emphasized principles and the memorization of great quantities of text and facts. Only modest advances were made in the use of the experimental approach for the teaching of the sciences. Whether the student followed the program in mathematics or philosophy (the French equivalents of our science and humanities programs) he was supposed to acquire a general cultural background and to learn how to learn. He was swamped with homework, had few opportunities to participate in sports, and lost what little leisure time he had when he was disciplined for minor infractions of the school's rules.

The *lycéen* had already learned at home and in primary school that everything there was to know had already been discovered by someone before him. Most of his professors confirmed this impression by displaying their own conviction that new facts were unimportant to a cultured person. (In France the man traditionally most admired was not the specialist but the cultivated individual who could respond brilliantly in a variety of contexts.) From Plato the student discovered that there is "nothing new under the sun," and from Descartes that the "natural order" of the physical world is similar to the "natural order" of human thought. The "mind," he was told, can control both "matter" and individual behavior by learning the principles that govern them. He was urged to apply these principles when he thought for himself, though he could easily become convinced that each generation finds itself confronted with the same problems as its predecessors, which, in most cases, had already found the best answers. Who was he to challenge the divine Racine in knowledge of the heart or the Cartesian method in the pursuit of scientific truth?

For over a century the baccalaureate diploma—which one prepared for in the *lycée*—has been a license for the more desirable jobs. As economic development and the Revolt of the Masses have reinforced each other, the proportion of youths between eleven and seventeen in the secondary schools has grown. In the academic year 1950–51 it was just under 19 per cent; in 1957–58 it rose to 28 per cent (with 16 per cent in liberal-arts programs and 12 per cent in technical schools), and the authorities estimate that this figure will be doubled by 1968. Between 1946 and 1958 the percentage of young men and women in universities and professional schools rose from 1.5 to over 3 per cent, and it is expected to double again by 1970.

France's institutions of higher education have produced an elite of scholars and professional people whose standards are among the highest in the world. Most of the universities give degrees in letters, science, law, medicine, and pharmacy. The fact that—until the late 1940's—there were over twice as many students in the law schools as in any of the others was an indication of France's technological and economic backwardness. In the past ten years this proportion has declined as the need for all kinds of professional and scientific personnel has convinced young men and women that they should prepare themselves in newer fields. Their choice of profession still lags behind the reality of opportunities in a changing economy, though. Many youths continue to seek entrance into the *grandes écoles*. For graduation from one of these prestige-laden institutions leads almost automatically to a coveted career in a top teaching post, advanced engineering and scientific research, public administration, or the officer corps of the army or navy. A *normalien* (from the École Normale Supérieure), or a graduate of the École Polytechnique or the École des Sciences Politiques is virtually assured of a brilliant future.

The principal drawback of France's traditional educational system was that it neglected the talents of the masses. Many Frenchmen now understand this, and educators have worked out an elaborate reform to make their schools more democratic and better suited to the needs of a modern industrial society. In 1958 they not only succeeded in raising the age of compulsory school attendance to sixteen but also in making it free at all levels. Beginning in 1960 all new pupils will be given a common course of study between the ages of eleven and thirteen to prepare them for one of three types of secondary school: (1) *école terminale* (general studies and vocational training); (2) *collège* (short program of general and technical studies); (3) *lycée* (long program of general and technical studies). It is hoped that these reforms will allow boys and girls to develop their aptitudes and intelligence to the limit of their capacity.

Another drawback of the traditional system was that students who failed the highly competitive entrance examinations for the *grandes écoles* had no place else to get the kind of professional training these schools offered. (In most cases they spent an additional year or two after having received their baccalaureate preparing for these examinations. The number rejected was sometimes as high as 90 per cent.) They can now attend special schools for Public Works, Building Construction, and Industry, as well as the newly created Institutes of Applied Sciences. These types

34

of institution may eventually fill France's pressing need for medium-level technicians and engineers—as they have for a long time in Germany. Both the state and some big corporations are also beginning to provide adult-training programs that will allow talented employees and functionaries to qualify for the lower ranks of the administrative hierarchy.

The main difficulties in implementing all these changes are the current shortage of teachers and professors and the lack of classroom space. Some of France's sixteen provincial universities have established branches in neighboring towns. Still, the various divisions of the mammoth University of Paris continue to attract more students than they have room for—and they already have over one-third of the total university enrolment in the country. Professors' salaries doubled between 1949 and 1959, so that they are now comparable in dollars to those of their American colleagues of similar rank. This is not saying much, but—since the average level of consumption in France is less than half what it is in the United States—it means that a professor in France lives better by French standards than a professor in the United States by American standards.

A major function of the public primary schools has always been to mold France's children into free-thinking, loyal republicans and patriots. Their laicism represents a tradition that is almost as old as Catholicism itself in France. Throughout the Middle Ages there were kings who tried to limit the power of the church. The chronicles and literature of the fifteenth and sixteenth centuries —Rabelais, for example—reveal a popular hostility toward monks, friars, and priests in a people that still wanted to believe in the teachings of Christ. In the eighteenth century gentlemen and scholars had begun to doubt the value of all religious practices. The charms of nature supplanted the supernatural for some, and new opportunities to visit and read about faraway places made them more cosmopolitan. By 1789 a large section of the middle and upper classes were Voltairians. They had adopted a laic outlook, which the Jacobins carried to extremes during the next five years.

After having been treated as a subversive influence during the 1790's the Catholic church (as well as the Protestant and Jewish churches) came under state sponsorship, an arrangement that lasted from 1801 until 1905. But throughout this period there was a heated struggle for and against the progress of laic ideas. Toward the end of the nineteenth century laicism meant militant atheism—sometimes combined with a positivist faith in science—for some Frenchmen. For others it meant restricting the activities of the priests to their churches. The Dreyfus Affair, the expulsion of the religious orders, and the final separation of church and state in 1905 marked the culmination of this offensive. Especially important in championing it were the Freemasons, many of whom were Leftist politicians.

Since the early 1900's laicism has persisted politically in the form of anticlericalism. While the attacks on religion as an absurd and dangerous survival have subsided, the school question persists. The issue is no longer whether or not religious instruction should be given in the public schools, but whether or not the state should give financial support to Catholic educational institutions. In 1951 and again in 1959 parliament reaffirmed the policy of providing funds for this purpose, although its opponents have not said their last word. (In June, 1960, the National Committee for Laic Action collected over ten million signatures on a petition to abolish these subsidies.)

One might think that since the majority of French children have been educated in state schools for several generations they would have completely absorbed the laic spirit. Its influence can certainly be seen in every facet of French life. Most people firmly believe in eliminating the church's authority in such fields as the regulation of public morals, censorship, and especially education. Every intervention of a bishop or *curé* in public life exasperates them, and they disapprove of any government that participates in religious ceremonies or that is accommodating to the church. Atheism is no longer as fashionable as it was at the turn of the century, but residues of former attitudes toward organized religion remain They include suspicion of the motives of the clergy and its friends, a mixture of mild contempt and ridicule toward priests and nuns because of their chastity and pious manner, and a belief that many Christian practices are akin to superstition.

Yet, Catholicism is far from dead in France. On the contrary, it has been undergoing a small-scale spiritual revival during the past few decades. The truly faithful are a minority, to be sure, but they have more dynamism than the majorities in other Catholic countries.

Out of a total population of forty-five million, about thirty-nine million Frenchmen are Catholics—at least in name. There are also about eight hundred thousand Protestants in the big cities and in certain rural areas—for example, in the Alsace and around an axis stretching southwest from Valence to Carcassonne. Over half of France's three hundred and fifty thousand Jews live in Paris, with sizable Jewish communities in Bordeaux and Strasbourg. Since the late 1940's the number of Moslems from North Africa has grown to over half a million, but most of these are not assimilated into French society.

Although most Frenchmen can be called Catholics because they have been baptized as such, this designation is largely a formal one. The majority of French families also go through the other three solemn acts of a Catholic life: solemn communion, marriage by a priest, and church burial. But the religious meaning of these acts escapes a large number of them, and there are working-class neighborhoods and rural areas (like the districts around Auxerre and Limoges) where many children are not baptized and many funerals are purely civil in character.

A practicing Catholic is required to take communion at Easter and to attend mass each Sunday. The number of Frenchmen who fit into this category varies according to geographical area, social class, occupation, age, and sex. They form a majority in whole regions of the Northwest, the East, the Massif Central, and provinces where the traditional language and customs are not French, such as Brittany, the Basque country, Alsace, and Flanders. In the north-central fourth of the country centered around Paris, and in the *départements* (counties) surrounding Bordeaux and Marseille, the proportion drops to one-seventh or one-tenth.

There are similar contrasts within the large cities. In Paris itself the proportion of practicing Catholics declines from one-third to one-fifteenth of the population as one moves from the West End to the East End. The well-to-do middle and upper classes in Passy go to church fairly regularly, while nineteen out of twenty workers in Belleville stay away. In the country as a whole, twice as many women as men attend church on Sunday, and the proportion of women rises in regions where the total number of practicing Catholics declines. Mass desertions from the church take place at certain times: both sexes (but especially boys) at the age of about eleven years and after solemn communion, and women when they marry or go to work.

In the past two hundred years the pattern of religious practices has changed markedly. All rural Frenchmen went to church regularly in the eighteenth century, while the nobility and the bourgeoisie had many dissidents. By the time of the Revolution, however, there was a major decline in religious practice in Paris and its neighboring *départements*. Most men in this area ceased taking communion at Easter, and many women no longer attended Sunday mass. In the 1830's and 1840's the pattern of the Paris region extended westward and southward, and in the 1850's it moved southeastward as well. The detachment of the rural masses was well under way by the late nineteenth century in the Southwest around Bordeaux, and in the Southeast around Marseille. Meanwhile, "dechristianization" continued in the central plain as far east as Dijon, as far south as Clermont-Ferrand, and as far west as Poitiers. Educated Frenchmen were abandoning religion for political and ideological reasons almost two centuries ago, but it was industrialization, mechanization, and emigration to the cities that destroyed the faith of the masses. As factories were built in the suburbs of northern towns, urban economic and social structures were transformed and the inhabitants' religious practices changed in the same way as they did in Paris.

The contrast between men and women in religious practice is a fairly recent development. At the beginning of the eighteenth century male peasants observed the outward forms as much as their wives and daughters, though the townspeople and the highest and lowest classes were less unified. A hundred years later there was a considerable change in opinion and living conditions, especially in urban communities. The nineteenth-century bourgeois (from whom the masses adopted many attitudes and norms for behavior) generally professed the belief that religious practice demonstrated and supported the morality of women, and that the main virtue of a man was independence. Everything worked to fortify this social dogma. Illustrious intellectuals (mostly male) affirmed that religious rituals were an affront to reason; public places like cafés, clubs, stadiums, and workers' exchanges did not cater to women; the sentimentalization of many forms of devotion seemed weak and feminine to most men. But after 1900 the attitudes and behavior of both sexes regarding religion changed again. While the progressive emancipation of women has weakened their religious motivation, or at least altered their manner of expressing it, the devout male is no longer exposed to the same kind of ridicule as he was at the turn of the century.

These changes are evident in every section of society. Until the early twentieth century most classes and their leaders were either hostile to religion as a conservative force or loyal to it as a traditional framework. Then, as rationalism gradually lost its prestige for the middle classes, many of them began to find a place for experiences of the spirit. The Second World War transformed the church into an asylum for the faithful, fashion has made it a meeting place again, and the improved quality of its music and art have attracted discriminating bourgeois Frenchmen who would have stayed away sixty years ago. Sincere devotion to Christ can be found in a small number of men and women in all social groups, including the urban workers. The proportion of zealous believers is probably the greatest in settings where routine piety has become an anomaly or where individual behavior is least regulated by custom and obedience. It should also be noted that rural areas increasingly follow urban models as local practices and beliefs disappear. The trend today is toward the domination of "global" practices and toward an increasing number—though still a small minority—of people who are active Catholics by conviction rather than because of custom, family influence, or other outside constraints.

Nevertheless, the majority of practicing Catholics have experienced all these pressures. Their family background is especially important. Only if religion is practiced *en famille* as well as in church—and is not a mere ritual of going to Mass on Sunday—is it really meaningful to most people. Religion comes alive for them through common prayers said before familiar pious images in their own homes at regular intervals and during certain holy periods like the month of the Virgin or the Sacred Heart. The general social milieu in which a person grows up also influences his religious belief and practice. How many Bretons who are far away from their native village church bells think of entering a Parisian church? The effect of class affiliations can be seen in the tendency since the late nineteenth century for the working classes to desert the church, while the middle classes clung to it or even returned to it.

Aside from the differences in religious practice between one part of the country and another, there are local variations in the same region. On the Breton coast, for example, there are two neighboring parishes of about one thousand inhabitants each. In each case, the men work on the sea, experience the same storms, and have the same cultural background. Both villages seem similar in every respect, yet one is very religious, and the other is indifferent. On closer examination one finds an economic contrast. In village A the "sailors" gather oily algae in one period of the year and cider apples in another. They work every day, including Sunday, during the "harvest" season, and their income is low and seasonal. In other words, they are a kind of non-urban proletariat. The men of village B, on the other hand, are professional seamen, with steady employment, comfortable incomes, and economic security. They leave the running of their households and the education of their children to their wives. These women have usually been taught by nuns. They instil religious principles in their offspring and then send them to parochial schools. At election time the Communist party gets almost twice as many votes in village A as in village B, for the former is proletarian and agnostic, while the latter is petit-bourgeois and pious.

There is an even greater difference between rural and industrial parishes that are a few miles apart. Such is the case on both sides of the Franco-Belgian border. It seems that identical socio-economic structures produce identical religious situations regardless of political frontiers. In towns that serve generally religious rural areas, indifference or non-practice prevails among middle-class merchants, artisans, and government employees, while the faithful are found mainly among small and medium farmers and, to a lesser extent, among white-collar workers. In a sense these regions are going through a change that others experienced one hundred and fifty years ago. Throughout the country the faith-less masses are found around big factories and big capitalist farms as well as among wine-growers, sharecroppers, greengrocers, and people engaged in animal husbandry.

The religious map of France also coincides with the map of social hierarchies, so that the largest proportion of practicing Catholics is found in those regions where the aristocracy and the clergy are still influential (as in the interior counties of the West) or where strong family ties are the rule (as in the extreme North). When no superior authority in the village or the home exerts pressure on individuals—and, of course, if they move away—they usually abandon religious practices. In those rural areas where at least 50 per cent of the inhabitants go to church regularly, the influence of religion on such matters as birth control and divorce is stronger than among the faithful in the cities. Urban Catholics are mostly to the Right politically, with some notable individual exceptions. At the same time, whole regions of rural Catholics vote for Leftist candidates, while others support the Rightists.

Whatever their economic, social, or geographical background may be, Frenchmen still show the influence of religion in their everyday behavior and attitudes. For practicing Catholics it is an important factor in family morals, the stability of the home, a high birth rate, relations between spouses, and the respect of children for parents and grandparents. The decline in the birth rate by *départements* closely paralleled the decline in the number of practicing Catholics after 1789 in the same areas. But other motives also explain the number of children a couple will have. Non-practicing Catholics have produced large families out of instinct or interest, irresponsibility or carelessness, patriotism or optimism, while some of the most pious Frenchmen have limited procreation because of avarice, selfishness, or despair.

It would be as risky to attribute contemporary social morality and attitudes in France to that country's long Catholic tradition as it would be to see the influence of the New England Puritans as the main factor in American norms today. Historically each of these religious traditions certainly set the tone, but in France as in the United States, there have been non-religious influences as well. In both countries the precepts of Christianity have often been ignored in the treatment of serfs, slaves, and industrial workers. "Good" Puritans were slave-traders in eighteenth-century America; "good" Catholics were black-market profiteers in the mid-1940's in France. Contrarily, a religious conception of justice moved American Abolitionists a hundred years ago and the Christian Democratic champions of the French working class in the twentieth century. The practice of Christian charity in France is evident in church-run institutions for the care of orphans, invalids, unwed mothers, and people with incurable diseases, and in daily acts of giving and service. But recent studies show how the treatment of refugees and the help given to war victims varied both among practicing and non-practicing Catholics two decades ago.

Until the end of the Second World War the majority of France's "good" Catholics were reactionary conformists of the type portrayed by the Comtesse de Ségur. More French children, especially girls, have probably read her stories than those of any other nineteenth-century author. She gives her young readers a vision of a perfect world that is threatened by the forces of Evil. (Like millions of "well-brought-up" French women, Simone de Beauvoir acknowledges the influence of Madame de Ségur in shaping her girlhood conception of a world clearly divided between good and evil forces in her *Memoirs of a Dutiful Daughter*.) In it God helps the police see to it that the upright, pious people are happy.

He is a kindly father who watches over his children and who punishes them when they disobey his commandments. If misfortune befalls a virtuous person, divine providence will find a way to extricate him from his predicament. Such is the case with Madame de Ségur's heroine Giselle in *Quel amour d'enfant*. Repentant in her widowhood and ruin, Giselle welcomes the return of her old suitor Julien as a support sent by God.

Madame de Ségur views the world as a *bien-pensant*—that is, as a "right-thinking" pious reactionary. Despite her qualified acceptance of the entrepreneurial spirit toward the end of the Second Empire, her sympathies are with the Old Regime. Her fictional children are well born, and their behavior teaches the lesson of *noblesse oblige*, particularly through acts of charity. Poor people should be content with their station so that the privileged classes can be charitable to them. In most of her stories Madame de Ségur ridicules ambitious bourgeois who try to "crash" high society. Thus, in *Les Vacances*, the Comte de Rosbourg buys back his chateau and town house from a *parvenu* at a ruinously low price for the latter. This transaction is shown as morally just because it restores the property of an impoverished nobleman and allows him to resume a style of life proper to his class. The story ends with the Comte de Rosbourg telling his wife the good news and kissing her hand. (After having read such tales, *bien-pensant* children are ready to take their place in those same south-western provinces where the liberal Catholic François Mauriac set his novels of bourgeois crassness and avarice.)

In one of her last books, *La Fortune de Gaspard* (1866), Madame de Ségur does find a place for "capitalists" in her traditional world. The hero of this story is a Christian industrialist who paternalistically supervises the men who work under him. They willingly accept their lot as God's will. The fact that they do not complain and are apparently satisfied removes the danger of revolution. This authoritarian defense against the "Red menace" appealed to pious reactionaries right up to the Vichy regime, when it was officially imposed on the whole country by Papa Pétain.

Another theme in Madame de Ségur's *bien-pensant* outlook is nativism. She sometimes portrays France's enemies as brave in battle, but always as incapable of resisting the superior commanders of the French. The Russians are treated fairly sympathetically in her novels, but she expresses ridicule and contempt for the English and the Germans. (She herself was born Sophie Rostopchine and moved to France after marrying the Comte de Ségur in the 1820's. Many reactionary Frenchmen shared her sympathy for her native country, which reminded them of their own beloved Old Regime. Her contemporary Jules Verne also lauded the virtues of tsarist Russia in his popular adventure story, *Michael Strogoff*.) When she wants to make a character miserly and dishonest, she has other characters call him a Jew. In this way she reinforces the Shylock-Fagin stereotype, which has been ubiquitous in most Christian countries. The Comtesse de Ségur's heroes are chauvinistic rather than loyal to any particular French government. Not all of them are courageous, but she usually contrasts the courage and uprightness of "decent" Frenchmen with the cowardice and vileness of foreigners.

As in many aspects of contemporary French culture, the residues of a traditional pattern of religious attitudes and norms continue to influence the behavior of people who have abandoned the church. The effect of these residues varies according to the geographical region and socioeconomic environment in which a child is raised. Even when he grows up and moves to the city or into a new occupational or social group, some of them stay with him. They can be seen in the preservation of practices associated with certain religious holidays, especially for children. The persistent superstition about having thirteen people to dinner was originally related to the story of the Last Supper and the death of the thirteenth person at that table. Prejudice against the Jews is in part a survival of medieval attitudes engendered by the Crusades, though more recent developments have nourished it. Some observers even maintain that the naïve faith of a doctrinaire Leftist in anticlerical propaganda—or of certain workers and intellectuals in the Communist party—is really a perversion of an earlier desire to believe in the Gospel of Christ.

The issue of laicism versus Catholicism can still arouse the passions of the champions of both sides to a greater extent in France than in other Catholic countries. Aside from the school controversy, debates over the deathbed beliefs of prominent agnostics are a recurring theme in French life. Soon after André Gide died in February, 1951, François Mauriac suggested that he had wavered at the end between doubt and belief and that he might have resolved his conflict in favor of the latter. Then a third novelist, Roger Martin du Gard, wrote a rejoinder recalling a statement of Gide's last days in which he had said that the idea of a "beyond" was unacceptable emotionally and intellectually. A similar debate occurred over the religious convictions of former Premier Édouard Herriot, after Pierre Cardinal Gerlier, Archbishop of Lyon, was called to his deathbed in March, 1957. In his speech as Herriot's successor in the French Academy, the biologist Jean Rostand made a discreet reference to his having taken the last rites of the church. Another "immortal," Jules Romain, then said that there was nothing to the suggestion that the renowned Leftist politician had died repudiating the conception of things he had held since his youth. Such arguments are rarely settled, but whether Gide and Herriot were believers or non-believers, they were children of the past.

Malthus and the Bourgeoisie

Only a handful of Frenchmen has ever heard of Thomas Robert Malthus, yet millions of them have traditionally viewed the world in a way that has been justly labeled Malthusian. The term is used loosely to describe a low estimate of the amount of goods, services, jobs, government posts, and all forms of wealth available to a given population. People who make this pessimistic appraisal believe that they should conserve what they have or, at most, try to get a bigger share of a total that is fixed for the whole community. There will never be enough of everything to satisfy everyone's needs; if one person or group seeks to obtain more for itself, it will be at the expense of others. This Malthusian outlook explains a good deal of French economic and social behavior. Although it has usually been associated with the bourgeoisie, it has affected other sections of French society as well.

Malthusianism has long been evident among big businessmen in France in their habit of producing for a limited market and their

3

reluctance to expand production in anticipation of a growing demand. It persists even today among the directors of the iron and steel trusts and the Michelin Tire and Rubber Company. (Michelin recently bought out the Citroën Automobile Company. On a smaller scale this action resembles Du Pont's gaining the controlling interest in General Motors.) During the first half of the twentieth century various factors favored monopolistic organizations that deliberately restricted gross output. Because mass production was less developed in France than in other industrial countries, until the past few years the tendency toward monopoly there was aided by the manner in which decisions were made by a few key stockholders and by the participation of the same persons or financial groups in several branches of a given industry, rather than by means of "rationalization" or financial unification. The activities of certain capitalists closely associated with the great banks were decisive in the steel, coal, chemical, electrical, and cement industries, and in some branches of wholesale food distribution. This kind of collusion resulted in an increasingly imperfect competition and, thanks to gentlemen's agreements and combinations of a more binding nature, the growth of cartels.

The limited demand for French industrial goods made monopolistic control easier than it was in Great Britain, Germany, and the United States. In these three countries the rural population was proportionately smaller than in France but it had a larger average income and bought more manufactured products. At the same time, the development of a mass domestic market in these nations gave them an advantage in international trade, since mass-production techniques lowered prices. Because the French Empire was mostly underdeveloped it added little to the total market for French industry. France's increasing isolation from the world economy until the early 1950's (except for the exportation of quality articles) further reinforced the tendency toward monopolistic organization and Malthusianism in her basic industries.

Strange as it might seem, the cartels wanted laws that would preserve small and middle-sized business units. Undoubtedly they did not hesitate to eliminate serious rivals, but they tried to preserve those enterprises that were too weak to compete with them. They had a political interest in doing this, since the small units were a stabilizing social factor whose widespread existence tended to obscure the power of the monopolies. Furthermore, the fact that the smaller employers could not pay their workers very much seemed to justify the low wages paid by the big industrialists and even made the latter seem generous when they granted slight wage increases. Finally, the large firms had an economic interest in preserving the little producers. Because the latter had to charge high prices in order to stay in business they kept the market price high and permitted the former, who were sometimes able to "rationalize" their production, to make huge profits.

Some of the government's policies also discouraged greater productivity and even increases in gross output in certain cases. By giving tax relief to small manufacturers and craftsmen, they condemned them to stagnation. For these people lost this benefit if their income rose above a certain level. On the other hand, the big firms were penalized by proportionately heavier taxes and by the burden of social security contributions. They had to pay these in full, since their accounts were easily controlled, while small employers could reduce their operating expenses by avoiding part of this cost—often with the complicity of their workers.

Like many artisans, the small wheat-farmer lost certain benefits when his production exceeded a fixed level. If he sold less than fifty quintals in 1958, he received the full parity price of 3,709 francs—less 64 francs in taxes—per quintal (100 kilograms). Not only did the bigger producers cease to receive this price after the first fifty quintals, but they were forced to help the government subsidize the smaller ones through a special tax prorated according to their own output. In other words, as their production went up, the price they received went down. After a certain point, it was too low to allow them enough profit to improve their efficiency. Meanwhile, the marginal producers were unable to switch to feed grains because they lacked the necessary capital. So they continued to grow wheat and to demand higher prices to meet the rising cost of living.

In addition to protecting the nation's agriculture and industry from foreign competition with high tariffs for over a hundred years, the French government helped to preserve inefficient units in domestic commerce. By limiting the growth of mass-distribution outlets and by winking (until 1954) at tax-evasion on the part of small merchants, the state subsidized an outmoded and costly retailing system. This system kept prices high and consumption low, and it weakened the country's productive capacity by wasting the energies of almost two million petty retailers. The pathetic aspect of their situation has been that many of them work longer and make less money than skilled workers. Even today a man and his wife will spend ten to twelve hours a day in their shop, and the total result of all these man-hours will be the sale of ten spools of thread, three pairs of shoes, or a half-dozen boxes of nails.

Many artisans have faced a similar plight. Handmade products from France have been famous since the seventeenth century, but the demand for them, despite their continued high quality, has decreased with the appearance of cheaper, mass-produced commodities. There is still an important national and world market for *articles de luxe*, and the persons who produce them can eke out a decent living. Most craftsmen, however, do not manufacture luxury goods; they make shoes, furniture, pottery, agricultural tools, watches, clothing, toys, and other items for everyday use. After spending five, ten, or twenty hours working on a particular article they find that the price they receive for it is little higher than that of a similar one made in a factory in a fraction of this time.

In January, 1959, the French government launched a series of financial reforms, which, among other things, cut down the state's traditional support to inefficient producers. The first stage in the movement toward a European Common Market went into effect at that time, and France had to face competition from her neighbors. Ceilings were placed on wages in order to avoid inflation at home, and the franc was devalued by 17 per cent, so that prices would be lower for foreign buyers who could make their purchases in French currency. In his effort to balance the national budget Antoine Pinay, the minister of finance at that time, also reduced the rates for certain categories of pensions and social security benefits. But the group that has suffered the most (and with the loudest protests) from this "austerity" program has been the small farmers. For, horror of horrors, the government abandoned its policy of maintaining agricultural prices at a guaranteed parity.

Although government investments have generally improved the productivity of industry since the early 1950's, their effect on agriculture is questionable. In many cases this form of assistance still tends to subsidize small, inefficient units. Rural electrification, the increased availability of tractors, and government-backed, long-term mortgages make it possible for almost five million farmers to stay in business and in some instances—like wheat, wine, and sugar beets—to produce more than the market can absorb. The consequences of this situation have also affected other sectors of the French economy. While the income the farmer receives has usually been too low to allow him to buy many industrial goods, the market prices of most agricultural products—after all the middlemen have added their charges—have been too high to compete in the international market.

Whether an economy is free or planned, prices must be close to real costs if its natural resources, capital, and manpower are to be effectively utilized for the common good. Real costs are those that express the scarceness of raw materials and the amount of human effort that is directly or indirectly necessary for their production or transformation. But the prices of many goods and services in France have been fixed by the state for a long time. In most cases, these have depended upon the] relative strength of pressure groups representing producers, distributors, or consumers. Thus, alcohol prices have been far above the real costs of production, while apartment rents and railroad fares have been far below the real costs of maintaining these services. The chronic shortage of milk and meat and the superabundance of wheat and wine have also resulted in prices that the state has supported at artificial levels.

Monopolistic enterprises have done their share in keeping prices high, but the government has also been responsible. By subsidizing marginal enterprises it has raised the prices of the things they sell. In addition, military expenditures, development schemes in Algeria and other parts of Africa, amortization, heavy investments, and a costly welfare program have steadily increased the public debt. Along with the large amount of commercial paper held by banks, these have created demand in the form of more money in circulation. By 1956–57 production was unable to keep up with this demand, and prices began to rise again after four years of relative stability. In order to curb this trend—and also to cut down the demand for imports, which was creating an unfavorable balance of trade—the government began to restrict the availability of credit. This measure aggravated another retardative factor in French economic growth—dear capital.

Certainly the monetary and financial disorders of the twenties and thirties made wealthy Frenchmen particularly wary of investing their money at home; but the low rate of investment in productive enterprises was also conditioned by the Malthusian view. In an economy where important sectors were controlled by cartels the producers' goal was to limit the supply of a given commodity to the point where its price would bring the highest total profit. There was therefore little incentive to expand the existing facilities of heavy industry in France. This non-expansion policy also discouraged new capital investments in the competitive industries that manufactured consumers' goods, because the means of production were too expensive to permit the low prices that would have created an expanding market.

Until the past few years the dominant tendency in France was to adjust supply to consumption at every stage in the production and distribution of goods. This practice was in marked contrast to the attempts of American manufacturers and retailers to increase the demand for their products by high pressure advertising, instalment buying, temporary price reductions, and a host of other promotional techniques. Such methods were virtually untried in France and there was much opposition to them. In addition to the aforementioned Malthusianism of the industrialists, the attitudes of the small shopkeepers also discouraged the mass production that would have caused an increased investment in industry. Except in a few large department stores and chain stores, the French marketing system was extremely old-fashioned. Most merchants insisted on exaggerated profits from a few sales, they often refused to accept responsibility for the quality of their merchandise, and they would let their stock lie and take a loss rather than get rid of it in a clearance sale. Such policies made mass turnover and, hence, mass production, virtually impossible.

The limited market, the conscious restriction of production in many producers'-goods industries, and the buying and selling habits of the French public all discouraged new investments. It was not so much a lack of savings (these continued to accumulate during the interwar years, though at a rate gradually decreasing from the pre-1914 level) as how they were used that was at fault. Millions of Frenchmen hoarded the money they did not spend; or, if they did not keep it in cash, they usually bought government bonds or sent it abroad. For the French had a static conception of wealth. They thought of money—especially gold—as having an intrinsic and permanent value, and they were reluctant to convert it into risk capital. Until the early 1950's even the workers viewed their wages in purely monetary terms rather than as purchasing power.

Despite the secrecy that has surrounded the policies of the great French banks it is possible to make a few generalizations about their influence in restricting capital investments in France. The banks have served as repositories for savings, which they have usually invested in short-term treasury bonds. After the First World War they extended less and less credit to productive enterprises, not only because of their Malthusianism, but also because of the increasing fusion of banking and industrial capital by "personal union." Since the same people were often on the boards of directors of the large banks and the monopolistically organized industries, the former tended to restrict their financial support to the latter.

But it was precisely the large industries that needed bank credit least, because of their ability to provide their own finances from their great profits and because of their voluntary restriction of production. Moderate-sized and small businesses, which might have expanded with the help of loans, found that the bank directors were either unwilling to subsidize competitors of the big firms with which they were connected or reluctant to finance competitive businesses whose profits were smaller and less certain than those of the cartels. Even so, it must not be thought that a simple change in credit policy would have altered the basic stagnation of the thirties and forties profoundly.

Credit is used only when there is a demand for it. This demand is affected by the interest rate, but it has also been determined by a wider range of factors. Just as French businessmen have opposed high-pressure advertising, mass production, and instalment buying, they have rejected the use of credit on a large scale. They have done this in order to avoid risking the bankruptcy that could result from a small decline in sales or prices. A writer in the April, 1948, issue of *Fortune* tried to explain the successful expansion of American capitalism in an article entitled "The American Genius for Bankruptcy." In France, however, bankruptcy has long been considered a disgrace, and most French entrepreneurs have clung to this view. Besides, if a Frenchman goes out of business, it is difficult to start another one, and he might lose his precious economic security permanently.

As in so many of their affairs, the French have been caught in a vicious circle regarding the level of their private investments. These have been insufficient because of their high cost, but as long as they remain so, their dearness will persist. The current volume of public and private investment in France cannot maintain an annual increase of the national product at its recent high rate. In proportion to the nation's total revenue, its investments are not inferior to those in the United States. But Americans can manufacture their means of production with existing equipment at prices that are relatively low in comparison with those of consumers' goods and services. In France this is not so. Until her productive plant becomes larger, her present rate of investment will not be enough to cover the needs of enterprises making both producers' and consumers' goods.

Only private sources can provide the needed increase in investment, for the state has so many other obligations that it is unable to help any more than it has in the past. Already pinched for revenue, it cannot raise taxes much above their present level, which is 23.6 per cent of the total national income; and if it did so it would further discourage business expansion. (French taxes on industry are already higher—and more complicated—than those in Germany and Great Britain.) The real problem is the chronic hesitancy of most people with savings to appreciate the returns available from investments in private enterprise. Forty years of bad experiences ruined their confidence in most forms of movable wealth as well as in the national currency. The restoration of the twenty-cent franc and the increase in exports in 1960 may bring back some of this confidence.

The Paris Bourse is only a small bridge between the mass of savers and the big companies. Early in 1958 the total value of outstanding stocks was less than one billion dollars, while Frenchmen owned over four billion dollars worth of gold. Local and regional banks have declined since the Great Depression, so they have lost much of their earlier financial importance. People are still hesitant to lend money on a long-term basis because inflation might reduce the value of their return. As a means of circumventing this obstacle the De Gaulle government backed its first national loan in 1958 with the price of gold, while a few corporations—like the Électricité de France—have linked the worth of their bonds to the price of some product. Yet, as long as the interest rate remains high, many companies prefer to provide their own risk capital from their profits.

The Malthusianism of French industrialists was not the only factor in retarding their country's economic development, for the workers, too, were reluctant to abandon their traditional ways. In the early twentieth century many of them still had family ties with relatives in the country and retained something of the peasant's view of the world. Artisans who gradually shifted their production to small factories also preserved some of their old habits. French industrial workers were especially able to resist new ways of doing things because the transition from the plow and the craftsman's workbench to the assembly line was less abrupt in France than in countries like Germany and the United States, which became industrialized in a shorter time. Certainly the working conditions of French coal-miners, mill hands, and railroad gangs differed little from those of other countries. But the survival, well into the twentieth century, of many small-scale, semihandicraft industrial units—particularly in the production of consumers' goods—allowed most French workers to resist the demands of industrial organization, such as bigness, pace, standardization, discipline, specialization, and occupational mobility.

By the time these demands were generally accepted—certainly not before the mid-thirties—many French workers had turned to class warfare rather than to confidence in increased production as the only way to better their lot. They saw the unwillingness of their bosses to keep up with technological progress and to grant them shorter hours, better wages, and social equality. Their ambiguous notion about their place in the economic system was also related to the fact that most other Frenchmen viewed them as a social class rather than an occupational group. Both the state

55

and the employers reinforced this view, the effect of which on the workers themselves was to obscure in their own minds their functional role in an industrial society, and, thus, to hamper their integration into the technological as well as the social and political structure of this society.

In a way, the industrial workers were imbued with their own brand of Malthusianism. Part of it came from the preindustrial outlook of forebears who were peasants and artisans, and part of it came from Marx (whom they *had* heard of). For Marx agreed with Malthus that the economic pie was limited in size, and with Ricardo that it was in the sky as far as the mass of wage earners was concerned. He correctly saw that the proletariat would acquire a feeling of solidarity when confronted with the predatory, unenlightened type of nineteenth-century capitalism. In France, as in other Continental countries, a large number of people continued to identify themselves with this class and to believe that their only course of action was to make a revolution and redistribute the existing wealth among themselves. Even today many of them are conditioned to being underprivileged and to being cheated out of their just share in an expanding economy.

The individualism and Malthusianism of self-employed Frenchmen (although the proportion of Frenchmen in this category is declining, it is still around 35 per cent of the economically active population) have also reinforced each other and have been expressed in these people's ambivalent feelings toward the state. Pride in one's craftsmanship, the satisfaction of being one's own boss, the cultivation of gustatory, amorous, and aesthetic tastes— as long as these delights have been possible, most French artisans, shopkeepers, and peasant-proprietors have not seemed to mind their relative lack of material comforts. For over a century they have believed that only through self-reliance could they get their modest share of the limited market for their goods and services and that shifting to wage-work would reduce them to the hopeless insecurity of the proletariat. (A few of their sons became policemen or soldiers and could thus look forward to steady employment and a pension. But one gave up one's independence when one worked for the government—and pensions might be made valueless by revolution or inflation.) Despite everything that the state has done to keep France's marginal producers and distributors in business, they have continued to view it as a threat to their economic freedom. It has always seemed ready to ruin them with taxes, to give some other group a larger portion of the economic pie, or to favor their more efficient competitors in some way.

Most small business men have resisted the introduction of new industries and new methods into their home communities. Recently a local *syndicat d'initiative* (chamber of commerce) tried to appraise the needs of a backward town in Brittany and reported them to the government with the hope of attracting new enterprises to the area. But this group is exceptional. In most instances, the people in underdeveloped regions neither expect nor want new industries or projects that might raise their economic level. If they do, they look to the state—that traditional dispenser of largesse—to take the initiative.

They are especially hostile to a modern-minded entrepreneur like Édouard Leclerc, who behaves as if one could sell more by charging less. This young food merchant's "revolutionary" method is to buy goods directly from the producer and to retail them at wholesale prices. By 1959 sixty stores throughout the country were using this system under his name. Local competitors have been forced to lower prices, and their tempers are rising proportionately. A "monster" like Leclerc threatens hundreds of thousands of middlemen in France's overloaded food-distribution circuits as well as uneconomic small retail outlets.

In almost all kinds of activities the French have resisted the imposition of other people's bright ideas on them. Let each person look out for himself to the best of his ability, they say. Knowing how to get out of difficulties and take advantage of opportunities—*se débrouiller*—is a much admired virtue in France. It has made French men and women resourceful, imaginative, and adaptable to unfavorable conditions. (They showed remarkable ingenuity in getting food, publishing clandestine newspapers, and sabotaging the enemy during the German occupation.) But it has held them back in a world where organization, large-scale planning, and discipline are necessary for economic and technological development. France has thousands of free-lance inventors whose talents are not co-ordinated by the big corporations or the

57

government. Instead of working in somebody else's laboratories they rent small apartments where they invent their gadgets. They apply for patents in Liechtenstein or Uruguay in order to avoid French taxes. Then they sell their rights to a French firm and receive royalties from it.

In France status has traditionally been as important as money to many people—and, like money, there has never seemed to be enough of it to go around. One of the most significant features of French society in the twentieth century has been the persistence of a system of stratification ill-suited to the needs of an industrial economy and an egalitarian ideal. By the end of the First World War there were numerous occupational groups in France whose status was not determined by birth or inherited wealth and whose interests often conflicted with those of other members of their class. Nevertheless, the majority of Frenchmen continued to identify themselves with one of the traditional classes. Political orators who extolled egalitarianism had to look back to the early 1790's for its Golden Age.

Technological, organizational, and political changes have modified—and, in extreme cases like Soviet Russia, redefined—the class structure in many places, but there has been much resistance to this process in France. There social, artistic, and intellectual aristocracies acquired a higher degree of prestige than in most other European countries. Although the hereditary nobility virtually ceased to participate in public life by the end of the nineteenth century, it retained its dominant position in high society and continued to exclude *parvenu* nobles and wealthy commoners from its inner circle. The plutocracy and the upper middle classes were also consciously exclusive. Even the middle and lower-middle classes, which championed the principle of social equality, were careful to distinguish themselves from the urban and rural proletariat. The workers, in turn, viewed themselves as a segregated minority group. As a result, they sometimes tended to identify their interests with their class rather than with the nation. All these attitudes made it difficult for Frenchmen to move up the social ladder.

By the eighteenth century the upper bourgeoisie had adopted the values of formal hierarchy and seniority and had tried to monopolize the professions and the higher civil service. In fact, some members of this class were so impressed by the prestige of the hereditary nobility—both before and after the Revolution—that they sought to imitate its style of life. The symbols of noble status were titles, land (with a chateau), and exemption from taxation. These could be bought, to be sure, but after 1750 (when hereditary offices ceased to be sold) it was more feasible for most rich bourgeois to displace the nobles than to join their ranks. They then set up their own "dynasties" and maintained their dominant position in French public life through their wealth, family connections, and access to higher education.

The business elite itself could not muster sufficient prestige to set the style for a whole culture. Consequently, the values of industrial capitalism never enjoyed the degree of "legitimacy" in France that they acquired in some other Western countries. Because of their own mixed feelings about modern capitalism French businessmen lacked self-assurance in the face of a hostile audience. The masses in France have never been taken in by Horatio Alger and Daddy Warbucks types, and these did not appear in popular fiction or films as models to be admired and emulated.

Dynamic entrepreneurs were suspect in France. The engineer-promoter Ferdinand de Lesseps organized the construction of the Suez Canal with great success in the 1860's. But the failure of his Panama venture and the resultant scandal in 1892 did almost as much to discredit men of his type as John Law's "Mississippi Bubble" had done a hundred and seventy years earlier. The French image of the successful capitalist in the nineteenth century was that of the financier Jacques Laffitte, who, according to popular legend, amassed his fortune by saving everything in sight—even pins. After the First World War the image was that of a banker with a country estate and a son holding a high post in the civil service.

Well into the twentieth century many bourgeois Frenchmen still preferred to be *rentiers* rather than entrepreneurs. They lived in provincial towns and rural chateaux (usually recently built copies of medieval models), put their investments in land, and arranged their children's marriages for the purpose of consolidating their holdings. Their preference for land over mobile wealth was partly a remnant of Physiocrat theory, partly a suspicion against speculative ventures, and partly an expression of snobbery. They viewed marriage as neither a sacrament nor a matter of love. To them it was a contract, signed in front of the town notary. Most property contracts were also simple enough for this functionary to formulate and register without consulting a lawyer. But there was much litigation over property rights, so lawyers were much in demand too.

The belief that money isn't everything can still be seen in the preference of professional people for a *situation* that assures its holder of a regular salary and a pension. A lawyer who had risen socially recently said that his mother-in-law often reproached him for not having an administrative post, even though he earned five times as much as his colleagues who worked for the state. She considered him an adventurer because, at the age of fifty, he ought to have been approaching retirement instead of entering the most creative period of his life.

"Bourgeois" is a vague term. It can include everyone who saves part of his income, in which case it is synonymous with the equally vague "capitalist." In addition, it can designate people who are paid for their services in fees or salaries rather than wages. Above all else, it is a state of mind expressed in a style of life by various economic groups.

When the Abbé Sieyès made his plea for the Third Estate in 1789, he was referring mainly to big merchants, enterprising landowners, prosperous lawyers and magistrates, bankers—in other words, "useful" members of society, who were neither noble nor poor. Since the Revolution the upper and middle ranks of the bourgeoisie have been augmented by factory-owners, high-ranking civil servants, and people in the liberal professions. These different groups included *rentiers* and entrepreneurs, apostles of science and progress and old-fashioned conservatives, pious Christians and agnostics. But psychologically and socially they all identified themselves as members of the same class. Beginning in the early twentieth century their feeling of solidarity increased as the industrial workers became more numerous and more restive. Once such issues as the Dreyfus Case, clericalism, and monarchism —which had divided them until that time—were settled, most of them closed ranks in order to defend their property and to maintain the status quo against its Left-wing attackers.

All sections of the French bourgeoisie possessing influence, authority, and power opposed changes that might have affected their status unfavorably after the First World War. The older generation maintained its hold on business, government administration, the army, and education, all of which lacked young blood. Heavy wartime casualties had created a dearth of young men in the country as a whole, but some talented ones did manage to achieve high positions and to challenge the established hierarchies. The resulting ambiguity and contradiction in the criteria of status classification caused significant strains in French society. It tended to create situations in which competing groups claimed the right to leadership roles without having gained general recognition as legitimate leaders. This conflict over leadership and status produced sharp divisions among France's bourgeois "dynasties," and it often made them shirk their responsibilities.

Malthusianism made France ill-equipped to compete with those powers that were forging ahead of her in economic and technological progress. Once the First World War had permanently changed France's pattern of development from conservation and leisurely growth to reconstruction and replacement, lack of dynamism in the bourgeois elite retarded and sometimes strangled business activity. At the same time, the collapse of the franc, after a century of stability, demoralized those social groups whose greatest economic virtue was supposed to be thrift.

The persistence of the nineteenth-century bourgeois family pattern also retarded French acceptance of industrialization. Most French businesses remained family-structured in a way generally associated with preindustrial economies. Family and firm constituted an economic unity, with the latter serving as the material basis for the prestige of the former. The desire to preserve this relationship accounted for many conservative business practices and the avoidance of risk and credit-financing.

Even though the continued importance of the family gave French social life a stability that was lacking in Germany, Great Britain, and the United States, this family-oriented system of loyalties worked against day-to-day identification with the interests of the community. Perhaps the French had received an overdose of nationalism under the Jacobins and the two Napoleons, and many of them were reacting against it. In any case, the disparity between ideals and reality that existed concerning the slogan of social equality was also apparent with regard to the symbol of the nation. France was a nation of patriots *ideologically*, but a feeling that has been rationalized into an ideology has already lost its basic emotional force. The survival of strong family ties in twentieth-century France has helped to compensate for the relative paucity of political values to which all Frenchmen could respond in unison.

During the interwar years the French bourgeoisie increasingly resisted social as well as economic change. Acting as one of its main spokesmen, the Radical Socialists (who were neither radical nor socialist) refused to enfranchise France's women, despite their contribution to the national economy during and after the First World War. These politicians defended their antifeminist stand on the grounds that most women would vote for the Rightist parties. But it also reflected the conservative notion—shared by those very Rightists whom the Radical Socialists said they feared —that woman's place was in the home and not in public life. As for the workers, the big businessmen believed (as some of them still believe) that any concessions to them would make them lazy and more demanding than ever.

The tendency of the French bourgeoisie to shirk its responsibilities to the nation reflected a demoralization of the spirit. At the turn of the century many bourgeois Europeans were already displaying a combination of complacency and hypocrisy, which has been so well described by Henrik Ibsen, George Bernard Shaw, Thomas Mann, Roger Martin du Gard, and André Gide. Recently Jean Anouilh showed the "sick" soul of a pre-1914 retired French general in *The Waltz of the Toreadors*. Although Anouilh is primarily interested in expressing his own views on love and life, the setting of this play and the attitudes of its characters reveal much about the upper-middle classes in twentieth-century France.

General Saint-Pé believes that a person can satisfy his vanity and his physical needs as long as he keeps up appearances. He explains his "philosophy" to his secretary—an ingenuous, idealistic youth—whom he tries to mold into his own image. According to the general, a man must keep swimming with the regulation breast-stroke toward an ideal he will never reach, but which he should never lose sight of. If he wants to relieve himself in the water, no one will notice as long as he continues to swim with the regulation breast-stroke. In another "lesson" the general says that life is like a long family lunch. One must observe the proprieties of this boring ritual, but behind the back stairs one can sleep with the maid. (The theme of the bourgeois husband taking advantage of the maid is still prominent in jokes, films, and anecdotes, though there are fewer young country girls to play the part in real life.) Such is the outlook of a man who has all the bourgeois comforts and an honorable military career behind him. He is still attractive to women, but he is bored and he is the prisoner of his nagging wife.

The *malaise* of Frenchmen like General Saint-Pé—including men in business as well as in the professions—developed into a selfishness and defensiveness against anything new during the interwar years. They hated everything from the Bolsheviks and the "Lost Generation" to the effects of technological change. Then, beginning in the 1930's, they split into two groups: a small one whose guilty conscience was stronger than its hatred of change; and a larger one, whose hatred of change was stronger than its guilty conscience. (The political stand taken by these two types will be discussed in chapter 6.) But in both cases the spiritual demoralization of these people, their Malthusianism, and their cynicism, made them unfit to lead their country along the path of social democracy and economic growth.

France's bourgeois elite bore the stigma of the military defeat and occupation by the Germans in the early 1940's; it lost some of its prestige, but not its status. The temporary eclipse of the pre-war politicians and the youthfulness of the Resistance and Fighting French leaders gave many young men the opportunity to hold high government posts in the Liberation period. Women, too, were claiming the right to participate as equals in the nation's economic and political life. They had played an active role in the underground, and they had substituted in all kinds of jobs while so many men were prisoners in Germany. The Radical Socialist party, which had been the main antifeminist group in the past, was too weak to prevent them from being given the right to vote in 1945. Furthermore, they were encouraged by the Communists, who championed the view that, as in Russia, women in France should have equal rights in all fields. Still, most women and younger men did not try to change French social habits and institutions. They merely sought their places within the existing system.

Five years of war and servitude failed to produce any new elite in French society. The country's upper social strata survived the Liberation unscathed. Neither the "purge" of the more notorious collaborators nor the nationalization of a few sectors of the economy dislodged them from their strongholds in the higher ranks of business and government administration. Workers and persons with fixed incomes were hurt by the postwar inflation, but most farmers, shopkeepers, and professional people were able to maintain a decent standard of living. No old economic class was wiped out, and no new one appeared to challenge the existing hierarchy.

Even today, old class distinctions persist, in spite of the rising level of consumption of most Frenchmen. The junior executive is afraid to drive a bigger car than his boss. He continues to treat policemen and waiters as inferiors and becomes indignant if they fail to show the proper degree of servility toward him. A skilled worker no longer tolerates such treatment. He now considers his segregated status as "separate but equal." Social revolution is becoming less and less of a threat as the material comforts enjoyed by the masses increase. Meanwhile, the upper and lower levels of French society are catching up with their counterparts in Great Britain and the United States in adopting the style of life of the middle group. This change is more cultural than social, and it has been going on for a long time. The French call it *embourgeoisement*.

In France the people who have been traditionally considered bourgeois have been those who work without getting their hands dirty and who can afford the basic material comforts without living beyond their means. The proportion of Frenchmen who consider themselves entitled to this label—at least with the word "petit" in front of it—now approaches three-fourths. Since the early nineteenth century individual men and women have sought to move upward socially through guile, education, and marriage. Julien Sorel, the hero of Stendhal's *Le Rouge et le Noir*, was an early prototype of today's "angry young man," and the novels of Balzac are full of ambitious characters who seek their fortune by moving from the provinces to the capital. But most "status seekers" stayed at home and practiced thrift and birth control.

The desire of petit-bourgeois Frenchmen to live within their means brought France's population growth almost to a halt by the mid-nineteenth century. (There were 37,000,000 people in France in 1846, while one hundred years later there were 40,780,000, of whom 1,670,000 were aliens. Only since the Second World War has the historical trend toward stagnation been reversed.) In contrast to England and Germany, her provinces did not produce more children than could be eventually absorbed into the existing economic structure, as either producers or consumers. Nor was there a mass immigration comparable to that which America experienced. Even after 1900 urban and rural workers in Germany and the United States continued to have large families. The French proletariat also had a high birth rate, but this did not offset the low fertility of the other classes. Hence, the demographic pressures that may have hastened industrializaton elsewhere were lacking in France.

Through conscious individual planning millions of men and women produced few children or no children at all in order to safeguard certain social and cultural values. Lagging population growth in France was not caused by famine, poverty, or emigration, but by the fact that French women of child-bearing age were having fewer babies. With the exception of a declining number of active Catholics most small peasant-proprietors practiced some form of birth control. Their purpose in doing so was to preserve the family patrimony as an economic unit capable of insuring the security and independence of their offspring. Petty functionaries, white-collar employees, shopkeepers, and people supplying various kinds of personal services also wanted small families so that they might maintain the standard of comfort and the genteel types of work that would give them the right to be treated with civility and respect.

Given France's modest rate of economic growth before the early 1950's, these people found themselves constantly competing for security, status, and independence with limited resources at their disposal. Since each child would have to be given all the social and educational opportunities necessary for achieving these same values, most middle-class parents restricted the number of children they brought into this competitive society, with its preindustrial view of the world. Despite the laws of church and state, they exercised foresight and self-control in the most calculating ways. It has been estimated that during the 1930's there was one abortion for every two live births—and most of these abortions were procured by married couples. This kind of behavior was carrying Malthusianism to extremes.

4

La Fontaine versus Einstein

The French habit of planning is based on a strong belief that man and nature can be tamed. This view of the world reached its earliest and fullest expression in the classical art and thought of the second half of the seventeenth century. At that time philosophers, scientists, and builders believed that they had mastered the principles governing physical forces once and for all—just as Racine and Molière had done for human relations. Their conception of the world as man-centered, orderly, predictable, and complete continued to sustain the self-confidence of ordinary Frenchmen and to influence the creative forms of France's high culture for over three hundred years. The most widely read and universally accepted version of this outlook is in La Fontaine's *Fables.*

Just as one turns first to Homer in order to understand the underlying assumptions of the ancient Greeks, one should look to La Fontaine for those of the French. No less a critic than Sainte-Beuve called him France's true national poet—her Homer.

Although the privileged minority of *lycée* students learned the Cartesian method of reasoning by analysis and synthesis, Descartes was only a name to most Frenchmen. He was, after all, an abstract theorist who wanted to reduce the whole universe to a rational-mechanical system that could be expressed in mathematical formulas. Even his famous initial doubt was less in keeping with the so-called skepticism of the French than the "What-do-I-know?" attitude of his sixteenth-century predecessor, Montaigne. Like Montaigne they valued truths of detail over ambitious theories, but La Fontaine came closer to expressing all their traditional beliefs about the world around them.

La Fontaine lauds the virtues of the open mind—imbued with its own weakness, yet passionately fond of philosophizing—which leads the good fight against prejudice and superstition. Whether he talks about lions and foxes, farmers and millers, or noblemen and judges, he teaches a lesson about life in general. He is a realistic observer with a strong dose of peasant malice and bourgeois caution. His *Fables* often show a spectacle of violence, ruse, vanity, stupidity, wickedness, and the triumph of injustice, though they implicitly suggest humanity and goodness. They preach neither the nobility of disinterest nor the heroism of sacrifice. Instead, they recommend a humble practical wisdom made up of prudence, moderation, and foresight. "Good sense," according to them, consists in recognizing that things are the way they are because they are that way and that God helps him who helps himself.

The French have been no different from other nations in clinging to a traditional fund of feelings, experiences, and common-sense knowledge. They have preferred La Fontaine to Einstein, whose name has come to stand for a world in which everything is relative to something else and therefore indeterminate. Ordinary language and logic do not help us to understand a universe so conceived. Since the late nineteenth century, scientists, philosophers, and artists have tried to formulate theories and invent signs that would explain some of its mysteries, but their incompleteness, openness, and variety frighten most people away. In the interwar years most of France's writers, painters, and composers, sharing their countrymen's fear of the dehumanizing effects of science and technology, salvaged what they could from their artistic tradition and approached the problems of modern life intuitively.

Their fear was relatively new. In the eighteenth and nineteenth centuries writers like D'Alembert, Condorcet, Comte, Saint-Simon, Taine, Renan, and Littré (and Jules Verne on a more popular level) expressed the belief that science and technology would bring unlimited progress and free people from their resignation to things as they are. Politicians like Ferry and Freycinet added faith in public education and confidence in material advancement to this outlook and made Positivism the semiofficial creed of the École Polytechnique, the École Normale Supérieure, and the Republic itself. But Positivism—with its determinist laws and its apparent denial of the mind as the true source of our actions—was too impersonal a philosophy to appeal to most cultivated Frenchmen. They were primarily concerned with the individual man and with an ethic that would keep their society going.

On the metaphysical "front" Henri Bergson led the attack against Comtian Positivism, Cartesian Rationalism, and the grip of mechanics, logic, and determinism on philosophy. He rejected these in order to do justice to the concrete, the immediate, the vital. For Bergson intuition was superior to thought in its power to see all things and to describe them accurately. He maintained that the history of the evolution of life shows us that the faculty of understanding is an appendage of the faculty of acting. It is an increasingly precise, complex, and supple adaptation of the consciousness of living things to the conditions under which they live. Eventually our intelligence will create the perfect relationship of our body to its environment and allow us to be one with it. Just as we understand time as a lived experience, so we will be able to "think matter" (*penser la matière*).

Bergson's "anti-intellectualism" was an effort to arrive rationally at a just appreciation of the actual roles of rationality and nonrationality in human affairs. To his many admirers (and opponents) Bergson seemed to be saying "feeling is all." But the power of reason has never been denied for long in France. What had happened by the end of the nineteenth century was that empirical science and human thought had become artificially set against each other. Facts were said to speak for themselves, and minds were allegedly committed to dry theorizing. Indeed, from a strictly empirical, behaviorist point of view, the "mind" was a philosopher's myth, "a ghost in the machine." While admitting the limitations of this "ghost," Descartes had insisted on its power to control action and will. He had believed that there was no distinction between the real and the intelligible and that science was relative to man. Reacting against the Positivists and the Bergsonians, a few French thinkers reaffirmed this Cartesian "good sense."

In 1865 Claude Bernard published his *Introduction à l'étude de la médicine expérimentale*, in which he set forth his famous experimental method. This method, which scientists still use today, combined the kind of empiricism that consisted in accumulating facts without trying to explain them with deductive logic, which consisted in reasoning without taking the facts into account. According to Bernard, experimentation is the application of rational methods with the definite purpose of varying or changing the processes of nature. Some simple observations must precede any hypothesis, but a crude fact is not scientific. In order to proceed scientifically, we must first have an idea and then summon facts (observations) to check this previously assumed idea. It is the experiment based on a hypothesis—and not the observations that preceded it—that prove or disprove it.

For the educated layman it was Planck and Einstein, rather than Bernard, who destroyed the assumption of nineteenth-century scientists (or, at least, men who philosophized about science) that the laws of nature existed somewhere "out there" waiting to be discovered. Still, Claude Bernard anticipated these men by a generation in pointing out the hypothetical character of all explanations of the workings of the physical universe. In opposition to the Positivists, he said that determinism was a convenient and necessary postulate, formulated by human beings, rather than an immutable force beyond our control. Far from reducing the phenomena of life to mere chemicophysical processes, he reasserted the power of reason to control and improve the world around us. Like Descartes, Bernard believed that we should doubt everything until it was demonstrated and that the first certainty was the fact of our thinking.

While Bernard reintroduced logical reasoning into science, Henri Poincaré stressed mathematical reasoning as well. In the true Cartesian tradition he maintained that scientific knowledge—far from being an artificial construction—is the natural result of an agreement between the hypotheses of the mind and what we observe. But he approached Einstein and Louis de Broglie by admitting the possibility that a particular theory can be useful even though it cannot be demonstrated empirically. According to Poincaré the important thing is not the existence of ether (or quanta or waves) but that, from a certain perspective, everything happens *as if* it did exist. In other words, the ether hypothesis (in Poincaré's time, at any rate) was convenient for the explanation of natural phenomena.

A third philosopher of science who tried to reconcile the subject and the object was Léon Brunschvicg. In the early 1900's he interpreted Einstein's Theory of Relativity as a confirmation of his own conception of the interdependence of reason and experience. He did not unconsciously project the human soul into God or into things, nor did he make it dependent on them. Descartes had needed God, but he had implicitly asserted the sovereignty of human reason. Brunschvicg spelled out this implication. For him the mind is completely free, and the sciences it has created are evidence of this fact. To know is to impose the analytical and synthetical forms of thought on reality, which is a part of the mind's inner development. Descartes had said, "Give me motion and extension, and I will construct a world." For Brunschvicg too, to know was to build.

While scientists and philosophers were reasserting man's power to create a better world, some of France's creative artists began to flee from modern civilization as it had developed by the late nineteenth century. They viewed urban industry and the rising masses as filthy monsters that would destroy art and thought

71

completely. In the 1870's Arthur Rimbaud voiced the earliest protest of the sensitive aesthete against the peculiar horror of life in big cities—their restlessness and unnatural routine, the swarming misery of their slums, the smoky anonymity of their brothels and bars. He announced the poet's isolation from and opposition to all forms of democratic organization and bourgeois culture. His rebellion against the established order led him to break also with the conception of language as a rational means of conveying thought. All poetry expresses emotion, but until Rimbaud it had retained its classical mold. What he did was to strip it of all connecting links—grammar, syntax, accepted meanings of words—that stood in the way of his poet's vision.

Rimbaud sacrificed everything in his quest for the unknown and the absolute. He opposed the culture that produced him, and revealed its instability and its materialism. Having written all his major poems by the time he was twenty, he renounced literature and Europe altogether and became a drifter in Africa. The frenzy and precipitation of his own short life dramatized modern man's burning for total satisfaction in an unsatisfying temporal existence. In his "Bateau ivre" Rimbaud uses a drunken ship as the symbol of his own destiny as a poet, which is to exhaust all the possibilities of poetic imagination and adventure and then choose death.

In the eighties and nineties the Symbolist poets tried to remove their poetry from all contamination by the vulgar, modern world. They took up Rimbaud's attack against the conventions of language and deliberately cultivated obscurity of expression. Stéphan Mallarmé wanted to "give back a purer sense to the words of the tribe." Along with the other Symbolists, he tried to create a form of speech that revealed our inner powers and that had its own value as pure sound. His ambition to write poetry that would live by itself and for itself was a form of exile, comparable to Rimbaud's real exile from European civilization. Mallarmé's sonnet, "Le vierge, le vivace, et le bel aujourd'hui," compares the poet imprisoned by the real world to a swan whose wings are caught in a frozen lake. It seems to be saying that the sensitive man is prevented from developing his personality fully in the crass, smug society of the 1890's.

Impressonist painters and composers used colors and sounds as evocative symbols in the same way that Mallarmé and Verlaine used words. Renoir, Monet, and Seurat "transmuted" the world they painted by dissolving its conventional forms and patterns into a soft haze and by suggesting its hidden beauties through nuances of color. (Gauguin, like Rimbaud, preferred to abandon the modern world altogether.) In order to express his vague, subtle impressions Debussy used unconventional harmonies and uneven rhythms, which seemed ultra-sophisticated in their day. His *L'Après-midi d'un faune*, based on a Mallarmé poem, was as far from the sordid, commonplace world as one could get without renouncing the European artistic tradition completely.

Then, around 1905, a new art appeared that broke emphatically with the recent past and tried to cope with the modern world in its own terms. The poet Guillaume Apollinaire took life as he found it and described it precisely and energetically. He was not afraid to talk about automobiles, airplanes, the Eiffel Tower, or "les becs de gaz [qui] pissaient leur flamme au clair de lune." The Cubist painters and sculptors stripped their objects of all adventitious aids to expressiveness and relied solely on the formal structure of their straight lines and curves, hard surfaces, and solid forms in constructing a sharp-edged, architectural art for the twentieth century.

In music, as in painting, a "primitive" foreigner came to Paris during the immediate prewar years and jolted French art out of the pleasant rut of Impressionism. For Igor Stravinsky, like Pablo Ruiz Picasso, had a greater impact on his fellow artists in France than any native son. Both men first gained notoriety by rejecting the egocentric cult of personal sensitivity and harking back to the expressive forms of prehistoric tribes. The riot that *Le Sacre du printemps* provoked at its first performance in 1913 was not just another manifestation of Parisian pique. It was a call to defend French culture from this monster that had come out of some primeval forest to destroy it.

Aside from a few "first-nighters" and cultivated dilettantes the French people had no vital contact with the innovators in their midst in the early 1900's. A handful of artists, scientists, and philosophers announced the bankruptcy of the traditional forms, theories, and beliefs that had given Europeans the illusion of dominating an ordered, recognizable world. They wanted to grasp a reality whose existence the average person did not even suspect. Poets, painters, and composers tried to fathom it by inventing new "languages." Physicists like Henri Becquerel and Pierre and Marie Curie were discovering that inorganic "matter," far from being inert, had radioactive properties whose powers could not yet be predicted. Bergson asserted that everything in nature was relative to something else and constantly changing. In place of complacency and sterile theorizing he urged his countrymen to seek direct contact with life and the surging aspects of experience in order to achieve a higher stage of evolution. But the majority of Frenchmen preferred to live like semiretired pensioners counting their blessings and cultivating their gardens. They still wanted to believe that La Fontaine provided all the answers.

Then the First World War and the accelerated pace of industrialization that accompanied it brought an increasing number of Frenchmen face to face with an unpeasant and unreasonable world in which their traditional outlook was an inadequate guide. Even those who tried to adjust themselves to it (following La Fontaine's precept of making the best of things as they are) were further discouraged by the assertions of many scientists that nothing was what it seemed to be. Einstein pointed out the possibility of transforming atoms into energy in the form of light and heat, and Max Planck said that energy was composed of grains of atoms and electrons, thus destroying the wave theory of light. In 1924 Louis de Broglie reconciled the wave and quantum theories as two different ways of looking at the same thing. Later revisions by other physicists contested the very principle of determinism in the movements of atoms. Meanwhile, cultural anthropology and Freudian psychology were showing that institutions and a strong set of personal habits established in early infancy stood between the individual and his learning of the truth.

While France's greatest contributions to science have been based on the use of mathematics, ordinary Frenchmen have been reluctant to let x equal anything they could not see with their own eyes. But since the "revolution" in physics at the turn of the century scientific achievements have no longer been an enlargement of operations that are part of the natural world and comprehensible to the senses. They are the result of theories and hypotheses constructed in rigorous mathematical terms. (In 1960 a young French physicist named Jean Charon made the latest attempt to find a mathematical function that would include the laws governing gravitational, electromagnetic, and nuclear forces. He was able to verify some of the constants he used—such as the elementary electrical charge and the mass of the electron—with the aid of electronic testing machines.) Mathematicians have viewed "matter" successively as a form of energy, a function, and now an activity. Although the physical things the French people know through everyday perception seem solid enough, their new *Encyclopédie française* tells them that a molecule or an atom is not a "thing" but an activity that is always going on, like a dance. The component parts of an atom are not substances either. They are rather like themes in a picture or a dance, visible as forms in space, though not subsisting in space.

For over sixty years French scientists, mathematicians, and philosophers have made various attempts to reconcile the immediately given with the universe of science and to show that scientific activity could benefit mankind. The mathematician Henri Poincaré said that, even though no ethical imperative can be deduced from the principles of science, a man who is in a position to feel the splendid harmony of the laws of nature will be disposed to conquer his paltry selfish interests. He believed that the same is true regarding co-operation and the striving for truth, without which no science can exist. During the interwar years the physicists Paul Langevin and Jean Perrin carried on a campaign for the moral and intellectual liberation of France through a kind of scientific humanism. Men like Émile Durkheim, Lucien Lévy-Bruhl, and Pierre Janet also stressed the humanistic goals of sociology, anthropology, and psychology. In an age of increasing specialization, the historian Marc Bloch urged social scientists to work together as teams in the field, instead of isolating themselves from one another and society. The logician and philosopher of science Gaston Bachelard said that scientific reason is not just an elaboration of the empirical but an autonomous power of construction.

Until recently, though, French scientists had little influence on national policy, and their talents were neglected by the government, industry, and the general public. Almost all Frenchmen tended to think of pure research as a separate compartment from practical affairs; their "logic" told them that these were two unrelated categories of activity. The scientists themselves did not usually challenge this view. Besides, they had their own battles to fight. Despite the fact that her Academy of Sciences dated back to the seventeenth century, no modern nation had been more unimaginative and tightfisted than France in providing the resources and accommodations that scientific activity requires. Everyone has heard about the deplorable conditions under which Louis Pasteur and the Curies made their famous discoveries. Until the Second World War research facilities were mainly confined to university campuses, where lack of space and funds made it difficult for French professors to train advanced students in their laboratories, as the Germans did.

After 1850 the French lost the century-old leadership they had held in European science during an age when most scientists worked in isolation from one another. As individual initiative gradually gave way to collective activity and state control, France began to lag behind Germany and England. Her manpower losses in the First World War hastened this decline. Petit-bourgeois opposition to government spending, and the backwardness of private industry in fostering research prevented France from creating new scientific institutions. In addition, her educational system neglected the experimental method in the teaching of the natural sciences. Finally, during the first half of the twentieth century certain social and intellectual groups, including many conservative Catholics, continued to devalue science as an approach to knowledge.

Clerical authoritarians repeated the arguments against science that dated back to Joseph de Maistre, Louis de Bonald, and Paul Bourget. In England and the United States the Fundamentalists were mainly non-intellectuals, and the educated classes in these countries were generally not antiscientific after the turn of the twentieth century. But French opponents of "scientism" have often been cultivated and articulate. They expressed in an extreme form the feelings of millions of *bien-pensants*. Until the Second World War most university students came from this background, and they tended to share their parents' indifference and contempt for scientific and technological achievements.

Even those Frenchmen who had studied the natural sciences and mathematics in school often continued to think of them as accumulations of facts and theorems that one memorized. For them "rationalism" was the philosophy of two and two makes four. They were bewildered by the multiplicity of original systems—non-Euclidean geometry, mathematical chemistry, etc.—that human reason could produce. These creations showed them the strange new lack of attachment on the part of scientists for any fixed perspective. This kind of freedom had nothing in common with that of a mind open to every event. The scientist prepared his own events. While he claimed to benefit from the possibility of switching from one system to another, outsiders found this kind of intellectual mobility hard to understand. How could science and mathematics have any value if they were not attached to certain basic elements: molecules, cells, rational numbers—anything?

Another line of attack on the value of science was based on the uses to which it was put, especially through technology. Aside from the obvious case of military weapons, this view was concerned with the bad cultural effects of technological progress. An article in the popular and influential magazine *L'Illustration* in January, 1929, charged that a few scientists and engineers invent machines and techniques that relieve the ordinary person from having to use his intelligence. It went on to say that the twentieth-century Frenchman is at the opposite extreme from the seventeenth-century *honnête homme*. Pushing aside culture, reflection, and well-ordered ideas, he is interested exclusively in sports, pleasure, and business (which, according to this article, the "good sense" of his seventeenth-century predecessor disdained). The article concludes with the prediction that society will eventually be divided between an elite of scientists and a mass of healthy automatons; and maybe someday thinkers can be dispensed with in a completely automatic, mechanized world.

Contemporary science has shown its ability to improve upon nature and to transform men, but there are people who argue that scientific knowledge cannot change human nature. As their country moved from a handcart culture to an IBM culture, the French clung to old-fashioned ways of doing things because they did not want to become robots. Their moralists, novelists, and playwrights had heightened their own awareness of human motivations and relationships and given them psychological insights that made them believe they knew most of what there was to know about human behavior. They recognized irrational impulses, but from childhood on these were institutionalized in harmless channels. Until recently most Frenchmen hesitated to admit the importance of an unconscious over which they had no control. They looked upon psychology as a pretentious discipline that tried to camouflage what everybody knew behind an incomprehensible jargon. (Today, however, the uneducated masses are beginning to acknowledge the usefulness of psychoanalysis—at least in a joking way. The typical cab-driver used to say to someone he disagreed with, "You're nuts!" Now he says, "Go get yourself psychoanalyzed, man!")

Perhaps the best-known foe of technological civilization in France is the novelist Georges Duhamel. How, he asks, can his country hope to maintain its humanistic values when factories operated by industrial cannon fodder turn out masses of goods that standardize the lives of those who use them? From his first attack on life as he saw it in the United States (*Scènes de la vie future*, 1930) to his recent allegory about hell (*Nouvelles du sombre empire*, 1960) he has rejected industrialization and its organizational techniques as a return to barbarism. Each morning the almost half a million readers of *Le Figaro* can watch him shed a tear over a patch of grass being replaced by a superhighway or a stream that must be diverted from its natural course in order to serve the needs of a hydroelectric power plant.

Other writers have also expressed their anxiety concerning the ruinous effects of science and technology. Georges Bernanos protested against them in his *La France contre les robots*, and Paul Valéry compared scientists and engineers to "a fleet of ships immobilized in a fog." The standard image in all these attacks is that of the sorcerer's apprentice who can no longer control the powers he has created. More recently Père Dubarle took up this line in his review (in *Le Monde*, December 28, 1948) of Norbert Wiener's book *Cybernetics*. Here the issue was the mass manipulation of human beings. According to Père Dubarle, stability of prediction regarding human behavior is unrealizable in a free society. Stabilization in a mathematical sense can be guaranteed only by the submission of the masses—either voluntarily or by being mesmerized—to a skilled "human engineer." "This is a hard lesson of cold mathematics, but it throws a certain light on the adventure of our century: hesitation between an indefinite turbulence in human affairs and the rise of a prodigious Leviathan. In comparison with this one, Hobbes' Leviathan was nothing but a pleasant joke."

While most French intellectuals have tried to follow the precepts of La Fontaine rather than admit their insignificance and impotence in the incomprehensible world postulated by contemporary scientists, a significant number of them have paid heed to that other seventeenth-century moralist, Blaise Pascal. Like Einstein, he too explored the eternal silence of the infinite spaces (he even constructed a computing machine). According to him, man might be merely a reed, but he was "a thinking reed." Yet Pascal was deeply pessimistic: "We wish for truth and find only uncertainty. We look for happiness, and find only misery and death." He believed that, while religion alone could redeem us from this fate, most men tried to console themselves with various forms of entertainment. They cannot find peace or pleasure in a room by themselves, so they throw themselves into conventional activities in order to blot out the unknown with the familiar.

Among twentieth-century Catholic philosophers Jacques Maritain preferred to return to the humanistic Christianity of Thomas Aquinas, but Maurice Blondel and Gabriel Marcel revived the tradition of Pascal (which really went back to Augustine). Blondel said that all our earthly actions and speculations leave us with a sense of incompleteness, which only the contemplation of God can overcome. Marcel spoke even more dramatically of man's despair when he becomes aware of the void that surrounds his existence. For him, the leap across this void to God was the only way to prevent ourselves from being treated as mere objects, which was the way he thought scientists viewed us. Another Catholic, Emmanuel Mounier, was more optimistic about man's place in the world. His philosophy of Personalism maintained that the human individual is not an object to be observed but a center of reorientation for the objective universe.

Religious philosophy, whether pessimistic or optimistic, did not make the world of science and technology palatable or understandable to most Frenchmen; nor were the *avant-garde* artists much help. Fauvism and Cubism had already begun to transform painting, just as depth psychology and mathematical physics were transforming science. Neoprimitivism was merely a stage in the development of modern art, and its products were meaningful only to those people for whom plastic forms are a symbolic language. Fetishes did not invade the factories, farms, or bourgeois living rooms of Western Europe until long after the artistic elite had abandoned them to the decorators. The one modern art form that reached the masses immediately was that last incarnation of storytelling: the movies. They might well ask: Who needs another Michelangelo or Delacroix when we have Jean Renoir and Cecil B. De Mille?

Despoiled—or relieved—of their secondary functions as portraitists and storytellers, European artists devoted themselves to experimenting with painting as a unique medium of expression. They sought the reality of life beneath or beyond conventional appearances. But if art is to be meaningful to the members of a given society, its symbolic forms must be derived from the real forms of their culture. When painters reduced factory chimneys, newspaper mastheads, or machines to symbols they were certainly trying to do this. It takes generations, however, for a new artifact to become a symbol in the popular imagination. Most people see modern "things" in a literally factual way, not as signifying anything.

Usually an object or a sign has to be related to a myth or a rite before it acquires symbolic meaning. Few Frenchmen have thought of the machines they use as sources of emotional or mental satisfaction, in the way that earlier craftsmen viewed their tools, or sailors their ships. The kind of work that most modern men and women do is not part of a meaningful pattern, nor do they find much vital import in the hackneyed symbols of nature or the state. Despite its continued importance for millions of individuals, religion too has lost its function of giving meaning to the life of the group through its rites. The forms associated with it have either been abandoned or converted to purely decorative uses.

When Picasso paints a picture of a nightmarish woman with eyes and nose shown from both the front and the side, sitting in a chair that is about to collapse, he may be offering us his vision of a personality disintegrating in the horror of a crumbling civilization. He may also be transferring the Einsteinian idea of simultaneity from the physical world to the visual one, where it shocks our psychological experience of what is "natural" even more. Or, as one wag says, he may simply be painting like Picasso. Perhaps he unwittingly reveals the archetypal images of some Jungian collective unconscious. If so, his monsters are Spanish, rather than French. For Picasso's art is that of a great civilized cave man of Altamira.

Henri Matisse comes much closer to the sensitive Frenchman's intuitive interpretation of modern life. He seems to seek the small, the select, and the luxurious aspects of things. By holding on to a fixed focus, a single line of sight, he paints passionately, swiftly, and intensely an image in which every detail is part of a visual whole. Aside from his early canvases like "Joy of Life," "Dance," "Music," and his murals of the thirties, most of Matisse's paintings show a seated woman or a still life bathed with light from an open window or a French door. He feels that "the space from the horizon to the inside of the room is continuous and that the boat which passes lives in the same space as the familiar objects around me: the wall around the window does not create two universes" (from a Vichy radio broadcast in 1942). Here indeed was the way the French would like to view their relationship to the world around them.

Matisse's style is essentially abstract, though his paintings are usually figurative in appearance. Except for his "Odalisques" of the twenties he treats his models as mere forms around which to arrange colorful clothes and objects. By the thirties his surfaces are completely flat, and he does not hesitate to distort parts of the body in order to meet the demands of his composition. Whether his women are looking at a bowl of goldfish, a Chinese box, or nothing at all, they seemed bored and inert in their clean, modern surroundings. There is no hint of war, death, or unconscious fears (which are so overpowering in Picasso) in Matisse's works. He deals with love and life and expresses his feelings about them exclusively through color and design.

Like many sophisticated Frenchmen, Matisse accepted modern *chic* in the arts, clothes, and interior decoration without being interested in the underlying technological, spiritual, and political transformations of the twentieth century. During the crises of the thirties he continued to paint his elegant mannequins and still lifes. In 1937 Picasso created his "Guernica" and Matisse his "Lady in Blue." There could be no greater contrast between two works and the kinds of feelings they suggest.

While Matisse continued to use the same symbolic forms throughout the interwar period, other artists tried to give expression to the world around them in more direct ways. In the 1920's Purists like Piet Mondrian, Le Corbusier (Édouard Jeanneret), Jean Arp, and Juan Gris declared that impersonal, standardized, modern objects should be the subject matter of artistic creations. Precise geometrical forms expressed the spirit of the age best for them. But this striving for "pure abstraction," like neoprimitivism, was also a way of taming the forces that threatened contemporary life, by reducing them to fixed conceptual images. An Arp statue and a Mondrian canvas resemble Paul Valéry's *Cimetière marin* (see p. 91) and the arid, neoclassical compositions of Stravinsky and his French disciples of the late twenties in their effort to "blot out the living."

Fernand Léger was the artist who most self-consciously tried to create an artistic style for the machine age. During the First World War he became impressed with what he thought was the sympathy of technicians and workers for the machine and their optimism toward it as an expression of human power. He conveys this feeling vividly in "The Mechanic" and "The Construction Workers." Like the Purists he believed that geometrical forms could be used as symbols of an industrial society, though he introduced representational details of the modern work-a-day world into his paintings. Between 1910 and 1924 Léger substituted tubes for cubes as the basic elements in the anonymous, constructive whole he wanted each of his pictures to be. He made his human figures somewhat more conventional in his later works, but he always presented them as objects in violent contrast with the mechanical objects around them. Actually, his non-representational "Compositions," with their dynamic, flowing forms and contrasting colors, are more expressive artistically than his glorifications of the working man, who was as unimpressed with Léger as he was with Socialist Realism and Surrealism.

The Surrealists tried to express the emotional climate of the interwar years by exposing specific unconscious feelings in an almost clinical way. Indeed, André Breton, the leader of this group, was a trained psychiatrist, in addition to being a poet. Yves Tanguy and André Masson were the main French Surrealist painters. They rejected the overintellectual approach of the Cubists and Purists and deliberately tried to evoke dreamlike feelings by combining photographic images with Expressionistic symbols. Their goal was to provide a kind of twentieth-century mythology of the unconscious. But true popular myths feed on a living tradition, not on the arbitrary symbolic language of artists—or the movies, animated cartoons, and advertising copy, all of which have converted Surrealist and Abstractionist techniques into mass-production formulas (Disney is the poor man's Dali). Thus, the *Sturm und Drang* movements of the twenties failed to create a style for contemporary civilization.

Georges Rouault was the major interpreter of the Catholic view of the world in modern French painting. He resembled the medieval friar who converted unbelievers by hitting them over the head with a crucifix. Unlike the German Expressionists, with whom he is sometimes linked, Rouault was neither a nihilist nor a revolutionary, although he too exposed the sordid side of life with satire and brutality. His mosaic-like clowns and saints express pain and humiliation, but through his artist's vision they are somehow saved. Merely pious Christians are repelled by Rouault, while those who still "see" the world through the "eyes" of a suffering Christ have compared him to El Greco.

Most French artists resembled Matisse—rather than Rouault, Tanguy, and Léger—in shying away from the "wasteland" of contemporary civilization during the twenties and thirties. Georges Braque was interested in the abstract beauty of a few objects on a table, and he painted them in the classical tradition of Chardin, Corot, and Cézanne. Miserly with his means and painstaking in his craftsmanship, Braque was the ideal painter from the traditional French point of view. He once said that he "liked the rule that keeps emotion in check," though his self-imposed restraint did not prevent his rich sensitivity from expressing itself in a lyrical manner. While Braque used a modified, humanized, Cubist style and small interior settings, Maurice Utrillo depicted rows of simple houses in an almost photographic way. Like Utrillo, Raoul Dufy was "representational," although the vivid levity of his landscapes and modern seaside resorts expresses a more satirical view of life.

By 1920 France had "domesticated" the Stravinsky of *Le Sacre du printemps*, and it was he, along with Erik Satie and "Les Six" (a movement of the early twenties, consisting of Darius Milhaud, Francis Poulenc, Arthur Honegger, Georges Auric, Germaine Tailleferre, and Georges Durey), who broke the main paths that French music was to follow during the interwar years. In their efforts to restore the sense of melodic and rhythmic pattern and to reintegrate traditional materials in untraditional ways they were reasserting the relation between the act of the creator and the world of creation, which is the *sine qua non* of all the arts in France. Only after the Second World War were some of the younger composers to experiment with the more revolutionary techniques of Arnold Schönberg.

Just as the paintings of Matisse and Braque seem tame compared with those of the German Expressionists, so the compositions of Stravinsky, Poulenc, and Milhaud between 1925 and 1940 sound classical and even flippant compared with those of Schönberg and his disciples. Leaving aside the technical aspects of the twelve-tone serial system, the uninitiated listener finds the compositions of the Viennese innovator grating, tense, and often frenetic. His Third and Fourth String Quartets have a strained, groping quality that suggests a tortured nightmare—a kind of coherent madness in four movements. Anton von Webern and Alban Berg were able to achieve purity of form and moments of lyricism, but their music, like that of their master, was meaningless to the French.

Unlike Schönberg, Satie, "Les Six," and Stravinsky salvaged isolated musical forms from the sunken concert hall of the post-Romantic era, dehydrated them, gave them artificial respiration, and tried to get them moving again. Motion, not life, is the main feeling these revived creatures convey. They avoid furtive caresses, feverishness, and miasma and concentrate on a kind of locomotive beat interspersed with fragments of dry lyricism and syncopation. Woodwind and percussive instruments were preferred to strings and brass in such works. Like the Purist painters of the same period, "Les Six" wanted to reduce their expressive forms to short, simple essays.

Many postwar composers in France and other Western countries were temporarily attracted to primitive and popular musical forms, and they borrowed themes and rhythms from carnivals, music halls, and Harlem night clubs. They added the trombone slides of American jazz to the percussive syncopation of jungle drums from Africa and Brazil. Perhaps this was their way of expressing an unconscious longing for lost innocence and naïveté. (Julian Benda would have said that they were abandoning their obligations to High Culture and succumbing to the Revolt of the Masses.) In any case the new aesthetic in French music was comparable to the use of factory chimneys and African masks in painting and the efforts of poets and novelists to borrow images from billboards, newspapers, and trains.

Arthur Honegger's *Pacific 231* combines primitive and ultra-modern feelings in a truly spectacular way, but, in general, he is more serious than the other members of "Les Six." There are still undertones of Bach and Wagner in his orchestral and choral works. His *Roi David* and *Jeanne d'Arc au Bucher* express dark passions, heroism, religious exaltation, animal joy, and even a little black magic. By the late twenties Honegger had abandoned the simplicity of Stravinksy and "Les Six" and was giving an architectural effect to his music. It is more intense and dramatic than that of Milhaud, Poulenc, Auric, Jacques Ibert, and Jean Françaix.

These composers wrote in a light, almost popular style, using simple melodic lines which they embellished with modern harmonies and rhythms. Françaix's suite *The Emperor's New Clothes* and his Concertino for Piano and Orchestra are slick, facile, and unromantic—like the "modernistic" style of French furniture in the 1930's. Much of Ibert's and Poulenc's music conveys the same feeling, though Poulenc is not always superficial. In his Concerto in G Minor for Organ, String Orchestra, and Timpani he combines lyricism, force, and repose with his usual Parisian wit and self-assurance. His cantata *Sécheresses* describes with a deadpan seriousness the effect of a plague of locusts and a drought on a once-thriving community. One suspects that Poulenc is gay and easy-going in most of his works because he wants to avoid facing the parched, futureless world he describes in *Sécheresses*.

Despite their notoriety, the compositions of "Les Six" and Stravinsky were less expressive of the kinds of feelings that appealed to most sensitive Frenchmen than the polished master-pieces of Maurice Ravel. Though he had written his best works by 1920, Ravel continued to compose until 1932; he died in 1937 at the age of sixty-two. At his funeral the minister of education, Jean Zay, summed up his accomplishments in the following way:

> If I call to mind the greatest names in our moral and artistic tradition
> . . . I am led to ask myself what is the common factor in all this genius,
> and what is essential to Ravel's genius; I think I have found it

throughout to be a supremely intelligent capacity to contemplate phenomena, however passionate or moving, and to submit such phenomena to the discipline of a style. No power of emotion is excluded from the French tradition. . . . [But] when we submit we do not go under.

Ravel displays in his music the same kind of controlled emotion that Matisse and Braque show in their paintings. His *Tombeau de Couperin* combines classic elegance with modern harmony and counterproint the way Braque does in his still lifes. The pagan, sophisticated hedonism of *Daphnis et Chloé* conveys feelings similar to those of Matisse's "Joy of Life" or his mural "The Dance" in the Barnes Foundation in Philadelphia. Ravel can be exotic, brilliant, or solemn, but he is always fastidious. Even when he is sensual he never wallows with his eyes closed. As a self-conscious Frenchman he wants to see and to direct the course of his enjoyment. The intelligence, craftsmanship, and fastidious sensuality of Ravel's music are highly valued qualities in French culture; so is his essentially non-romantic view of the world. Although his works offer an unfailing charm and elegance, they lack what Gide once said he missed in the French novel, "the virile *élan* of adventure and exploration, the salty breeze from the sea and the wide horizons and open spaces."

La Valse (1920) consciously suggests the disintegration of pre-war European civilization, but Ravel sees this event in a very French way. His expression of it is no Wagnerian *Götterdämmerung*, nor is it like T. S. Eliot's "The Hollow Men," for whom the world ends with a whimper. Like Matisse's "Lady in Blue," *La Valse* seems to show the relentless depersonalization and decay of a once-beautiful woman through a series of face-liftings. She wants to die in style.

After 1920 Ravel tried to keep up with the times by incorporating dissonance and jazz into his works. In his lyrical fantasy *L'Enfant et les sortilèges* (1925) a persistent and fine boring drill pierces the wall of a prison which all the furies of *La Valse* had hardly touched. Ravel repudiates thematic development and the continuity of recitative in this little opera in an effort to be "modern." Even so, the enchanted world he creates satisfies the same kind of escapist aestheticism that Jean Giraudoux cultivated in his plays and novels (see p. 98).

Ravel's final work, the Piano Concerto in G Major (1931), has a last movement that calls to mind an old prima ballerina who has starved herself so she can fit into a size twelve dress, has put on a pound of rouge, and has tried to make a comeback in a fast-stepping revue. Because she has real talent and is used to learning new routines, she gives a spectacular performance; but she collapses after the curtain comes down.

Though six years Ravel's senior, Albert Roussel successfully made the jump from "the pleasant grooves of the Gallic modernists, with their Impressionist twilights and misty, pagan afternoons, their poetic nature-painting and their sensuous but well-bred ironies, and landed . . . in the strange new world of the ultra-moderns, where tonalities whose families do not speak try desperately to occupy the same space at the same time and keys lie side by side without love" (Lawrence Gilman in a New York Philharmonic Orchestra program book of 1935). In his Third and Fourth Symphonies and his *Bacchus et Ariane* suite—all written in the early 1930's—Roussel developed a new manner that showed how a twentieth-century Frenchman who was over fifty could be as up to date as Stravinsky, Honegger, and Bartók and still preserve a humanistic and aesthetic approach to life. His late works express the kind of human energy that produced the ocean liner "Normandie," crack railroad trains, the dam at Kembs, the International Exposition of 1937—and the Maginot Line! In the arts as in other fields, some of the "modernists" in France were willing to move forward, but no further. Though they recognized the relativistic and fragmented character of the world, they wanted to order the fragments in a meaningful frame.

5

Humanists in a Wasteland

During the interwar years many of France's literary "modernists" did not want to move forward into what they considered the wasteland of contemporary civilization. Instead, they made themselves the officer corps of a rear-guard defense against its dehumanizing aspects. A number of the older "generals" went on "sick call" and withdrew to rest havens where they could play at art until the white barbarians passed them by. Others sulked in their tents, nostalgically recalling images of a glorious past. The more revolutionary "junior officers" issued naïve manifestoes about how things should be in the future. Some of them tried to project humanist values into Marxism, while others turned to action for its own sake. But all these poets, novelists, and playwrights wanted their countrymen to continue the struggle.

In trying to salvage what they had most cherished in the pre-1914 era, the French were not essentially different from other Europeans. But the First World War was a cataclysm from which Europe was never able to recover completely. It had unleashed forces that were soon to destroy what was left of the liberal, parliamentary, humanitarian tradition. Nationalism and socialism, which had apparently been tamed by 1914, were to assume unbelievably virulent forms in Germany and Russia, the two major wartime losers. Instead of assuring a return to the good old days, the war aroused mass passions that made it possible for Lenin, Mussolini, and Hitler to set up totalitarian regimes and to destroy the decency and freedom that the Europeans thought they had been fighting for.

The First World War did not *cause* the decline of France and the European civilization she exemplified. It only hastened the end of the reign of flamboyant individualism that had already begun to succumb to anti-intellectualism, apathy, and the flood of collectivist philosophies by the turn of the century. The poet and essayist Paul Valéry saw and described the crisis of the humanist tradition immediately after the war. His analysis is worth considering not only because it is full of insights but also because he was France's unofficial poet laureate and a spokesman for the French Academy during the interwar period.

In his essay *La Crise de l'esprit* Valéry reviewed the familiar development of modern European civilization from Greek, Roman, and Christian values. By the twentieth century the people who had made this civilization had become intellectually "modern," like the Romans in Trajan's time or the Greeks in Alexandria under the Ptolemies. This "modernism" was characterized by an empty eclecticism. The mind of each cultured person had become a crossroads for all species of opinion. Each thinker was a world's fair of ideas.

After describing the thoughtful European's state of mind in 1914, Valéry turned to the immediate postwar period. Paraphrasing the graveyard scene from Shakespeare's play, he created a humanist Hamlet meditating on the ghosts of past controversies, achievements, discoveries, knowledge, and glory. His Hamlet felt incapable of renewing the boundless activity that had created his civilization. He was tired of producing new ideas. Besides, the world had abandoned thought for action. Should he, too, follow the movement of the times like Polonius, who ran a big daily newspaper, like Laertes, who was an aeronautical engineer, or like

Rosenkrantz, who had joined the Communist party? He concluded his monologue with the observation that the world had no more need for individual creative minds. In a few more years modern progress would have created the perfect ant-heap society.

Paul Valéry and his literary spokesman Monsieur Teste resembled many twentieth-century French intellectuals in their desire to withdraw from a world that was hostile to reason. Monsieur Teste (from the Latin *testis*, meaning "witness") detached himself from it in order to understand it intellectually and to judge it objectively. He wanted to reduce all reality to clear ideas and thus avoid being duped by any illusions. His watchword was "Worldly things interest me only as they are related to the intellect."

Here was the twentieth-century inversion of the humanist credo: I am a man, and nothing human can be alien to me. It preserved only half of the traditional outlook of humanism—the rational half. For the complete humanist also glorifies the emotional, intuitive, and religious side of man, as Augustine, Pascal, Rousseau, and Bergson had done. Valéry, on the contrary, wanted to free his mind as much as possible from the deterministic aspects of existence. He was therefore at the opposite pole from the Existentialists as well, since they put existence first and insisted that the intellectual must commit himself (*s'engager*) to it in some way in order to assert himself as an individual.

In Valéry's greatest artistic creation, *Le Cimetière marin*, a poet looking at the Mediterranean Sea feels the need to think. The sea is a symbol of the mind for him. Its active surface is unchanged by the waves with their pendular rhythm of flux and reflux. Valéry finds in this image a perfect expression of thought, which is transparence without transcendence, an exercise without an object, balancing life against death, being against nothingness, and which leaves on the shore a few hard ideas and solid verses like beautiful seashells, sonorous, sparkling, and cold.

According to Valéry, individual liberty is possible only in the realm of ideas, which alone is capable of revealing our existence to us and giving us a few joys. This view was widespread among French writers in the twenties (and was to reassert itself during the early forties under the German occupation). Valéry was pessimistic regarding the future of the belletristic tradition of humanist culture—a tradition compelled to specialize more and more and driven further inward on itself by industrialism and democratic education. He believed that as language became more international and more technical, it would become less capable of supplying the symbols of literature. Just as the development of mechanical devices was compelling us to resort to sports in order to exercise our muscles, so literature would survive as a game—a series of specialized experiments in the domain of symbolic expression and imaginative values attained through the free combination of the elements of language.

Valéry was probably right in relating the development of extremely difficult and subtle literary works written in a complicated style—and hence forbidden to most readers—to the increase in the number of literates and the consequent production of mediocre and average works. His prediction that this trend would be permanent was to be disproved by the realistic writings of the 1930's and 1940's. But in the 1920's many sensitive people—in France and elsewhere in Europe—were especially hospitable to an esoteric literature that was indifferent to action and unconcerned with the group. They seemed to feel impoverished and exhausted as a result of the war and to lose confidence in the possibility that political action could solve their problems. Some of them became skeptical about all attempts to organize men into social units—armies, parties, nations—in the service of some common ideal or for the accomplishment of some specific purpose.

Like a number of writers after the First World War, Valéry suffers anguish over the existence of death in living persons. In *Le Cimetière marin* he says:

> La vrai rongeur, le ver irréfutable
> N'est point pour vous qui dormez sous la table,
> Il vit de vie, il ne me quitte pas!

For him the true death is not that of corpses in their tombs—they have lost consciousness—it is that of living persons who die and who know they are dying. He sees not only himself but his world being eaten away by an "irrefutable worm."

"Concierge," photograph by Robert Doisneau, from Rapho Guillumette Pictures, New York City, reprinted from *Vogue*, Copyright © 1951, The Condé Nast Publications Inc.

Under the watchful eye of the apartment-house concierge. . .

Maurice Utrillo, "Impasse Trainée, à Montmartre,"
courtesy of the French Embassy Press & Information Division,
New York City.

. . . or behind the closed shutters of their individual dwellings, most Frenchmen have traditionally valued their personal privacy.

Hôtel des Invalides,
courtesy of the French Embassy Press & Information Division.

The slightly faded grandeur of earlier times is still an important part of the Parisian landscape.

La Maison de la Radio under construction,
courtesy of the French Cultural Services,
New York City.

But the construction of ultra-modern buildings like the Maison de la Radio (now completed) is rapidly altering the appearance of the French capital.

The countryside is also being transformed. Here is a view of the Donzère-Mondragon hydroelectric power plant on the Rhone River.

The Donzère-Mondragon hydroelectric power plant,
courtesy of the French Embassy Press & Information Division.

The destruction of the Bastille in 1789 marked the beginning of the Revolt of the Masses.

"Les Grandes Journées Révolutionnaires—Démolition de la Bastille," contemporary engraving, courtesy of the French Embassy Press & Information Division.

"Sire, ce linceul vaut bien la croix!" *image d'Épinal* (1837), courtesy of the French Embassy Press & Information Division.

But until the late nineteenth century the Napoleonic legend stirred more French hearts than the democratic tradition. In this image d'Épinal *a dying soldier thanks the Emperor for giving him his own cloak and says that it is worth more to him than any medal.*

"At the Theater," drawing by Constantin Guys,
The Bettmann Archive.

*The upper
classes . . .*

*. . . and the
masses a
century ago.*

Honoré Daumier, "A Third-Class Railway Coach,"
The Bettmann Archive.

"Procession de Notre-Dame de Boulogne-sur-mer," photograph by Goursat, courtesy of the French Embassy Press & Information Division.

Religion is still an important part of the lives of many Frenchmen.

"Fête Dieu," photograph by René Messager, Rapho Guillumette Pictures.

Catholic magazines and newspapers in France,
courtesy of the French Embassy Press & Information Division.

*Today the Catholic press uses all the techniques of the mass media.
Its comic books—*Âmes Vaillantes, Coeurs Vaillants, Bayard, *and*
Bernadette—*have a combined sale of almost a million copies.*

Georges-Pierre Seurat, final study for "Un dimanche d'été à la Grande-Jatte," courtesy of the French Cultural Services.

At the end of the nineteenth century most bourgeois Frenchmen were oblivious to new developments in science and the arts.

Pablo Picasso, "Nus,"
courtesy of the French Embassy Press & Information Division.

*Well into the twentieth century they found no meaning in new expressive
forms like this one.*

A country road sixty miles northwest of Paris,
courtesy of the French Government Tourist Office, New York City.

France can be seen as a land of balance or a land of contrasts—
depending on one's point of view.

A steel plant in Lorraine,
courtesy of the French Government Tourist Office.

Honoré Daumier, "Les gens de justice,"
courtesy of the French Cultural Services.

*In the nineteenth and early twentieth centuries the legal profession
attracted more university students than any other.*

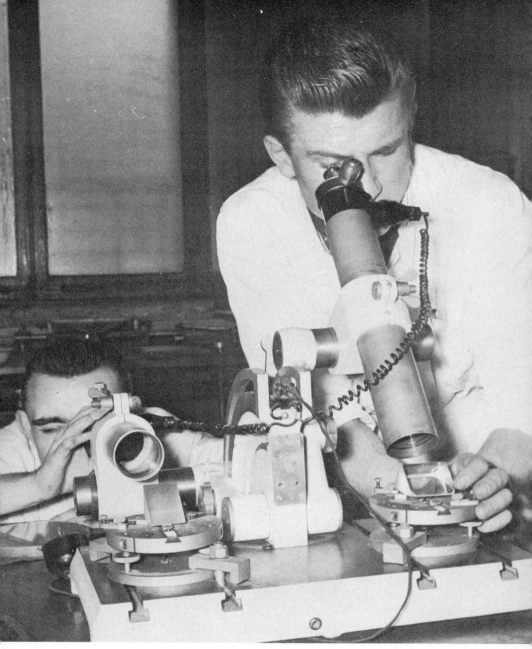

Students in a laboratory of the Collège Technique d'Optique in Paris,
courtesy of the French Cultural Services.

Today a scientific or technical career has more appeal.

The Tour de France in 1952,
courtesy of the French Embassy Press & Information Division.

A rugby match between France and Ireland in 1960,
courtesy of the French Embassy Press & Information Division.

*Millions of fans love to watch the professional athletes exert themselves
in the Tour de France and in international rugby matches.*

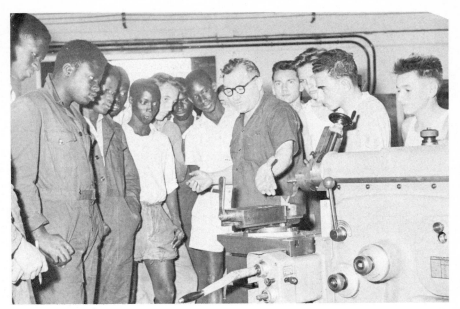

A class in the Lycée Delafosse in Dakar, Senegal,
courtesy of the French Embassy Press & Information Division.

*In France's former colonies in Africa there is no distinction between
Frenchmen and natives. Here an instructor explains the operation of a
machine tool to students in a Dakar high school.*

Candidates about to enter the examination building
of the University of Paris,
courtesy of the French Embassy Press & Information Division.

*Every year more and more candidates for advanced degrees take the
long and highly competitive examinations given at France's overcrowded
universities.*

The peristyle of the Grand Trianon at Versailles,
courtesy of the French Cultural Services.

Harmony and elegance in French housing.

Moderate-income apartments at Drancy,
courtesy of the French Cultural Services.

During the interwar years many French painters evoked the colorful façade of modern life.

Henri Matisse, "Deux jeunes filles,"
courtesy of the French Embassy Press & Information Division.

Raoul Dufy, "Deauville—La sortie des cinq mètres,"
courtesy of the French Cultural Services.

Bernard Buffet, "L'atelier,"
courtesy of the French Embassy Press & Information Division.

*Today an important group of them seems more interested in showing
isolated objects in their concrete nakedness.*

Some of Jean Gabin's best films of the late thirties expressed a fatalistic attitude toward the sordidness of life.

La Bête Humaine,
courtesy of the French Cultural Services.

Huis Clos,
courtesy of the French Government Tourist Office.

In the mid-forties Jean-Paul Sartre's play No Exit *showed how we are all in hell together.*

Lack of love and understanding lead a Parisian boy to juvenile delinquency in this scene from the 1959 film The 400 Blows.

Les 400 Coups,
courtesy of the French Cultural Services.

Jeanne Moreau portrays a present-day Madame Bovary—bored, and longing for glamor—in this scene from the 1959 film The Lovers.

Les Amants,
courtesy of the French Embassy Press & Information Division.

Edouard Manet, "Le dejeuner sur l'herbe,"
courtesy of the Louvre Museum.

Lunch on the grass, nineteenth- and twentieth-century style—or, The Revolt of the Masses.

"Sunday on the Banks of the Marne," photograph by **Henri Cartier-Bresson**, copyright Magnum Photos, New York City.

"Strip-Tease," cartoon by J. Sennep,
copyright *Le Figaro*, SPADEM, French Reproduction Rights, 1960.

*A famous Right-wing cartoonist entitled this drawing "Strip Tease."
In it he shows Paul Ramadier, Pierre Mendès-France, André Le Trocquer,
Pierre Pflimlin, and Félix Gaillard "taking off" the Fourth Republic.*

Cartoon by Vicky,
copyright *London Daily Mirror.*

MAY, 1958

*Thoughts of grandeur
while waiting for
"the call."*

JUNE, 1958

MARIAGE DE CONVENANCE

High-school students leaving Paris on their vacation,
courtesy of the French Cultural Services.

Today's city-dwellers are enthusiastic campers.

"Les Sables d'Olonne—camping," photograph by Robert Doisneau,
Rapho Guillumette Pictures.

But they often bring their city comforts with them.

Professional wrestling reassures its fans that, basically, everything is understandable and right always prevails, despite the complexity and ambiguity of the modern world.

"Catch-as-catch-can," photograph by Robert Doisneau, Rapho Guillumette Pictures.

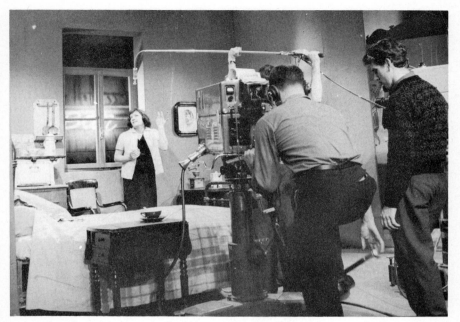

Colette Renard on the television program "Magazine de la Chanson,"
courtesy of the French Cultural Services.

*Television also tends to avoid controversial topics and to make
everything seem familiar and friendly.*

"Tourists at the Apache Dance," photograph by Robert Doisneau, Rapho Guillumette Pictures.

As in other modern countries, the authentic popular culture of the lower classes has become commercialized for middle-class tourists in France. Here a night-club audience watches a professional performance of the Apache dance.

Since his earthly self is full of death, Valéry wants to eliminate it and find a "super-self" that endures. His proud intellectual isolation and self-contemplation is apparent in most of his writings before the 1930's. Monsieur Teste, who expresses Valéry's reflections in several volumes, wants to "blot out the living." He is outside society and he almost succeeds in dissociating himself from human relations altogether. Monsieur Teste spends his dying years in bed analyzing and classifying his ideas without any real hope that his work will last. In this respect he resembles Proust, who also tried to add a word or polish a phrase in his novel until his lonely death in 1922.

Marcel Proust spent the last years of his life shut up in a suite of rooms at the Ritz Hotel in Paris, where he finished his long novel *À la recherche du temps perdu*. Many critics have noted elements of snobbery in this work and they have blamed these on Proust's social pretensions and on the decay of the prewar aristocratic society in which he moved. While it is true that with Proust we always feel as if we were reading about the end of something, his writings contain more than penetrating social commentary and aesthetic insights. In trying to recapture the past he was really looking for his basic self beneath its superficial and changing aspects, so that his book could also be called *À la recherche du moi perdu*. In an extreme way it expressed France's search for a cultural identity in a world where old values and norms were losing their meaning.

Along with other European writers, Proust was obsessed by the presence of death—in the sense of a meaningless existence—in living persons who know they are dying. Whether the demon that makes life meaningless takes the form of Death, Nothingness, Nonsense, or Abstraction, the anguish is the same. The reaction to it may be crime, perversion, sensuality, or other versions of what psychologists call "neurotic" behavior. Although most neurotics may be sick because of flaws in their individual life histories, the prevalence of morbid subjects and distorted forms in the arts after 1919 seems to have been symptomatic of a widespread social *malaise*. Writers like Proust cannot be dismissed by the criticism that they were merely projecting their personal maladjustments into their artistic creations. If the arts have meaning for the historian—if they help him to understand man in a cultural setting—they cannot be viewed as reflecting only the personality of the artist. They must be interpreted as symbols of human problems and aspirations.

The basic human problem that Proust struggles with is: How can the individual enjoy life and experience it as part of a bright and perfect existence that escapes the ravages of time and is in some sense eternal? In *À la recherche du temps perdu* the narrator and all the characters suffer from some form of unsatisfied longing or disappointed hope. The lovers who fix their aspirations upon other human beings are frustrated, because love, according to Proust, is a fatal drama leading to inevitable catastrophe. It is played by people who seek each other out, establish momentary relationships, wound and irritate their partners, separate, and forget them. Love cannot last, not only because time destroys it, but because each person is imprisoned in his own world, which is isolated and impenetrable.

Love is a spell, as in a fairy tale. The initial physical attraction is fortuitous. Love really takes hold only as the result of an internal crisis caused by the fear of losing the person that interests us. Thus, Swann did not fall in love with Odette until the evening she failed to appear at a rendezvous and he, distraught with anxiety, searched for her in the cafés and streets of Paris. The narrator too did not totally suspend his normal activities in order to devote himself to Albertine until he learned of "her" attachment for Mademoiselle Vinteuil.

Eventually the causes of the enchantment lose their force, and habit sets in. Then jealousy appears, and it revives the anxiety over losing the loved one. Here the pathological side of love is most evident. Speaking of Swann's feelings toward Odette in later years, Proust says: "Regrets over a mistress and persistent jealousy are physical diseases like tuberculosis or leukemia." No individual can satisfy the emotional needs of another. Even those characters who pursue evil and perversity for their own sake, like the Baron de Charlus near the end of the book, are disappointed when their satisfaction depends upon others.

Proust pushes his analysis of human frustration even further by maintaining that it is impossible for man to know and master the physical world. This is true because it, too, changes through time, which destroys everything. Time is the world's fourth dimension, and the ultimate units of Proust's reality are events, each of which is unique and can never occur again. His early experiences, his characters, love, society, and the world, are constantly changing during the course of his novel. In it he tries to recapture these events in a gigantic dense mesh of complicated relations with innumerable cross-references between different groups of characters. Since Proust felt that it was hopeless to seek his true reality in his ever changing consciousness and the continual transformation of the world, he looked within himself. What he found in his unconscious he tried to preserve in a work of art, which might possibly endure.

Obviously this form of sublimation was not accessible to most people and it was therefore not a constructive answer to the problems of twentieth-century France. Yet Proust's conception of time as the great enemy was shared by many Frenchmen who felt that life had been more pleasant in the past. Even government policy in political, social, economic, colonial, and international affairs often reflected a hostile, non-adjustive, attitude toward time. The French postponed reforms that its passing required but they knew that it would continue to work against them. They could not escape from the world—they could only keep it waiting.

In the 1920's different people were trying to escape from or rebel against different things, and they did this in a variety of ways. While some regretted the disappearance of old cultural values, others wanted to destroy what was left of them. There was a revolt against the traditional order almost everywhere. The war had shown that nothing lasts, and in France the postwar generation, particularly the youth, was disoriented and maladjusted. It abandoned eternal and universal values and found nothing positive with which to replace them.

Until the mid-twenties André Gide expressed this spirit of revolt in his novels, plays, and essays. The message of *Les Nourritures terrestres* (*The Fruits of the Earth*) was anti-intellectual and anti-historical. It was free of all moral ballast and opposed to all traditions and values. Gide warned his fictitious pupil Nathanaël against memories and affiliations of any kind. He must not stay anywhere; nothing should be more pernicious to him than his home, his family, and his past; he is to forget his past and burn his bridges behind him. The nihilistic hero of *Les Caves du Vatican* (*Lafcadio's Adventures*) is motivated by a facetious compulsion. His wanton misdeeds are all forms of *l'acte gratuite*, the disinterested gesture in its purest form, pushed to its utmost, paradoxical extreme. He is aware of all the risks involved in his actions, but to him danger furnishes an additional attraction.

In *Les faux monnayeurs* (*The Counterfeiters*) Gide's youthful protagonists are also driven to gratuitous acts by the demoniac whispers of their inner voices. (In real life the notorious Loeb and Leopold affair in this country was a classic example of the gratuitous act.) If the unconscious is the devil's retreat, we must lift the darkness from this hiding place. Those characters who openly admit the presence and the power of the demon are better adjusted than the others who deny or conceal their own basic motives.

Gide's attempt to rehabilitate the instincts seemed to challenge the classical humanist tradition, which championed the dignity of man. In other countries preoccupation with the baseness of man's unconscious strivings was related to the vogue for psychoanalysis and was expressed by dramatists like Eugene O'Neill. But Gide's approach was cultural rather than psychological. Furthermore, his fervor and his sincerity prevented him from debasing man completely. Gide was also deeply concerned with moral problems, and his flaunting of old values was part of an attempt to bring some order into the disordered postwar world.

Gide felt that French social and religious values and institutions were meaningless because they no longer worked. With pitiless irony he transformed the family cell into a prison in which his heroes found themselves isolated from their closest relatives and alone in a world of artificial groups organized around economic and political interests. But French society as a whole remained conservative in the decade after the war, and talented and respectable writers like Henri Bordeaux, Jacques de Lacretelle, and Georges

Duhamel continued to describe its nostalgia for the nineteenth century. In their novels the family circle kept its place as the basic social unit—the microcosm of many facets that refracted and filtered all human feelings. The family still had meaning for most Frenchmen, but, as Gide, Roger Martin du Gard in *Les Thibaults*, and other authors showed, it could no longer adequately shelter the individual from the disintegrating forces of war and industrialism.

Les faux monnayeurs and *Si le grain ne meurt* (*If It Die*), which were written in 1925 and 1926, respectively, still depicted a bewildered and confused generation reacting against a rigid society whose values were losing their meaning. The heroes of these as well as Gide's earlier novels captivated the imagination of reckless young Frenchmen, who imitated them in rejecting bourgeois moral standards, savoring new experiences, and asserting their independence. (Meanwhile, bohemians and flappers in London, Berlin, and New York were also trying to forget ethics, science, and history in their pursuit of fleeting pleasures in sex and sport.) But Gide's apparent exaltation of the gratuitous act was more than an expression of irresponsible rebellion. It was the individual's protest against the apparently senseless regimentation of contemporary civilization and an assertion of his own validity as a person.

Gide's credo as a youth was: "One must dare to be oneself"; yet, throughout his career he tried to lose himself in something higher. His personal life and his works ranged over the complete scope of modern man's experiences, obsessions, uncertainties, and dilemmas. Gide felt the twentieth-century intellectual's contradictory longings for individualist freedom and comforting submission to authority—his conflicting impulses toward self-protection and self-dissolution. In *Les faux monnayeurs* there is both the devil of self-assertion and the angel of self-loss. Beginning with this novel, however, the demon that had formerly obsessed Gide's characters gradually withdrew and was superseded by a more rational inspiration. The author's voyage to the Congo in 1925 made him conscious of the problem of social injustice, and his feeling of guilt about the exploitation of the natives he saw there attracted him to communism for the next ten years.

While Proust, Valéry, and Gide led the offensive against the destructive forces of machine-age culture, others sought a refuge behind the lines. Those Frenchmen who chose this alternative found pleasure in the writings of romantic and elegant patricians like Colette, Jean Cocteau, and Jean Giraudoux. Colette seemed to be impervious to the historical disturbances of her time. The events in her personal world—and in that of her heroines—were the passing of the seasons, the color of the days, the adventures of her pets and her friends, her childhood memories. Her main concerns were self-mastery, acceptance of experience for its own sake, and—above all—love, which she describes with a disarming earthiness and with an imagery that appeals to all the senses.

Giraudoux was also a master at evoking fragile images and subtle sensations, which he did by contriving theatrical settings of pure fantasy. In his plays he exorcises the tragedy of human existence with a pseudo-serious gaiety that is full of irony and unexpected twists of plot and mood. Cocteau too was capable of expressing the despair of his generation in a pure and moving way in a comic play like *Les Enfants terribles,* though the main concern of this *grand couturier* of French letters was to glorify the poet in an unpoetic age. In doing so, he sometimes mixed the magic of poetry with the brilliance of sheer effects. Along with Colette's descriptions of the game of love and Giraudoux's gay stoicism, Cocteau's poetic *tours de force* offered a refuge from the harshness and meanness that sensitive people saw around them.

By the 1930's some of France's outstanding writers began to face the problems of man and society less pessimistically and to seek positive rather than negative answers. Aside from the Catholics and the Marxists, who had their own solutions, some authors tried to rehabilitate man as an individual with a *raison d'être.* The literary generation of the depression years was primarily an ethical one. Its members asked: How can one live in order to justify living? They differed from their Existentialist successors in the 1940's, who posed the same problem but sought the answer through metaphysics. Many of them, however, already felt that literature could no longer remain a game or a document; they wanted to provide a formula for salvation—a key to life. Their writings prescribed energy, commitment, liberty, and conscience.

Antoine de Saint-Exupéry took the way of the adventurer who chooses a cause and sticks to it. He began his career as a professional pilot in the 1920's, when commercial aviation was still in its pioneering stage, and he died in 1944 on a reconnaissance mission over France for the Free French forces. Saint-Exupéry used his heroic and aristocratic virtues in the service of a high sense of duty. He was a "man of quality," and throughout his life he stressed the duties rather than the rights of the great man.

For Saint-Exupéry the greatest virtue was a sense of responsibility—to his mission and to his comrades. He also felt that his work was related to the destiny of all men. Here was a Frenchman who was doing something constructive; he was part of a venture in modern technological progress that was made possible by a combination of individual prowess and co-operative effort. His *Vol de nuit* (*Night Flight*) deals with the tragic adventure of one of the pioneers in night flying over South America. Like all Saint-Exupéry's novels it has an authentic epic note. As Gide says in his famous introduction to this work: "Each of the characters in this book is whole-heartedly, passionately devoted to that which duty bids him do, and it is in fulfilling this perilous task, and only thus, that he attains contentment and peace." Toward the end of the story the director of the airline, after having told the lost pilot's wife of her husband's disaster, thinks to himself: "The goal, perhaps, means nothing, it is the thing done that delivers man from death."

Some people would call this attitude a rationalization of an action that has no meaning. It resembles the outlook of the general, the explorer, and the scientist who experiments with human life. How different it is from the introspection and moral soul-searching of the typical French intellectual! Saint-Exupéry was a relativist. In *Terre des hommes* (*Wind, Sand, and Stars*), which describes his adventures and reflections as a pilot in North Africa, he denies that "the truth about man" can be demonstrated.

If orange trees grow solid roots and bear fruit in this particular plot of ground, then this plot of ground is the truth of the orange trees. If this religion, this culture, this scale of values, this form of activity . . . brings out man's fullness and the nobleman whose presence in himself he ignored, then this scale of values, this culture, this form of activity are the truth of man.

Although Saint-Exupéry found a "scale of values" that justified his life, the values that give meaning to the functioning of a whole society must have their roots in a culture or a religion—preferably both. The scientist, the explorer, and the adventurer can improve man's material comfort, safety, and health and open up new lands for development. In doing so they realize their own individual potentialities, but their discoveries and their inventions must be integrated into an old or a new cultural pattern before they mean anything to the group. The wings of Daedalus, who, like Saint-Exupéry, escaped from the labyrinth by flying, would have been useless to the masses.

A poet rather than a social philosopher, Saint-Exupéry wanted to bring out the greatness in men, which, for him, expressed itself through individual courage and comradeship in a common cause. He had no use for the ideologies of his time and he found little meaning in traditional Catholicism. Like the great humanists of the past, he saw a budding genius in every man. Even the most modest role, according to him, could make a person happy if it gave his life a sense of direction. But at the end of *Terre des hommes* Saint-Exupéry says that what torments him most when he observes the world's masses is the Mozart that has been assassinated in them.

Saint-Exupéry was a "great man" because of his devotion to duty, his heroism as a pilot, his literary talent, and his self-reliance in the face of danger. In Nietzschean terms he was a superman. Unfortunately, the economic, technological, political, and social foundations of twentieth-century civilization do not seem to lend themselves to the world view of heroes and artists. Saint-Exupéry's creative humanism had little appeal for the older ruling groups, who were becoming die-hard conservatives, or the wage-earners, who seemed to be looking for salvation through the state rather than the individual.

André Malraux is also a humanist. Even in the 1930's, when he apparently favored what Saint-Exupéry called a "popular soup," Malraux was more of an artist than a Communist propagandist. Aside from Gide, he was the most "intellectual" French novelist of the period, though, as a poet, he felt his ideas more deeply than he analyzed them. He believed that they should be "lived, not thought." His most self-consciously political novel, *L'Espoir* (*Man's Hope*), in which he tries to glorify the Communists in the Spanish Civil War, contains episodes and characters that contradict his basic thesis. In 1937 Malraux wanted to prove that man's hope lay in the success of the proletarian Revolution, but he was really more concerned with man's fate—*La Condition humaine*. The most sympathetic people in *L'Espoir* are men whose tragedy is based upon a conflict between ideals and the necessity for action, rather than those who sacrifice their personal values in the interest of Communist discipline.

Malraux's characters represent types of temperament—aspects of human nature in the face of a tragic destiny. Contrary to Saint-Exupéry, Malraux saw a basic absurdity in man's effort to transcend his destiny through action. According to him, the value ascribed to this kind of behavior was the source of Western man's conflict between dream and reality; it gave rise to his basic anxiety. Although Malraux sought an adventurous life and wrote stories that glorified acts of heroism, he knew that he could rescue his heroes from their inevitable destruction only by creating poetic situations that somehow turned defeat into victory. Hernandez, the scrupulous Loyalist army officer in *L'Espoir* who is executed by Franco's soldiers, attracts the reader's sympathy more than the successful Communist Manuel. In *La Condition humaine* (*Man's Fate*) Kyo Gisors and Katow die in the Shanghai insurrection of 1926 because the Comintern lets them down. But the circumstances of their deaths are described in such a way as to persuade us that, despite defeats, the power and glory of being a man lifts the individual above his fate.

Of the characters in *La Condition humaine* who escape from Chiang Kai-shek's Nationalists, Clappique symbolizes the hedonist, Ferral the elegant entrepreneur, and old Gisors the irresolute intellectual. Their destinies show us the power of the absurd. At the end of the novel Gisors says to his dead son's wife:

> Marxism has ceased to live in me. In Kyo's eyes it was something voluntary, wasn't it, but in mine it is a fatal destiny. I accepted it because my anguish regarding death was a kind of fatalism. Now there is practically no more anguish in me, May. Since Kyo died I am indifferent to death. I have been delivered from both death and life.

In *L'Espoir* Alvear, the bereaved father of the blinded Jaime, also manifests the intellectual's apathy when confronted with the absurdity of action. Malraux expresses in each of these books his own inner conflict over values through several characters, no one of which is his official mouthpiece.

Nineteenth-century nihilism was based upon a value judgment—bourgeois institutions and values are bad—but Malraux was tormented by the impossibility of judging the value of anything. He reflected the moral relativism of his environment and the wish of many people to resolve their difficulties through action. Something is viewed as being absurd when it cannot be related to any accepted meaning or norm. To view life itself in this way indicates the breakdown of the whole value-system absorbed from one's culture. As always, the creative artists, religious thinkers, and social reformers of our time have been among the first to sense this breakdown. Malraux was especially significant because he spoke not only for the French but for all mankind.

The values and problems Malraux dealt with are universal: suffering and solitude, humiliation and human dignity, the constant imminence and irrevocability of death, the absurdity of life. In transposing his experience into art he was particularly sensitive to the relations between politics and the prevailing anxieties and ideological conflicts of the contemporary world. The paradoxical aspects of his novels seem to express modern man's confusion regarding the inconsistency of his own motives and goals in trying to adapt himself to a culture in which several value-systems are openly competing. Georges Bernanos and Graham Greene see paradox as "the heart of the matter," but find solace in the Catholic religion. Malraux did not have their faith. His view of the world was a tragic one. Neither religion nor any existing social system offered him the means of transcending the absurdity of life, though in the thirties he sought to do this through heroism and an idealized form of communism.

In effect, writers like Malraux expressed an increasing distrust toward logic as pointing the way to human happiness. These people wanted to break with traditional intellectual values and find the salvation of man through an act of will in the 1930's. They were part of a small artistic elite that sought to free itself from both traditional and mass cultures and reassert the value of the human person as a free agent. Saint-Exupéry and Henry de Montherlant spoke openly of a superman—that Nietzschean answer to the devaluing of all values—though Saint-Exupéry would have constrained him to serve all men.

In *Terre des hommes* Saint-Exupéry tells how he bought freedom for a Moorish slave and tried to help him recover his human dignity. He would also like to show all of the world's office clerks and shopkeepers how to free themselves from their dull, rational, and unimaginative lives. Even the simple peasant, according to him, has a fuller life than they—despite his tradition-bound existence—for he finds meaning in his work and he is close to the physical world, like the pilot in the sky. But Saint-Exupéry's solution to the dehumanization of modern civilization was essentially that of self-reliant adventurer, and most Frenchmen were still too strongly committed to logic to put their faith in heroism. They were unprepared to accept the leadership of latent Saint-Exupérys in all fields of endeavor.

Malraux too believed that the old ruling groups had succumbed to a hopeless routine. In *L'Espoir* he said that man's hope lay in the working class, and more than any other writer of his generation he expressed the spirit of the Popular Front. Here was an ideology that might have united millions of people in a constructive effort. But it too had to be led by an elite, and this elite, for Malraux in the 1930's, was the Communist party. His later support for

General de Gaulle was not really an about-face. It showed that he was more concerned with positive action than with any party or intellectual system.

Many writers besides Malraux felt an emotional and humanitarian attraction for communism in the 1930's, and in France Louis Aragon remained loyal to the party as man's only hope. André Breton and the Surrealists became associated with the Trotskyite heresy in their efforts to serve the Revolution by probing man's subconscious. Aragon, on the other hand, adopted the official Soviet watchword of Socialist Realism in his poems, novels, and criticism. He used current political issues and overemphasized the scandalous side of French middle- and upper-class life as backdrops for his glorification of the working class. In this way he tried to expose what Marx called the defensive superstructure of bourgeois culture.

Unlike Malraux, Aragon wants to be sure that his readers know who his heroes and heroines are. He does this through the characters themselves—especially in his trilogy of novels called *Le Monde réel*, which he wrote in the 1930's—rather than by creating revolutionary situations in which they personify specific political theses. Malraux is interested in mankind, while Aragon is concerned with individual French men and women in a bankrupt society. Aragon had resolved the cultural crisis by becoming a Communist, and he did not often project his inner conflicts into his writings. Communist humanism, which other intellectuals abandoned as a fraud, never lost its enchantment for him. He translated this utopian myth into terms that were meaningful within the tradition of class antagonisms in his own country. What he did in literature the Communist party tried to do in its propaganda. Millions of Frenchmen continued to view the French social structure as an organized form of class interests. Using this belief for their own purposes, the Communists did much to perpetuate it, both among the workers and among people who considered themselves bourgeois.

Catholics also wrote about the bankruptcy of bourgeois society and the wasteland of twentieth-century civilization, but some of them were more pessimistic than others about the future of modern man. It has been said that Charles Péguy (who died in 1914 but whose influence was still strong), Paul Claudel, and François Mauriac are Easter-Sunday Catholics, while Georges Bernanos is a Good-Friday Catholic. The first three are Christian humanists; they emphasize the alliance between God and man in Christ, who was incarnated and resurrected. Bernanos, on the other hand, recognizes no power other than the crucified Savior, who redeems his miserable creatures supernaturally. While the Easter-Sunday Catholics have a faith that lets them enjoy this world, Bernanos is obsessed with the invincible evil of men, which is symbolized by the Crucifixion. Like Christ, his country priest (in *Le Journal d'un curé de campagne*) suffers poverty and humiliation at the hands of "respectable" people. But he will get to heaven, says Bernanos, for heaven is the address of saints, not men.

Bernanos, like Malraux, was protesting against the values of moderation, prudence, compromise, and mediocrity, which were associated in his mind with the traditional French bourgeoisie. During his lifetime he adopted successively the ideas of the Action Française, the Christian Democrats, the Resistance movement, and finally, the professional anti-Communists. But basically Bernanos hated every value and institution of the modern world beginning with the Renaissance. He was more reactionary than any other French writer—even Charles Maurras—for his poetic utopia existed somewhere in the twelfth century. It was expressed by certain stained-glass windows that showed a medieval and chivalric France, composed of nobles and peasants who were loyal to a paternal—though impotent—monarchy and to simple parish priests who instilled in them the moral virtues of the early Christians. Bernanos blamed the rise of capitalism and democracy for destroying the natural hierarchy and humble faith of this utopian France and substituting the ignoble and absurd tyranny of money.

In literature, as in politics, one answer to the intolerable aspects of the twentieth-century world was reaction. Many sensitive Frenchmen were prepared to see materialism as the source of the current crisis. While Saint-Exupéry and Malraux proposed unselfish heroism as an alternative, the Communists (who attracted the largest following) tried to reorient a basically materialistic outlook by reorganizing the social structure. Men like Montherlant and Louis-Ferdinand Céline built a bridge between reaction and fascism, and some people started to cross it. The majority stayed where they were, a significant minority kept their Catholic faith, but those whose cynicism was stronger than their indifference became increasingly receptive to fascist shibboleths.

It is ironical that Henri Bergson, whose thought is more difficult to classify than that of almost any other twentieth-century philosopher, should have given birth to an "ism" that was bandied about by publicists and critics. In *La Trahison des clercs* (*The Betrayal of the Intellectuals*) Julien Benda mistakenly identified "Bergsonism" with all the things he deplored among his colleagues: a taste for the emotional, a return to instinct, and a catering to mass passions. Actually, Bergson was not betraying the function of the intellectual. He was recognizing an aspect of reality—irrationalism—and trying to cope with it; he was not proposing it as a justification for all kinds of partisan political doctrines, as Benda claimed. What Benda objected to was the intellectuals who succumbed to the values of mass culture and abandoned their true humanist calling. Like Ortega y Gasset, he deplored the Revolt of the Masses.

Benda blamed the intellectuals for spreading nationalism, fascism, and communism, and for the prevailing materialism of the times. These writers, according to him, had prostituted knowledge and reason in the service of the nation, conflicting social classes, and economic interest-groups. What was worse, they then tried to justify the new, antihumanist values fostered by these organized forces. Benda charged that, by abandoning ideas for ideologies, the intellectuals betrayed their true role, which is the dispassionate study of abstract principles and the expression of universal human experiences.

Julien Benda cherished the ideals of the classical education that he himself had received and he wanted to preserve the type of academic humanist who disdained the vulgar world and was uncorrupted by it. Most of his professors had been uninterested in anything but scholarship and scholars. Like the Chinese mandarins, they had had to make a special effort in order to realize that other people existed and needed to be considered. In contrast to them, many current *clercs* were abandoning the search for eternal verities and climbing on the bandwagons of worldly and violently partisan mass movements. According to Benda, "It can be said in advance that the intellectual who is praised by ordinary laymen is a traitor to his function." His use of the word *clercs* implied a monastic order of men who had set themselves apart from secular considerations to live in the cloisters of the spirit.

There were many such scholars and academicians in France. Despite the vocal minority of publicists that openly advocated various forms of revolt and reaction, most French men of letters were usually conservative and traditionalist in their responses. Bergson, Freud, Marx, and Maurras were popular with some of the university students, but the majority of the educated adults clung to the humanist and rationalist values instilled in them by the French educational system.

Some French intellectuals behaved like celebrities and were viewed as such by the public. In the interwar period many Frenchmen were more interested in what certain well-known journalists, novelists, professors, and even artists thought about current issues than in any cross-section of opinion. The fact that the state controlled most of the institutions dispensing honors, posts, and recognition also created crises of personal vanity among academic and literary people. They were constantly competing for these rewards and easily embittered if they did not get what they felt they deserved. Their habits of boasting, professional jealousy, and dependence upon special attention and publicity were almost reflexive. Sometimes they acted as if they had to subscribe to some doctrinaire political position in order to be recognized, even though it was not integrated with their personalities.

Intellectuals with doctrines that could be popularized have had a special role in modern French life. Most Frenchmen knew nothing of their manifestoes, feuds, and schisms, though, indirectly, these "squabbles among monks" provided rationalizations for popular prejudices of various kinds. They produced no Lutheran

Revolt, but in a few cases—like communism and reactionary nationalism—they furnished ammunition to discontented sections of the population. The *philosophes* had not caused the Revolution of 1789, though their names and slogans had been widely cited by the active participants in the events; this had also been true in 1848, 1871, and, to some extent, during the Dreyfus Case. In the twentieth century there were no comparable mass upheavals. Students, veterans' groups, and labor unions demonstrated in the streets in the name of watered-down social philosophies that were attributed to professors, editors, and café philosophers, but the intellectuals themselves had little direct influence on public policy or private behavior.

6

The Failure
of the "Isms"

Since the politicians as well as the intellectuals have championed various "isms" from time to time, it is not surprising that most other Frenchmen tended to think about current issues in ideological terms. Temperamentally they might favor Order or Movement —which supposedly distinguished the Right from the Left—though sometimes it was the Right that wanted change, while the Left tried to preserve the status quo. (The most recent examples of this kind of paradox were the respective attitudes of the Rightist and Leftist parties toward the rebellious European settlers in Algeria in May, 1958, and January, 1960.) In addition to this kind of inconsistency, these two "families" have rarely agreed among themselves on all questions. Indeed, it can be stated as a constant of French politics that the lines of division on diverse problems have not coincided. Even when these lines of division were adopted merely for tactical purposes, the habit of expressing them as ideologies added to the general confusion.

The basic level of confusion has been between means and ends.

Ideologies are systems of ideas (whether associated with specific interest groups or not) that can determine the choice of alternative paths of action for achieving a specific set of values. They differ from myths, which express the values themselves. Democracy—the sovereignty of the people—is a myth, while egalitarianism, republicanism, parliamentarianism, and plebiscitarianism are ideologies. Social justice—to each according to his needs—is a myth, while socialism, syndicalism, communism, and fascism (which often pretends to promote this myth) are ideologies. Order—a hierarchical society in which everyone keeps his place—is a myth, while authoritarianism in all its forms, from monarchism to statism and conservative republicanism, is an ideology. The Nation is a myth, while nationalism, veteranism, imperialism, and colonialism are ideologies.

In France there has been a persistent belief that the way to make one or more of these myths prevail is to change the political system. Until recently the peculiar feature of the French genius seemed to be to do something before anyone else and then to keep doing it over and over again in the same way. Between 1789 and 1815 Frenchmen experimented with every form of government they were to know thereafter: constitutional monarchy, popular democracy, bourgeois republic, plebiscitary dictatorship, and military empire. In the 1820's Charles X tried to follow the same policies that had caused his brother Louis XVI to lose his head as well as his throne. Then the Revolution of 1830 forced the last of the Bourbons to make way for Louis Philippe, and the whole cycle of experiments was repeated during the next forty years. When the Second Empire collapsed, advocates of all the earlier regimes were on hand. Any one that was adopted would have been number three of its kind.

Not all Frenchmen wanted a Republic in 1870. In fact, the majority of the delegates they elected to frame a new constitution were monarchists of one sort or another. As in 1815 and 1940, military defeat made millions of France's citizens momentarily accept Order as the price of Peace. But the democratic tradition could not be suppressed for long. In June, 1789, the delegates of the Third Estate had met in an indoor tennis court and proclaimed themselves the National Assembly. With this act they had first combined the myths of the sovereignty of the people and the Nation. Because the Bourbon, Orleanist, and Bonapartist monarchs in the nineteenth century refused to accept such an arrangement, French democracy came to be identified with republicanism and parliamentarianism and a deep-rooted distrust of a strong executive in any form.

The Third Republic may have been the political system that divided Frenchmen least, but it failed to reconcile the reactionaries who wanted to restore monarchical rule or the revolutionaries who wanted social justice for the workers. During the first thirty years of its existence the separate tasks of governing the country and defending the regime became permanently confused for this reason. In the face of a disloyal opposition, the members of successive Center coalitions neglected needed social and economic reforms. Wrapping themselves in the tricolor, they took up the sacred defense of the Republic as malcontents on the Extreme Right threatened to overthrow it. For after the partisans of Order lost control of the Chamber of Deputies in 1877, some of them tried to gain their ends by more subversive means. Their effort to use the Boulangist movement in the 1880's was a preview of the way in which ideological confusion was to produce negative results in France for the next seventy years.

Although General Boulanger's main attributes were his habit of talking too much and his handsome appearance on a black horse, he came to symbolize a different "ism" to each of the groups that backed him. The Bourbon and Orleanist monarchists saw him as General Monk (the man who would restore the king), while the Parisian masses saw him as General *Revanche* (the man who would restore Alsace-Lorraine to France and punish Germany for having taken them in 1871). Some former Bonapartists saw him as an *ersatz* emperor, others as a dictator installed by a popular plebiscite. The miners and metal workers of the Nord *département* believed that he would give them labor reforms and elected him as their representative in parliament. Unfortunately for all his backers, Boulanger lacked the audacity, the will, and the character to carry out a *coup d'état*. He passed up his chance to storm the presidential palace in January, 1889, when he was at the height of his popularity. After he fled the country three months later, his cause soon collapsed.

The failure of the Boulangist movement was an obvious triumph for the republicans, yet it gave those Frenchmen who longed for Order the idea of adopting the formerly Left-wing ideology of nationalism (which had come to mean an aggressive foreign policy and repression of dissent at home) as a means of achieving their purposes in the future. By charging that the parliamentary regime was incapable of protecting "the Nation in danger" they hoped to gain popular support for overthrowing it. For they learned that they had to have the backing of a significant section of public opinion in an age of universal suffrage, political journalism, and partisan leagues specializing in street demonstrations. The Dreyfus Case prompted them to add anti-Semitism and the honor of the army to their stock of slogans. Authoritarian republicans like Poincaré and Clemenceau temporarily displaced the *bien-pensants* by making nationalism respectable and even official from about 1910 to 1923. Then, when liberals and "pacifists" like Herriot and Briand returned to power in the mid-twenties, the reactionaries took it up again and tried to revive the wartime spirit of the trenches by nurturing organizations of veterans. By the 1930's they were also sponsoring leagues of discontented youths.

In the crises of the depression years the reactionary nationalists again found that the people who momentarily joined them in attacking the regime had goals different from theirs and sometimes viewed a riot as an end in itself. Street demonstrations had become the classic means by which the Extreme Rightists sought to contest the results of universal suffrage that displeased them. The most notorious example of this tactic was their attempt to storm the Chamber of Deputies on February 6, 1934. Though this was a sensational event, it was a riot, not a revolution.

Most of the demonstrators did not actually want to seize power, which would have embarrassed them once they had it. They wanted to force the legally constituted cabinet out of office because of its alleged involvement in a financial scandal. A Russian-born Jew named Alexandre Stavisky had sold some bogus securities to insurance companies with the complicity of a few high civil servants and Radical Socialist politicians. Hence, when Édouard Daladier's new Radical Socialist government presented itself to the Chamber of Deputies on February 6, several leagues of war veterans, Right-wing youths, disgruntled taxpayers, and even Communists joined forces in the Place de la Concorde and tried to cross the bridge leading to the Palais Bourbon (where the Chamber was in session). Over a hundred thousand Parisians gathered in this great square to watch the battle with the police who were defending the bridge. Neither the leaguers nor the onlookers shouted, "We want a dictator!" Their battle cries were, "Down with the thieves!" and "Throw the rascals out!"

The largest organized forces consisted of ex-soldiers—especially a group called the "Croix de Feu." (Although the "Croix de Feu" units were not in the Place de la Concorde but on the same side of the Seine as the Palais Bourbon, they did not try to storm it.) Their veteranism was dedicated to the Nation they had defended with their blood. They had known discipline and unity in the face of the enemy and they found the slowness and the seemingly endless discussions of the parliamentary process incompatible with the imperatives of the national interest. Despite the fact that there was no immediate threat of aggression from abroad, the emotion of "the Nation in danger" played an essential role in forming the psychological climate that led to the attack on the Chamber of Deputies.

Since the insurrection of February 6 was viewed at the time as fascist-inspired, it should be noted that Hitler and Mussolini did not gain power by sending undisciplined college boys into the streets to throw rocks at policemen. They succeeded because of their leadership qualities, their ability to "stretch" their ideologies in order to appeal to diverse social groups, and their national parties, which were well represented in parliament. The rioters in the French capital had neither dynamic (or even well-known) leaders nor a unified plan of action. Only the neo-monarchist Camelots du Roi had a consistent program. The young rowdies in the other leagues were half-hearted fascists, preferring arm bands and berets to storm-troop boots, hissing members of parliament to beating up Jews and Communists.

As in so many other political crises in France, ideological confusion divided the attackers and temporarily united the defenders of the current "system" in 1934. There was considerable bloodshed on February 6, but the police held the mob in check. The rioters did not get to throw the deputies into the Seine. Law and order were restored in Paris within a few days, and the rest of the country remained peaceful. After the Radical Socialist cabinet resigned, the conservative nationalist Gaston Doumergue formed a new government and promised to reform the regime along authoritarian lines. While he was unable to do this, his presence as premier temporarily placated many Extreme Rightists. In response to the continuing threat from that quarter, the Communists abandoned their antiparliamentary tactics and began trying to form a Popular Front of all the Leftist parties.

Most of the participants in the February 6 riots had simply been expressing their disgust and their discontent. Although they knew what they did not want better than what they wanted (aside from a desire for moral dignity and national grandeur), their aspirations expressed themselves spontaneously in the form of "isms." Some of these were old, others were making their first appearance; and their momentary alliance in 1934 gave the events of that time their real meaning. The participation of an antitax league added a note of Poujadism twenty years before this "ism" actually appeared. Reactionary nationalists and fascists also gave racism and hatred of foreigners new ideological forms with which they tried to gain popular support during the next two decades.

For all their ideological pretensions most Extreme Rightists in France were moved primarily by hate and fear in the mid-1930's. It is difficult to say which of these two feelings was the stronger with regard to the workers, the Jews, the Soviet Union, the Communists, Socialists, and liberal republicans—and, of course, the democratic regime itself. The fact that the Republic could fall into the hands of a man like Léon Blum made it suspect even to some conservatives who had formerly supported it. More than any other public

114

figure in twentieth-century France, Blum symbolized everything the Right hated and feared. His Popular Front government seemed like a prelude to Bolshevism.

Politically the Popular Front was an electoral alliance and a parliamentary coalition of Radical Socialists, Socialists, and Communists, which supported the Blum cabinet from June, 1936, to June, 1937. Socially it was a temporary *rapprochement* between the workers and the middle-class liberals in the face of a threat to democratic liberties and institutions. It also stood for a program of economic reform. Finally, it was a tactical and propaganda device which the Russian-controlled Comintern used to forestall possible German and Japanese aggression against the Soviet Union. In this respect it was related to the international conflict between fascism and communism.

Various sections of French society supported the Popular Front for different reasons. Its most numerous and most enthusiastic backers were the workers, who wanted better wages and social recognition. The farmers with small holdings felt the pinch of falling prices because, like the workers, their income had rarely allowed them more than a modest standard of living. At last the majority of Frenchmen seemed to notice how close its minimum level of subsistence was to actual poverty. The problem for most people was not unemployment, bankruptcy, and lost savings, as in the United States. Instead, members of the lower-middle and lower classes in France found that, even though they were working, they could not make enough money to live decently. They turned to the Popular Front for economic reasons—with the exception of the minority that went fascist.

Like the farmers, small merchants, and white-collar employees in America, Frenchmen in these occupational groups temporarily abandoned their social conservatism and sought help from the state. The parallel between French and American farmers during the depression years is especially interesting. Few of the former lost their farms, but they resembled the latter in making scapegoats out of the symbolic figures of big business: Wall Street bankers, the "200 families," the munitions manufacturers, and the wholesale distributors. In Iowa and Auvergne the image of the greedy capitalist evoked the same resentment, though in neither area did the majority of the people want socialism. They wanted "social justice" —by which they really meant economic security for themselves. For the workers in their own country or the victims of aggression abroad they cared little. In France, particularly, the lower-middle class sought to keep what it had, and the workers tried to get what they had always wanted.

Political democracy was threatened in France as it never was in the United States, so it too was a value to be defended against its enemies. The followers of the Socialist and Radical Socialist parties, regardless of their economic and social status, momentarily saw the Popular Front as its best defender. Radical Socialists like Daladier and Chautemps, who had been attacked at the time of the Stavisky scandal, were also seeking revenge against the Right. This pattern of behavior—by which French liberals temporarily aligned themselves with the Extreme Left after having been recently manhandled by conservatives and reactionaries—had been evident during the Dreyfus Case and was to appear again after the Liberation in 1944. It was not surprising then that "the Republic in danger" became a meaningful slogan for millions of Frenchmen in the mid-1930's.

The lower class and much of the discontented middle class sought to find political expression through the revival of the traditional symbols of the Left. In addition, the Popular Front ideology was a potentially new faith with new symbols that might yet help the French adjust their way of life to the twentieth century. As in other parts of the world, workers and bourgeois intellectuals were rallying to the welfare state and the defense against fascism with this hope in mind. In France the movement had its roots in the traditions of 1789, 1848, and 1871. The conservatives saw it as a Communist front—which it was in a sense—but the Communists did not lead it. They could only support it or abandon it, and they did both in turn. From the summer of 1935 to June, 1937, French liberals believed that the Popular Front could regenerate them. They also thought that the Soviet Union would gradually become democratic, that the French Communists could be domesticated, and that France might once again provide the world with moral leadership.

For the workers the Popular Front electoral victory in May, 1936, promised the end of their underprivileged status. Since the late nineteenth century they had developed a set of attitudes which in French was called *ouvrierisme*. ("Workerism" is an impossible word in English. *Capitalisme* was adopted without the *e* in England around 1850, but it had been used long before that in France.) At that time they expected no improvement in wages or working conditions from their unenterprising, anti-union employers or from the government. Social discrimination antagonized them as much as economic injustice, and they saw little chance of avoiding either one through collective bargaining or personal advancement in the social and industrial hierarchy. They viewed themselves as a minority group, segregated from the rest of the nation.

Scorning the outside leadership of Socialist politicians, the militant workers sought to better their lot through purely occupational organizations. They founded local federations of trades, called Bourses du Travail, which served as employment agencies, workers' clubs, and educational centers. By 1902 these Bourses were also performing the functions of central labor unions, and they merged with the CGT (Confédération Générale du Travail). Most of the CGT members before 1914 were skilled workers in small and middle-sized shops. They preserved the preindustrial craftsman's resistance to discipline and authority, thus hampering their national federation in dealing with employers on an industry-wide basis. For they distrusted their own union bureaucrats almost as much as those in the government.

Revolutionary syndicalism became the official doctrine of the CGT, though it was often contradicted in practice. Many workers who subscribed to its principles of the general strike and antimilitarism were expressing their *ouvrierisme* without committing themselves to specific actions. They preached class solidarity, but they refused to pay sufficient dues to make their unions financially independent and they quarreled among themselves over discipline and tactics. While the reformists believed in the possibilities of dealing with the employers and the government, they were divided on the issue of working with the Socialist party.

One reason for which organized labor rejected parliamentary action through the Socialists was the apparent hopelessness of trying to persuade republican politicians that every demand for change did not threaten the regime itself. Across the Channel, David Lloyd George's Liberal government got the British parliament to pass a series of laws favoring the workers beginning in 1909. In France, on the contrary, the "Radical" Georges Clemenceau emphasized the gulf of property rights that separated his party from the Socialists at that time. Aristide Briand, his successor as premier, had recently left the Socialist party himself, and he used military and police troops to put down a wave of nationwide strikes in 1910.

The social conservatism of the peasants and the lower-middle classes also acted as a drag on labor reforms. Since the Radicals—who represented these sections of society in the early 1900's—were indispensable in all parliamentary coalitions, this drag became a political force opposing all state responsibility for social security. It also confirmed the workers in their *ouvrierisme* and their belief that they were being discriminated against as a class. Meanwhile, the middle and upper-middle classes continued to take the revolutionary declarations of the CGT militants at their face value and opposed the granting of any concessions to labor before the First World War.

After almost five years of loyal co-operation with the government in achieving victory and peace, the French trade-union movement announced that it would return to its "normal" means of getting what it wanted. It disobeyed Clemenceau's order not to revive its traditional May Day demonstration in 1919, and it launched the first in a wave of strikes a month later. Although the railroad strike of February, 1920, failed, it dramatized the conflict within the CGT between those who believed in collective bargaining and those who wanted to impose Communist control on the working class as a means of achieving the value of social justice. Undaunted, the minority CGT leaders launched a nationwide general strike in May, but the morale of the strikers declined quickly in the face of government repression and general public hostility. They gained nothing, and many of the CGT militants were arrested.

The CGT was defeated, discredited, and even temporarily dissolved by the government in January, 1921. Hope for a solution to the labor problem waned rapidly thereafter. During the first eighteen months after the end of the war the total membership of the CGT had risen by 500 per cent to two and a half million, but this newly found strength was largely illusory. The new recruits, despite their eagerness for higher wages and better working conditions, lacked the philosophy and zeal of the prewar syndicalists. They deserted the CGT after the failure of the general strike, and by the end of 1920 its membership had shrunk to the 1914 figure of less than 600,000. Normal trade-union activities were further curtailed by a demoralizing internal struggle that led to an open schism when the revolutionary wing, inspired by the Communists, broke away from the CGT in 1921 and formed the CGTU (Confédération Générale du Travail Unitaire).

While this strife within the CGT had little meaning in the eyes of the employers, it did help them to retain their dominant position. They believed that all union leaders were committed to class warfare and violent revolution and that any labor legislation would be a mistake. International communism served as a bogeyman with which to frighten the general public, and it divided the champions of the workingman. Most of the workers resigned themselves to their isolation from the rest of society, but the more militant ones began to express their resentment over this situation by supporting the Communist party during the next two decades.

When the Popular Front was being formed, the CGTU showed its adherence to the new party line in its efforts to co-operate with the CGT. The process of reunification began in 1935, and by early 1936 the members of the two national unions—250,000 in the former and 750,000 in the latter—were united for the first time in fifteen years. This reconciliation, along with the spectacle of French Communists defending patriotic and democratic values, did much to increase the party's popularity with the working class. The Communists obtained seventy-two seats in the Chamber of Deputies as a result of the sweeping Popular Front victory in May, 1936.

Rightist fears of an economic and social revolution were fed by the nationwide sit-in strikes beginning in late May. When Blum took office on June 5, almost two million workers were on strike and three-fourths of them were occupying the factories in which they were employed. According to all reputable observers, these "sit-ins" were spontaneous. Wages were low, but the demand that they be increased was not the main one put forth by the strikers. What they wanted most of all was recognition of their right to organize and to conclude collective trade agreements. On the one hand, the members of the labor movement wanted to be integrated into French society; on the other hand, the employers persisted in refusing to take official notice of the organized trade unions and in viewing the workers as a dangerous social class.

In May and June of 1936 the French workers hoped that their sit-in strikes would achieve the goals of their *ouvrierisme* and allow them to abandon it. They were not bitter, nor were they filled with class hatred. With a large section of the lower-middle classes momentarily on their side, they felt that they were at last a part of the nation. The men in the strike-bound Renault auto works demanded such things as shower baths on the premises, while the women wanted enough money to buy pretty clothes, like those worn by bourgeois ladies. Everyone looked forward to the forty-hour week and paid summer vacations. The atmosphere in the factories and shops was like that of Christmas in an orphanage, when underprivileged children expect special concessions on "their day."

But the real "masters" did not believe in Christmas, especially when it was decreed from below. From their point of view the "orphans" were getting out of hand, and it was up to the public authorities to restore order. Rightists from all social strata called for martial law and the forcible evacuation of the plants. Even the Radical Socialists in Blum's newly formed cabinet put pressure on him to safeguard private property.

The sit-in strikes forced Blum's hand. He was not ready to propose sweeping social reforms immediately but he was also unwilling to oust the workers from the factories. Consequently, on the night of June 7 he called the major leaders of management and labor to his official residence at the Hotel Matignon. Under considerable pressure they signed a series of agreements there. In addition to recognizing the right of the workers to organize, the employers agreed to the appointment of shop stewards and to an immediate wage increase of from 7 to 15 per cent, plus additional raises in abnormally low wages. Both houses of parliament promptly passed legislation embodying the fundamental principles of the Matignon Agreement, and they soon supplemented these with paid holidays, a reduction of the workweek to forty hours without a decrease in weekly earnings, and a government arbitration system.

Most French employers felt that they had been forced to capitulate to the "class enemy" and, henceforth, they sought revenge for Matignon. The workers were slow in calling off their strikes because they were afraid of being driven into a disadvantageous position once they resumed work. Their fears were justified, for after the strike movement did die down in late July, the gains it had achieved were threatened by the industrialists and by inflation. A mass exodus of gold from the country also hindered economic recovery. Rich people preferred to purchase whole streets of business enterprises in Switzerland rather than convert their wealth into devalued francs and invest these in French industry—especially while Léon Blum was in power.

Despite its good intentions the Popular Front failed to meet the challenges of the depression and German aggression. Its social reforms, its economic program, its handling of extremists at home, and its foreign policy consisted of half-measures and false starts. The leaders of the movement had proclaimed the advent of a New Deal and a moral regeneration, but they could not achieve these goals because, like most Frenchmen, they did not really want to change the nation's basic way of life. Except for the minority—for it was a minority—that seemed ready to embrace communism or fascism, the French lost their vigor for adventure. Instead, they viewed the Popular Front's policies ideologically and thus prevented even modest gains in most cases.

Except for the active Communists, the working class was dissatisfied but apathetic after all the strikes, alarms, and dashed hopes since the summer of 1936. Prices had risen so much faster than wages that a worker's income in 1938 purchased no more than it had in 1935. The forty-hour week and paid vacations were real social gains, and they permitted Frenchmen who had never left their industrial slums to breathe the fresh air of the seashore or the countryside for a few weeks each year. But these benefits did not affect the unemployed, and they would cease for everyone in the event of a war. Besides, by 1938 many workers were abandoning the trade unions, which were the only agency that could protect their interests effectively.

The Popular Front was doomed to failure when the social groups and political parties whose interests had seemed to coincide in 1936 drifted apart. Higher prices and the temporarily increased spending for food by the workers appeased the farmers. They then joined the bulk of the middle class in worrying more about growing Communist strength and continuing industrial unrest than about fascist aggression. The Radical Socialists disapproved of Socialist schemes for nationalization and of the Communist demand for intervention in the Spanish Civil War, while the Socialists and the Communists split over foreign policy, parliamentary tactics, and competition for working-class votes.

Once again, the attempt to ally conflicting ideologies produced negative results—that is, in all but one respect. For, despite its other failures, the Popular Front saved Democracy. It was the menacing activities of the Rightist leagues and the impulse toward republican defense that had prompted the Radical Socialists to rally to it in the first place. Without the threat of fascism—both at home and from the outside—the Communists would probably have continued to sabotage the democratic system, and millions of impoverished petit-bourgeois Frenchmen might also have turned against it. Anticommunism might have become an irresistible slogan for them as the depression continued. It is true that the various reactionary and fascist movements in France were weak and divided. Still, one of them might have succeeded in setting up an authoritarian government, if there had been no alliance among the Leftists.

Since the Communists ceased to denounce the parliamentary

regime (though they often opposed the current government), the main threats to it continued to come from the Extreme Right in the late 1930's. Some people in this camp toyed with the slogan "Better Hitler than Blum," but none of their demonstrations or conspiracies toppled the hated "system." It was only after the Armistice in the summer of 1940 that parliament itself voted the Third Republic out of existence. It came to an end "not with a bang but a whimper."

Not only did some Frenchmen confuse a particular ideology with the end it was supposed to achieve; in many cases the two were viewed as incompatible by other Frenchmen. This level of confusion was especially apparent regarding the myth of the Nation. Under the German occupation, which was the best way to save the *patrie*? Marshal Pétain said that it was by purging it of its internal enemies—Jews, Communists, Freemasons, and "corrupt" politicians—by setting up an authoritarian state, a paternalistic economic order, and a God-fearing society, by collaborating with the Nazis when necessary but remaining aloof from the diplomatic and military conflict until it was clear whether the Allies or the Axis would win. Inevitably this approach became known as Pétainism.

The National Committee of the Resistance held completely opposite views. It said that true patriots should sabotage Germany's war effort and kill her soldiers, co-operate with the Allies and with General de Gaulle's Fighting-French forces, and work for the restoration of democratic liberties, the extension of social justice to everyone, the nationalization of the big economic enterprises, and the punishment of traitors—by which they meant the followers of Pétain. Inevitably this approach was dubbed Resistantialism by the Pétainists.

Both the Vichy-sponsored National Revolution and the Resistance Charter confused constitutional, social, and economic issues with national survival. So did the various subgroups that identified themselves with Vichy or the Resistance. Pétain's supporters included reactionary neo-monarchists like Charles Maurras, conservative republicans like Pierre-Étienne Flandin, trade unionists like René Belin, and fascists like Joseph Darnand. Despite the marshal's image of himself as the incarnation of a Nation struggling to survive, his regime was a congeries of divided factions to which the ideology of the National Revolution provided an imposing but detached façade. The National Committee of the Resistance represented an even wider range of ideological opinion. It was headed by a Christian Democrat, Georges Bidault, while the largest group in the "federation" it spoke for was controlled by the Communists, and the leader the whole movement backed was a rebellious brigadier general who also saw himself as the embodiment of the Nation. The Resistance Charter could not possibly reconcile so many divergent views and temperaments.

By late 1944 the Resistance was a myth for most Frenchmen. They wanted to believe in it, but its leadership, its clandestine activities, and its norms were meaningful only to the initiated. In reality the French people were divided not so much between those who had resisted and those who had collaborated as between a vigorous, but anonymous, minority and an inactive majority. The former thought of itself as a fighting elite, and its members, regardless of their political beliefs, looked to General de Gaulle as the champion of a self-liberating France. But the majority knew that it was the forces under General Eisenhower's command that had liberated them. For the liberation of France, like that of Italy or Poland, was only a phase of a world war in which the last of the great European powers—Germany—was being crushed by outsiders.

Although the Resistance was a myth, the renaissance it was supposed to bring about was only a slogan. Without greatness as a nation the French were not ready to change. Insofar as the idea of a renaissance had any meaning for them, it implied a nostalgia for the good old days before the war. A "has-been" can only make a comeback by catching up with the current stars—in form, in looks, and in vigor. But the French people were psychologically unprepared for Americanization or Bolshevization, especially after four years of refusing to imitate Nazi Germany. As they had done so often in the past, they settled for a political shake-up rather than a moral overhaul.

The Resistance movements that were demanding the purge of

collaborators assumed that all true Frenchmen were Left-wing, socialist, and revolutionary. This was not so, of course, but many people acted as if it were. The fact that the Communists had become the main standard-bearers of the Resistance ideology in most people's eyes made them more popular than they have ever been before or since. In addition to card-carrying members and voters, they attracted a large number of "sympathizers" from all social strata. The party rarely used its own name in its efforts to increase this following. It usually called itself the "Patriotic Republican and Antifascist Union" and cried louder than any other group for a French renaissance. These were magic words in 1945.

Priests, professors, and peasants became fellow travelers; concierges and society ladies voted Communist; and a few gangsters and industrialists sought party membership in an atmosphere where anyone who was known not to have resisted was open to suspicion as a collaborator. The Communists had other motives aside from punishing those people who were guilty of France's misfortunes. For them the purge was also a means of getting hold of the citadels of power. In the end, their unprecedented popularity was to be instrumental in creating a widespread, though never co-ordinated, opposition to them.

At first the purge was also a means of legitimizing De Gaulle's authority. Just as the Pétain regime had prosecuted the leaders of the Third Republic, the Provisional Government tried to prove that anyone who had been associated with Vichy was a traitor. In each case a humiliating national experience led to a search for scapegoats—which a large section of the population supported at first —but neither of these purges brought about a national revival.

Pétain's National Revolution failed because it had little meaning to a defeated people living under a foreign occupation; the Resistance Charter had a wider appeal. Its application would have been possible only if the movements that sponsored it had formed a strong political party after the Liberation, but by that time they no longer represented any existing reality. Hatred of the Germans had united patriots from all social and political camps. When they were gone, these people had nothing else in common.

Though most of them did hope for some kind of French renaissance, they could not produce a leader to rival General de Gaulle or an organization to match that of the Communist party. But the fact that this militant minority soon became powerless cannot be blamed on De Gaulle and the Communists alone. It proceeded to form new federations and splinter groups at a rate unprecedented in a society noted for this type of behavior. Simultaneously, late joiners and other opportunists were destroying what little meaning the word "Resistance" still had left. Disillusioned and bewildered, the bulk of the population turned to the professional politicians and parties, which had begun to reappear in the summer of 1945. (De Gaulle himself retired from office in January, 1946.)

It was hard for most Frenchmen to take France seriously, with its makeshift government, its paper army, and its apparent lack of purpose as a nation. Communism and Christian Democracy had a purpose, but they were soon to become mere ideologies sponsored by political parties, not movements of moral regeneration. Their parades, rallies, and Sunday outings sustained the enthusiasm of the faithful but did not affect non-members. Existentialism was the only new, non-political response to the immediate postwar world in France. Most people simply retired into their private lives and knew nothing of Sartre and Saint-Germain-des-Près. The behavior of those who called themselves "Existentialists" was far from typical, yet it reflected a widespread desire to "exist" without responsibility to a society that made moral demands.

The extinction of the Resistance myth also prevented the passage of basic economic and financial reforms (aside from the nationalization of a few key enterprises) and the creation of a workable political system. In the elections of 1945 and 1946 the majority of the French people still voted for the "Resistance" parties—Communists, Socialists, and MRP (Christian Democrats)—and assumed that the constitution they produced would surely be republican, progressive, and "to the Left, but no further." But, with the Nazis out of the way, the ideological differences among these three parties prevented them from agreeing on anything more than a patched-up version of the Third Republic. In October, 1946, the new constitution was submitted to a national referendum. Slightly less than nine and a half million Frenchmen voted for it, while almost eight million voted against it, and about this same number abstained from voting at all. The Fourth Republic began its existence with the approval of only a minority of the electorate.

The Second World War was the last ideological binge of Western civilization. As long as fascism was viewed as the main enemy and Communists were resisting it in the name of Democracy, Leftists everywhere felt that they were moving foward toward a better future. The fact that three of the five major Allies had conservative nationalist leaders (Churchill, De Gaulle, and Chiang Kai-shek) seemed to unite patriots and champions of social justice in a common cause. Then, less than two years after the last shot was fired (the atomic bomb made most "isms" seem as archaic as TNT), the Communists went their own way, and the Cold War against them turned into a defense of the status quo.

In France the ideologies of the Left came to express essentially a negative view of the restored social regime and the ideas that tended to perpetuate it. They lost the positive, forward-moving *élan* of the Popular Front and the Resistance. Even the Communists began to suffer from this sclerosis of the doctrine, and their ideological influence dwindled as a consequence. (The circulation of their daily newspaper, *L'Humanité*, declined from almost 500,000 in 1946 to 121,000 in 1957.) Until 1958 almost one-fourth of the electorate continued to vote Communist in protest against the conservative order, but most of these people did not expect the party to accomplish anything constructive.

Under the Fourth Republic the political leaders of the non-Communist Left were too concerned with getting government portfolios to worry about their doctrinal purity. This kind of behavior was reinforced in 1947 by the removal of the three Communist ministers from the government and the appearance of General de Gaulle's antiparliamentary Rassemblement du Peuple Français (RPF). De Gaulle came out of his self-imposed seclusion to save his country from the Communists, who were becoming frankly subversive and leading labor strikes against the Marshall Plan. In defending itself against these dangers from two extremes, the self-styled Third Force lost what dynamism it had had at first. It was the story of the early days of the Third Republic all over again—defense of the regime crippling positive solutions to problems. Paradoxically, the Fourth Republic began to lose ground at the time (1952) when it had acquired a certain political stability and undertaken a remarkable economic revival. For it showed itself incapable of resolving the most formidable problem of all, decolonization—in Indo-China beginning in 1946 and in North Africa beginning in 1952.

The Fourth Republic died because of this failure, but it also showed weaknesses similar to those of the Third. From its inception it was plagued by ministerial instability. Of the twenty-five governments between De Gaulle's retirement as premier in January, 1946, and his return in June, 1958, only two lasted more than a year. This situation was aggravated by the combined efforts of the extremist parties in parliament to overthrow the current cabinet, followed by their refusal to join a new one. As a result, the increasingly rapid succession of governments caused their growing loss of authority, especially overseas. It also created indifference and even hostility toward the regime by a large section of public opinion—larger than at any time under the Third Republic.

Frequent *crises de conscience* within the non-Communist Left added to the regime's immobilism, even though tactical considerations usually triumphed over ideological commitments (which sometimes involved internal contradictions anyway). The evolution of Georges Bidault from the Left-wing head of the National Council of the Resistance to a Right-wing colonialist is a case in point. He had shared the office of foreign minister with his fellow Christian Democrat, Robert Schuman, almost continuously for nine years after the Liberation. Although nominally committed to cooperation with the Socialists in the "Third Force," he did not hesitate to break with them over the issue of subsidies to parochial schools in 1951 and to remain in the foreign office in the conservative cabinets of René Mayer and Joseph Laniel in 1953 and early 1954. When Bidault and his party finally ceased to be prominent in the government he said: "Everything is falling apart; that is why we must hold firm. I feel myself becoming a fascist." Instead of building for the future (it was he who had said that his country would have a "revolution by law" in 1944), he became a defender of the past. Even here, he was inconsistent, for, as a Christian Democrat, he still championed European union. He wanted "to make Europe without unmaking France and her Empire."

The failure of the "isms" on all levels was nowhere clearer than in the stormy career of Pierre Mendès-France in the mid-1950's. Nominally a Radical Socialist—which meant a man who put politics first—he was, in his own way, as unadaptable to the requirements for success in the parliamentary arena as General de Gaulle. Unfortunately for him, many of the major problems of the Fourth Republic came to a head while he was premier from June, 1954, to February, 1955. It was he who had to pull France out of Indo-China and begin the liquidation of her North African empire. He carried out these tasks with daring and swiftness, but made implacable enemies of the colonialists. It was he who had to make the deputies come to a decision on the proposal for a European Defense Community. Whatever decision they made, the divisions it caused would have weakened the regime. Mendès-France himself was torn between his aversion to rearming Germany and his loyalty to the Western alliance. By trying to remain impartial when presenting the EDC treaty to parliament, he antagonized both the neutralists and the "Europeans." Finally, his fiscal reforms threatened businessmen and farmers with the loss of their subsidies and tax immunities. None of these issues except the EDC was an ideological one. Mendès-France's enemies brought down his government for selfish political and economic reasons.

After his fall as premier Mendès-France—who had been so dogmatic when he had no dogma—tried to revive the spirit of the Popular Front in electoral politics. As the 1956 elections approached, he and his friends in the four "republican" parties (Radical Socialists, Socialists, Christian Democrats, Democratic and Socialist Union of the Resistance) and the rump liberal Gaullist group known as the Social Republicans launched the *Front Républicain* as a campaign slogan. There was no contract and no program to bind these "allies." Without the Communists they could have succeeded only if they had been completely united. But the *Mendèsistes* (for the last irony was to turn this unclassifiable man into an "ism")

129

were actually a minority within their own parties and were thus handicapped by having to list their names on the ballot under their party label, rather than as members of a new movement. Like so many electoral alliances before it, the *Front Républicain* collapsed as soon as the returns were counted. The brilliant young politicians who had joined it nursed their dashed hopes with the newest archaic ideology—*Mendèsisme*—while intellectuals like François Mauriac and Maurice Duverger began to turn away from all political leaders of the non-Communist Left. Their whipping boy for their feeling that these politicians were betraying their ideals was the Socialist Guy Mollet, who was premier from February, 1956, until May, 1957 (a record term, but the last of its kind under the Fourth Republic).

Guy Mollet and his party were divided on both ideological and tactical issues. Their internationalist tradition should have made them good "Europeans," but, although Mollet himself approved of the EDC, the majority of his colleagues helped to defeat it by voting against it. Then it was his turn to abandon socialist principles. For it was he who instigated the Anglo-French invasion of Egypt in November, 1956. This action was counter to his party's professed pacifism and a challenge to a very socialistic measure, the nationalization of the Suez Canal Company. Mollet had also become converted to the cause of "French Algeria" (which the Socialists should have opposed because of their traditional anti-colonialism) by being pelted with tomatoes when he appeared before the Europeans in Algiers in February, 1956. Finally, it was he who persuaded over a third of the Socialist deputies to vote for the return of General de Gaulle as premier on June 1, 1958, despite the fact that Socialists had always opposed a strong executive.

Rightest attacks on the "system" were even less concerned with ideologies than those of the Left. The real danger from the Right was overseas, where some military and civilian officials and private citizens in France's colonial territories began to behave as if the Paris government did not exist. They were too busy defending their practical interests to bother with "isms." At home the Gaullist RPF and Poujadism were not systems of ideas; they were ephemer-

130

al, heterogeneous movements supported mainly by people who were fed up with politics and who were looking for a champion to save them from the Communists in the late forties and from Mendès-France in the mid-fifties.

When General de Gaulle sponsored the RPF between 1947 and 1953, millions of his admirers tended to see him as another Napoleon. Although Bonapartism was a nineteenth-century ideology, it continued to have meaning for large numbers of Frenchmen. Its goals were to establish governmental authority within a democratic framework through a national hero elected by a popular referendum. This strong man would end the chronic anarchy, silence the garrulous deputies, and prevent a return of the old regime or a proletarian revolution. A vigorous nationalism in foreign and imperial affairs completed the Bonapartist outlook. If De Gaulle suggested an "ism," this was it.

De Gaulle may have dreamed of becoming a prince-president, but he was too proud and too high-principled to stoop to the kinds of subversion and intrigue that Louis-Napoleon had used a hundred years earlier. He demanded the dissolution of parliament after the RPF got 40 per cent of the votes in the municipal elections of October, 1947. The deputies—even those who had rallied to him—were unwilling to commit political suicide in this way, and the general refused to consider a *coup d'état*. By the end of 1948 the isolation of the Communists and the economic benefits of Marshall Plan aid were clear. After that the RPF began to resemble a conventional opposition party rather than an ideological movement. Like the Radical Socialists and the Christian Democrats, it was divided on social and economic questions. Its only unifying feature was the personality of its leader. When he went into his second retirement in 1953, it simply disintegrated. Gaullism represented a man, not an ideology.

The other major Rightist movement under the Fourth Republic, Poujadism, began as an antitax league composed of disgruntled shopkeepers and artisans and led by a low-brow bookseller from south-central France. Pierre Poujade's "program" was almost completely negative. It was essentially an exasperated protest against an overcomplicated world symbolized by an incomprehensible fiscal system, a hollow political jargon, and inaccessible—and, hence, dangerous— technical experts. Poujade and his associates refused to accept any unpleasant reality. They misunderstood the nationalist developments in France's overseas territories and they ignored the necessity of making financial and military sacrifices to deal with them. Their economic proposals—such as guaranteeing a 20 per cent profit margin to the farmers, but "with due consideration for the other toiling classes"—showed how they wanted to have everything without sacrificing anything. If politics is the art of the possible, then Poujadism was a caricature of it.

With his apolitical "program" Poujade hoped to increase his following by catering to all Frenchmen who made the existing regime the butt of their grievances. Not only did he attack the parliamentary system, big business, and "meddling Jews" like Mendès-France, he also exploited the slogans of chauvinism, militarism, and nativism. Poujade's anti-intellectual outlook was the antithesis of an ideology. For him the "two Frances" were really two different physical and moral races. On the one hand were the decadent, cosmopolitan, supercilious intellectuals; some of them lounged all day in smart Left-Bank cafés, while others—the hated technocrats—thought up ways of squeezing the taxpayers. On the other hand were the hardy, diligent, clean-cut, down-to-earth "Gauls"—common people with common sense. These two races embodied the opposition between Paris and the provinces, Einstein and La Fontaine, the *distingués* privileged classes and the anonymous, insecure little men.

Poujade's enemies dismissed him as a rabble-rouser and a clown, but to his admirers he was a "regular guy," who "called a spade a spade," talked their language, knew their problems, and fought for their interests. As he worked himself up at a public meeting, he took off his coat, rolled up his sleeves, and opened his shirt. In this guise he became the rugged ex-halfback, the big brother who was ready to defend his "family" against the degenerate, blood-sucking, corrupt officials who threatened it. To the ladies he appeared as a stalwart champion who would save them from the evil clutches of the lecherous villain who had come to foreclose the mortgage. For Poujade was an authentic popular hero—a Hercules who spoke slang, a Mussolini with muscles, a Lone Ranger without the mask.

In France, however, political popularity is as unpredictable as women's fashions. Poujade was at the height of his career when forty-four of his candidates won seats in the national assembly in the 1956 elections. Soon afterward many of these deputies fell out with their leader, and, having failed as a party, his movement reverted to the behavioral pattern of the prewar leagues. By 1958 the Poujadists had become ambulance-chasers running after other peoples' lost causes. They tried to win support among the fascist-inclined colonists in Algeria and among French farmers who were staging demonstrations in protest against the government's slashing of price supports.

Poujadism was one expression of a trend toward racist nationalism among millions of petit-bourgeois and working-class Frenchmen after the fall of Dien Bien Phu in the spring of 1954. (Even Socialist officials like Robert Lacoste and Max Lejeune had caught this virus, whose symptoms they showed in their treatment of the Algerian nationalist rebels.) General Jacques Massu championed this outlook between 1958 and 1960, and his ex-supporters remain the most serious threat to French democracy today. They include army officers, veterans, and Europeans in Algeria.

Veteranism has taken on new meaning among the former soldiers who fought France's losing battles to hold Indo-China and North Africa. Unlike the mass leagues of the 1930's, today's most politically active veterans' organizations are restricted to officers, many of whom seem to want direct rule by the army. A number of their colleagues on active duty in Algeria have come to fancy themselves a progressive, revolutionary force, which can win over the Moslems and "resurrect" the Fatherland. These men were prevented from seizing power in May, 1958, only by the investiture of General de Gaulle as head of the government. They have twice allied themselves with extremist mobs of Europeans in Algiers. But it is significant that neither "French Algeria" nor military dictatorship is presented to the public as an "ism." Most Frenchmen now accept the failure of the "isms" to change their political system or to give them a new national myth.

From Anguish to Atomization

French intellectuals have abandoned the "isms" more reluctantly than politicians and ordinary citizens. Many a cultivated person adopted one or more of them as an emotional response to his class or professional status. Those whose guilty conscience was stronger than their fear of change turned to the ideologies of the Left; those whose fear of change was overwhelming were attracted to the ideologies of the Right. A significant number of literary writers, historians, social scientists, and journalists who received their higher education in the 1930's continued to express certain Marxist assumptions in their professional works. Sometimes they did this almost unconsciously, as in the use of epithets like "fascist" and "capitalist" in the writings of Leftists. Both Rightists and Leftists seemed to take the bourgeoisie and the class struggle à la Marx for granted. But they usually gave ideas more importance as forces than the master himself, who had made material conditions the basis of everything else—including ideas—which he called mere "superstructure."

7

The recent decline in the ideological temperature of France (and the world) is evident in the announcement in early 1960 of a "Parallel History of the United States and the USSR from 1917 to 1960" to be written by two famous literary men, André Maurois and Louis Aragon. A dozen years ago such a collaboration would have been impossible between Maurois, the grand bourgeois and advocate of enlightened capitalism, and Aragon, the Communist who has remained loyal to the party for over a quarter of a century. For the ideological and moral battles of the prewar and wartime periods were still being fought in the literature and drama of the middle and late forties.

Simone de Beauvoir's novel *L'Invitée* (*She Came To Stay*), which was published during the German occupation, shows that the human condition is meaningless and that it is impossible to be a part of someone else's life. The plot concerns the wrecking of what seemed to be a perfect liaison by a capricious, irresponsible, and petulant girl—the invited guest who stayed permanently. Both Pierre and Françoise, the lovers, are established and successful members of the prewar Paris theatrical world. She is a writer, and he is a producer. Though conscious of the threat of World War II, they find meaning in their work and in their relations with other people. Their own common-law marriage seems to be completely adult and "modern." They have no secrets from each other and they believe themselves to be incapable of jealousy, suspicion, and duplicity. Then they befriend Xavière, who, by her very existence, challenges everything upon which their lives are based.

The story is told mainly from the point of view of Françoise. She is thirty, self-confident, and proud of her maturity and talent, which set her apart from the frivolous and frustrated women she knows. In a sense, this was the kind of image that many educated Frenchmen wanted to have of themselves. Like Françoise, they learned that outsiders saw them quite differently, and that their view of themselves and the world was unreal. In Simone de Beauvoir's Existentialist language this discovery comes about through the realization that "others" are beyond our control.

Neither Françoise nor Pierre is able to control the thoughts and behavior of Xavière. Her incorrigible stubbornness and perversity are reminders that she exists—that she is "the other one." Françoise, in turn, discovers that Pierre, too, is an "other one" whose life she cannot share completely. For he falls in love with Xavière, and Françoise becomes an outsider to this new relationship. After she sees that all of her virtues—even her generous effort to assume a new role as a friend to Pierre and Xavière—are either wasted or misinterpreted, she kills her young rival.

This final action is not to be interpreted as one of banal vengeance. It is, rather, a means of exterminating Xavière's vision of Françoise as a domineering, jealous, older woman, a vision that the heroine dreads to accept as valid. Though *L'Invitée* deals primarily with interpersonal relations, it could also be viewed as an allegory about collaboration and resistance, with the Germans as "the other one" who came to stay. In this sense it has a moral: Life in France may be absurd and without purpose, but the occupation is an affront that Frenchmen should not bear without an act of protest.

Another novel that seemed to express the absurdity of life during the occupation period was Albert Camus's *L'Étranger* (*The Stranger*). Actually, Camus rejected the belief that nothing makes any sense and that one must therefore despair, but most readers of his *L'Étranger* interpreted its meaning in this way. Just as the "lost generation" of the twenties had seen only nihilism in Gide, so many bewildered young Frenchmen of the forties misread Camus. They linked *L'Étranger* with Kafka's *The Trial* and *The Castle* as an evocation of the nightmare world in which they seemed to be living.

There is no conventional plot in *L'Étranger*, and there is little dramatic conflict, suspense, or character analysis. The hero is a young office clerk named Mersault, and the narrative begins with his trip from Algiers to a nearby home for the aged to attend his mother's funeral. He seems to be completely unaware of the emotional responses that are expected of him in this and every other situation he finds himself in throughout the book. The people who observe him find him cold, sometimes heartless; but he is never overtly cruel or mean in his behavior.

His relations with a girl he picks up at a public swimming pool seem to lack any emotion aside from physical desire. When she asks him if he loves her, he finds this question meaningless. He tells her he "supposes not," but he consents to marry her anyway. Mersault also confounds his employer by his lack of interest in a promotion. The reader begins to wonder if this unheroic hero has any feelings at all. He seems to have no roots, no beliefs, no loyalties, no past, and no concern for the future. Some critics have viewed him as an exaggerated prototype of modern mass-man.

The action that precipitates Mersault's downfall is his murder of an Arab on a deserted beach. He is walking in the hot sun after having eaten a heavy lunch. The Arab appears, and Mersault shoots him without caring what he is doing. He acts without premeditation and without reason. His victim is a stranger who seems menacing but who does not precipitate a "your-life-or-mine" situation. Mersault kills him as he would have swatted a fly.

At his trial Mersault follows the proceedings with the dispassionate curiosity of a casual onlooker. He sees no connection between the references to his previous social behavior and the crime with which he is charged. When the judge asks him if he loved his mother (since he had shown no grief when she died) he answers: "Yes, like everybody else." This matter-of-fact reply antagonizes the jury, though it also shows that Mersault is not a conscious rebel. He simply does not understand that society expects him to give it answers that do not force it to question its basic beliefs. It therefore sees him as a monster, a creature devoid of conventional emotions and responses. After he has been convicted and sentenced to death he resigns himself to "the tender indifference of the world," from which he feels completely alienated. But he hopes there will be a large crowd of spectators at his execution, so that he will feel less lonely.

All sorts of interpretations have been placed on *L'Étranger*. Some critics claim that Camus is attacking society for being more hypocritical and unjust than Mersault is guilty. Others say that he is trying to prove that man has a history, and that it is an absurd one. Still another view is that Camus is condemning modern civilization for being so impersonal, so artificially organized, that a drab office clerk like Mersault has no roots in it. In a preface to a recent edition of *L'Étranger* Camus himself says:

> Mersault, for me, is a poor and naked man, in love with the sun which leaves no shadows. He is far from being deprived of sensitivity for he is animated by a passion, profound because it is tacit, the passion for the absolute and for truth. It is still a negative truth, the truth of being and feeling, but a truth without which no conquest of the self or the world is possible.

Camus uses Mersault to illustrate an attitude of negativism pushed to extremes. He does not make his protagonist in his own image, as Simone de Beauvoir does with Françoise in *L'Invitée*. Like Kafka's K, Mersault is a colorless "little man" who is a stranger in an alien world and a stranger to himself. In *L'Étranger* Camus seems to be saying that this has always been the human condition. Most people accept it without question, take their brief moments of contentment for granted, and want simply to be let alone. Mersault was like this until he committed the "error" of killing the Arab. For in doing so he "destroyed the equilibrium of the day, the unusual silence of the beach" where he had been happy. According to Camus, man must recognize his physical solidarity with the existing world (as Mersault did just before he died) and not give way to despair or irresponsible acts because life seems cruel and meaningless.

In the Liberation period many sensitive Frenchmen experienced a feeling of guilt for not having fought back during the occupation. This response was expressed in several plays and novels in which an individual or a community defies an apparently overwhelming force. In Jean Anouilh's *Antigone* the heroine dies rather than conform to the established order as represented by King Creon. Mathieu, the hero of Jean-Paul Sartre's *Les Chemins de la liberté* (*The Roads to Freedom*), is killed in a futile attempt to stem the German advance in June, 1940. Camus's *La Peste* (*The Plague*) and Simone de Beauvoir's *Les Bouches inutiles* show how a group of people threatened by plague and starvation fight the evil that besets them and, in doing so, find a new sense of human solidarity. These are some of the best examples of the so-called Resistance literature. Their authors, however, were troubled by more than the specific problem of the German occupation. They wanted to find a cure for their basic moral anguish by committing themselves to some cause or principle.

Of the aforementioned writers Anouilh is the least interested in commitment. His battle is for purity, and his enemies are vulgarity, meanness, and materialism. In most of his plays it is pure love and sincerity that his heroes and heroines seek. They are usually thwarted in this quest by the hypocrisy of other people and by the absurdity of contemporary society. Anouilh resents these things as much as Sartre and Camus, but he is more concerned with showing the ridiculousness of human behavior than with ideological or moral theorizing. In *Ardèle ou la Marguérite*, *La Valse des toréadors*, and *L'Hurluberlu* the chief character is a retired general who is victimized by a world he does not understand. The martial Don Quixote in *L'Hurluberlu* (*The Fighting Cock*) even makes a ludicrous and futile attempt to re-establish a vanished order of life based on honor and glory.

Anouilh's most typical heroine is a simple, idealistic young woman confronted with antagonists whose social or political status is high, but whose behavior is hypocritical and often mean. Only in *Antigone* and *L'Alouette* (*The Lark*—a patriotic play about Joan of Arc) is she faced with the authorities of the state as such. *Antigone* was viewed as a "Resistance" play when it was first performed in 1944, but Anouilh's heroine rebels out of sterile pride, not as a protest against political injustice. He distorts Sophocles, not only by dressing his players in modern clothes but also by transforming the whole substance of the quarrel between Antigone and Creon, who, for Sophocles, symbolized divine justice and human law, respectively. Anouilh's Creon is an amiable, skeptical man who is playing his role as king according to the rules. His Antigone is an egotistical girl who wants to have everything she demands, and right now. Since life is not organized to satisfy her wishes, she says "no" to it and goes through with the forbidden act for which she must die.

The Existentialists could not accept this negative brand of rebellion; like the Communists, they tried to construct an ideology that would justify their actions. Since most of them were intellectuals, or would-be intellectuals, they were unable to form a mass movement. They had no organization with a collective myth and they prescribed no norms for behavior. Yet they expressed the "morning after" feeling of a significant number of Frenchmen who despaired of finding any effective cure for their postwar hangover.

In its narrow sense Existentialism is a pessimistic philosophy that denies existence to everything we are not immediately and indubitably aware of. It need not lead to atheism, as can be seen in the writings of Gabriel Marcel, Nikolai Berdyaev, and Reinhold Niebuhr—not to mention Augustine, Pascal, and Kierkegaard. But owing to the dominant influence of Sartre and to the number and activity of his disciples, it became the label for a whole literature whose initial assumptions were the death of God and the contingency and absurdity of the world and its history.

French intellectuals with this outlook struggled fitfully in the quagmire of anguish, seeking a way out through a new kind of humanism. They tried to understand man in strictly human terms, without recourse to the superhuman or the subhuman. Inevitably this approach left some ambiguities unexplained, but the Existentialists maintained that these were part of life itself. In the tradition of Proust and Valéry, they meditated on the problems of individual liberty and communication with other people.

Existentialism was actually more important as an articulation of a prevailing mood than as a philosophical system. In France it found its most effective forms of expression in the novel and the drama. Sartre and his followers showed little interest in the fields of study that have concerned most philosophers: knowledge, the physical world, the good society, man's nature. They rejected these as "essences." All that these writers "knew" was that they existed and that they were trapped with other men and women in a hell from which there was no exit.

Sartre's play *Huis clos* (*No Exit*), which was first performed in the winter of 1944–45, is perhaps the best example of the philosophical drama in which interpersonal relations are shown as *the* contemporary problem. The characters are "dead souls" who find themselves thrown together in a sealed room and discover that they will be there forever. This is their hell. In itself, this situation would not be intolerable; what makes it so is the lack of a basis for meaningful relationships with the others.

Garcin is a coward and a military deserter whose actions have caused the death of his wife; Ines is a lesbian who has abused her lover so much that the poor girl turned on the gas one night and killed them both; Estelle is a vain, faithless wife who has murdered a baby she had by an illicit sweetheart. Each of these three damned creatures becomes the other's hell. Ines is attracted to Estelle, despite her awareness of the fact that she will be hurt and frustrated by this ravishing young woman. Estelle, in turn, wants Garcin to make love to her simply because he is the only man available, though she despises his cowardice. Garcin is tempted to respond to Estelle's coquetry, if she will think well of him. But Ines taunts him by reminding him of his own guilt feelings and convinces him that Estelle loathes him, though she would tell him that he was God in order to possess him. The three protagonists go on torturing each other for eternity.

Huis clos is not completely consistent, for it introduces evil— or sin—as the reason for which Garcin, Ines, and Estelle are forced to suffer. What Sartre is apparently trying to say is that everyone is locked in a room with no exit. There is no "other place" where one might be "sent" if he behaved in a "better" way. Furthermore, there are no valid norms that could tell him how to behave. Man's fate is to live in a hostile society, surrounded by other people whom he can neither love nor trust. Like Kafka and Faulkner, Sartre in *Huis clos* describes a world that is absurd and threatening.

These three writers were especially popular in France right after the Liberation. Although they represent separate cultures and are of different temperaments, they all ask the same question: How is personal happiness possible in a world of meanness, conflicting ideologies, atomic bombs, and concentration camps? In the mid-forties millions of Frenchmen were worried about these threats. The military defeat and the occupation had been traumatic experiences comparable to those of the heroes in Kafka's novels and Sartre's *La Nausée*. After the physical liberation of the country the old issues and anxieties remained. Its primary effect was to allow people to think about them again and to become devoted to those writers who dramatized them.

Sartre wanted to give a social function to purely subjective events. Political commitment seemed the way to do so during the Resistance period, but he became less certain of this solution in the late forties. For a decade he flirted with communism as the answer to an otherwise absurd existence. Like so many other intellectuals, however, he could not permanently close his eyes to the basically immoral methods of the Communists. (Simone de Beauvoir's novel *Les Mandarins* describes very well the dilemmas of French intellectuals after the Second World War.) He wanted a "clean" revolution—just as some people wanted a "clean" hydrogen bomb. If he had to dirty his hands, he did not want to take part in any political action, for then he would still feel the guilt he was trying to assuage. Sartre developed this theme in his play *Les Mains sales* (outrageously mistranslated as *Crime of Passion*). It haunted many Frenchmen during the postwar years.

In his two recent plays, *Le Diable et le Bon Dieu* and *Les Séquestrés d'Altona*, Sartre shows that he is a moralist at heart. These are ethical dramas. They involve conflicts of duties, rights, and classes, and their central characters discover that the only way to redirect their lives is to make a meaningful choice. Good faith dawns on them when they prove themselves capable of inventing their own course of action. The Existentialist credo is still behind their freedom to choose. For they learn that history alone will judge their actions, since God does not exist.

The postwar works of Camus expressed the dilemma of many thoughtful people in France and throughout Western Europe in an especially moving way. He was active in the Resistance and he later engaged in polemics with Sartre and the Communists. All the while, he was struggling with the basic mysteries of life that have always haunted artists and philosophers. Like Descartes, he reduced everything to an initial doubt in order to build a moral system that was not founded on illusions or threatened by dissolution into chaos. In his essay *Le Mythe de Sisyphe* Camus maintains that the only thing we can say about the world is that it is not reasonable. What makes it seem absurd is the clash of this irrationality with man's desperate desire for clarity. Sisyphus knows that each time he rolls his rock up the hill he is wearing himself out in an effort that can never bring final victory. Even so, he is somehow victorious, for the struggle toward the top is a form of happiness.

Camus was revolted by the cold-blooded, rationalistic organization of collective violence implied in the very structure of the modern state. The Nazis merely carried this to extremes. It was bad enough that the forces of nature could be cruel and destructive, but for men to add social injustice to this was monstrous. Though less resigned than the ancient Stoics, Camus resembled them in his desire to reduce human suffering on earth. This basic theme of his later writings struck a new note in French literature. He believed in the positive quality of life itself, which brings occasional moments of earthly joy. These are as real and important a part of human existence as the symbolic plague in *La Peste*.

In *L'Homme révolté* (*The Rebel*) Camus sought a new philosophy to overcome the dehumanizing aspects of modern mass civilization. This essay shows how he moved toward a secular humanism, stressing the classical Greek virtue of moderation, defying all absolutes, and opposing all transcendental justifications for abuses against men. By the early 1950's he had become a reformer who was unwilling to sacrifice freedom and the possibility of present happiness in anticipation of some ideal future. For this reason, he opposed the Marxist philosophy of history, which makes the historical process itself an idol and postulates its inevitable "march" toward communism. In 1952 Sartre criticized Camus for his stoical resignation. Then the two men engaged in a literary debate that pointed up the major issues confronting many postwar intellectuals.

The hero in Camus's last novel, *La Chute* (*The Fall*), is more concerned with his own guilt than with the evil in the world. Jean-Baptiste Clamence had been a successful Parisian lawyer before his "fall," which was precipitated by his failure to try to rescue a girl who had thrown herself into the Seine. After that he gave up his law practice, his social position, and his comfortable life. He became a derelict, confessing his sins in an Amsterdam bar to anyone who would listen to him. During the course of a monologue he carries on in the presence of a particular stranger he also comments on the state of modern civilization. Speaking of Nazi mass-extermination techniques as a logical outcome of its dehumanizing features, Clamence says, "When one has no character, one *has* to apply a method."

Most people today are characterless and bored, according to Clamence. They commit themselves to certain pastimes—sports, art, politics—as a means of escaping boredom and dramatizing their personal passions. "Something must happen, even loveless slavery, even war or death. Hurray then for funerals!" Here the Camus of *L'Étranger* seems to be speaking, but most of *La Chute* deals with the problem of a man trying to escape from his sense of personal guilt. Unless we assume that Clamence, like Mersault, represents an attitude pushed to extremes, rather than the author's mouthpiece, this book is hard to reconcile with *Le Mythe de Sisyphe* and *L'Homme révolté*.

In making Clamence a false prophet crying in a wilderness he refuses to leave, Camus is describing a certain type of postwar intellectual—the erstwhile humanitarian who is morally shaken and haunted by guilt. This interpretation seems justified by the following remark of Clamence:

> Most often . . . we confess to those who are like us and who share our own weaknesses. Hence, we don't want to improve ourselves or be bettered, for we should first have to be judged in default. We merely wish to be pitied and encouraged in the course of action we have chosen. In short, we would like, at the same time, to cease being guilty and yet not make the effort of cleansing ourselves. Not enough cynicism and not enough virtue.

Clamence himself goes through the motions of publicly cleansing himself in a way that contaminates his interlocutor with his own sense of guilt. Thus, his role as a penitent gives him the right to judge others.

Although Camus was probably attacking the Existentialists specifically for being like Clamence, the above quotation seems meant for modern man in general. Camus was an artist rather than a systematic philosopher, and he was not always consistent in his thought. He sought an "inner" or "higher" truth than that which logic alone can give. Yet he made it plain that he disapproved of those French intellectuals who behaved like mandarins, clinging to a special set of norms, resenting criticism, and thriving on flattery. According to him, these people could not even cure themselves, let alone society. ("Not enough cynicism and not enough virtue.") Camus had still not found the cure for his moral anguish at the time of his terrible death in an automobile accident in early 1960. But he had repudiated all systems that prevented the individual from finding it through personal conscience.

Throughout history men have tried to create gods and worlds in their own image and to find an essence or principle that would give meaning to their lives. Human mastery over self, others, and nature was the special aim of art, science, and philosophy after the Renaissance. Even the scientists who studied "forces" of which man was not the measure, did so in order to control them for his benefit. Religion alone has resisted the drive to explain and organize the world in strictly human terms, though some "modernists" have tried to "accommodate" traditional dogmas and rituals to modern man's "needs."

The experiences of the twentieth century have made men lose confidence in their power to be the masters of themselves, society, and the physical world. They have concentrated on controlling the last of these and reached a point where their ability to manipulate atoms and microbiological organisms can destroy everything. Meanwhile, wars, depressions, revolutions, and individual and group aberrations—all well publicized by the mass media of communication, which present only the appearance of things and behavior—have made the rest of us skeptical about human mastery over ourselves and others.

Frenchmen have been especially stricken with this anxiety. They responded more desperately than Britishers and Americans to the First World War, the depression, and the threat of extremists to their political institutions in the 1930's. Then, their military defeat, the occupation, and the implications of new types of warfare since 1945 made them feel more powerless than ever—as a nation and as individuals. Although France produced scientists and technicians who found positive solutions to specific problems, many of her writers and philosophers were still struggling with the general problem of man in a hostile and alien world during the 1950's.

The self-styled Existentialists and their successors of the "beat generation" offered nothing that resembled a cultural reorientation. They merely played up the worst aspects of the traditional French way of life and the mechanized, war-ridden world that threatened it. Some of them said that each person should make his own choice —to commit himself to something. But commitment for its own sake could lead to gratuitous forms of "self-expression." Jean Genêt explained his compulsive stealing in this way (though he can be profound and moving in a play like *The Balcony*); so did the "jitterbugs" in the Left-Bank night clubs and the heroines of Françoise Sagan's novels. By the mid-fifties the "beat" youths wanted to avoid "involvements" of any kind. They frequented wild parties, though, unlike their American counterparts, some of them lived in elegant "pads" and were not averse to being smartly groomed or to mingling with the "squares" at fancy seaside resorts.

On a more intellectual level some authors became so despairing of man's lot in contemporary society that they denigrated man himself. They portrayed him as guilt-ridden, tortured, alienated, immobilized, and capable of regressing to a murderous beast and even to simple protoplasm. Not only does he have no spirit, his very existence as a rational being is called into question. Henri Michaux and Samuel Beckett curse the universe of terror and ice that they expose. After vainly seeking salvation through simulated madness, Beckett finds himself in a meaningless world in which all words say the same thing. Michaux tries drugs and wish-fulfilment through imagined violent acts and ends by saying, "Then, in silence and exhaustion, I return to my paralysis, the only and the undeniable reality." (The artistic merits of Michaux's poems and Beckett's plays and novels are not being questioned here. I am only concerned with the kinds of feelings they express.)

Surely most Frenchmen did not lie awake nights "waiting for Godot." (This was the title of one of Beckett's plays.) They were not consciously worried about their identities or their place in society. Like their contemporaries in other countries they kept busy, made money, had relations with other people, and behaved as if they had some control over their lives. Nevertheless, many of them felt in an incoherent way what their more pessimistic writers expressed—a dual anxiety about their own future as persons and that of the world around them.

The current *avant-garde* in France has abandoned the big ethical and ideological issues of the postwar years. It assumes that the reasons for our acts and our emotions lie beyond our ken—all that we can know and express are concrete bits of objective reality. Painters, composers, and writers do this in a variety of ways, but their common goal seems to be the elimination of the individual personality as the main subject of artistic expression. They believe that we can understand the feelings and objects around us only by ceasing to assume that these exist exclusively in relation to ourselves. Therefore, they consciously avoid traditional conventions and use forms that are as simple and precise as possible. The critic Claude Mauriac has given the name "aliterature" to the attempt to write without being literary. The same negative prefix could be attached to some of the painting and music of today's *avant-garde*.

Although France's best-known authors continue to write in older literary traditions (André Maurois and Maurice Druon in biography; Jean Giono, Marguérite Yourcenar, Henri Troyat, Jules Roy, Roger Vaillant, Hervé Bazin, and Romain Gary in the social and psychological novel—sometimes with philosophical undertones; René Char and Jacques Prévert in poetry; Marcel Aymé, Jean Anouilh, and Marcel Achard in urbane, satirical plays), the "new novelists"—Alain Robbe-Grillet, Nathalie Sarraute, Claude Simon, and Michel Butor—reject these and seek to be "objective." Robbe-Grillet carries this effort the farthest. He renounces the psychological approach of his predecessors and (as far as he can) the subjectivity of his own observations in order to reflect the world as it is—neither meaningful nor absurd, but *present*. His conception of himself is: I am a camera. Only immediate sensations count for him. He reduces man to a robot and the mind to a machine that registers impressions. No incident is given any more importance than another for his heroes, whose feelings and thoughts are never described directly.

In Robbe-Grillet's novel *La Jalousie* we learn that the "hero" lives on a tropical plantation, that he thinks his wife is having an affair with a neighbor, and that he is constantly watching her actions. This man has no name, he never speaks, and he has no distinguishing characteristics. He is an empty space at the heart of a world of objects that take form in relation to him. But, since every emotional and physical relationship begins and ends with this void, it eventually becomes as concrete as the things around it.

With this technique Robbe-Grillet succeeds in dehumanizing one of the most intense human emotions: jealousy. There is no chronological sequence of events or thoughts. Every image is in the present for the narrator. The field of his perception constitutes the universe, here and now. By the end of the book the reader understands that what has been described—without ever having been *mentioned*—is a passion whose victim forgets nothing. The jealous husband loses all conception of time and all sense of proportion regarding specific incidents. Is he inhuman or only insane?

Like the other "new novelists," Robbe-Grillet constructs his novels meticulously and repeats certain images and incidents in order to illustrate his ideas. At least ten times in *La Jalousie* he describes the *apéritif* hour on the terrace and the dinner that follows. In each case the invisible narrator listens to the same banal conversation between his wife and her supposed lover Franck; he also watches the same centipede climb the same wall. On one occasion Franck crushes the insect during the meal, and the image is so overpowering that it needs no explanation. Throughout the book such interferences are presented. They unite indifferently animals and things, things and human beings, feelings and images, past and present, time and space. Robbe-Grillet's universe is no more inhuman than that of science, which it resembles (only in a different way) in being unrelated to the world of qualities and values that man gives to it.

Michel Butor also takes up the theme of subtle changes in an apparently static situation in his *La Modification*. Unlike Robbe-Grillet's heroes, the narrator of this novel is a conventional human being—a Parisian executive who is taking the train to Rome in order to bring his mistress back with him. The "modification" takes place on four different levels. First, there is the simple movement in space between the two cities. The passing countryside, the discomforts of the voyage, and the other passengers—all of which are described in minute detail—stimulate the mental images of the hero and imperceptibly make him change the decision that prompted him to take this trip. He also modifies his conception of his love for Cécile and gradually sees it as merely a symbol for his fascination with the Eternal City. Finally, after these three modifications have been made, he decides at the end of his journey to recapture the process by writing a book about it.

The characteristic that links Butor with Robbe-Grillet is the way in which he tries to discover the reality that is hidden by conventional appearances. He maintains that "the exploration of different forms of the novel reveals what is contingent in the things we are used to, unmasks it, delivers us from it, and allows us to rediscover beyond this precise narrative all the things it hides or is silent about." In some respects Butor is developing the function that writing served for Kafka and Proust, but he consciously adapts his style to the mid-twentieth-century world. Since everything changes so fast now, the novelist, according to him, must concentrate on little bits of feelings and impressions and make them as objective and concrete as possible.

Nathalie Sarraute is primarily concerned with discovering and expressing previously unverbalized feelings. Unlike Robbe-Grillet, she deliberately probes beneath surface appearances and dialogue in her quest for what *is*. There she finds a seething, frantic, subconscious world in which organic instincts become the true basis of our relations with each other and our environment. Her first book, *Tropismes*, is a series of disconnected descriptions of anonymous beings—you, him, they—who are attracted or repelled by the most elemental kinds of stimuli. Even when she gives her characters a name, as in her later novel, *Martereau*, Madame Sarraute always keeps them in that state of frightened ambiguity in which they both seek and unmask themselves at the same time. Her domain is that of dizzy individual inanity, the domain of all of us insofar as we have no other existence but a kinesthetic and social one. It is in these regions of sensitivity, which everyone knows and neglects, that Nathalie Sarraute's analytical power reigns.

According to her, contemporary man is suspicious of all the conventions and trappings of fiction. A factual, first-hand account (or at least this form of presentation) appeals to him more than the ordinary novel or film. He no longer believes in the traditional types of characters, which hide rather than reveal the psychological realities of the world today. Hence, Madame Sarraute rejects stock figures à la Balzac and Zola for nebulous personages who exhibit those "unexplored conditions that we find in ourselves." Her realism is a precise description of the most imprecise and evanescent feelings and thoughts. She maintains that the novelist should capture "bits of reality by forcing himself to cheat as little as possible—not to cut corners or smooth things over in order to resolve contradictions and complexities—to scrutinize these with all the sincerity of which he is capable and with the greatest degree of perspicacity his powers of observation will allow." In an age of manufactured personalities, brain-washing, and organization men, who can deny that Nathalie Sarraute's world is the only real one left?

Some of France's best young painters are also turning toward a new kind of atomistic realism. Until now the traditions of abstraction established by Matisse, Braque, Picasso, and Jacques Villon have influenced the major artists working in Paris. Since the war their inspiration has become more emotional and spontaneous than that of their masters; but the works of Hans Hartung, Pierre Soulages, Alfred Manessier, Pierre Tal Coat, Gustave Singier, and other postwar abstractionists are still calm and ordered. Theirs is a subtle art of organized transience, which concentrates on the creation of light through color. On the other hand, Bernard Buffet, André Minaux, and Bernard Lorjou no longer think that the purpose of painting is to create a purifying incandescence in which a motif is reduced to the signs that suggest it. They also reject the current French vogue for abstract expressionism and the portrayal of human anguish, frailty, and corruption in brutal images like Jean Dubuffet's "Dhotel with Yellow Teeth." Their goal is to paint concrete, depersonalized objects.

These three painters resemble the writers of the *nouveau roman* school in several ways. Although some critics have linked them with Existentialism, they are more interested in objective than subjective reality. They empty their objects of personal associations and give them an existence of their own, just as Sarraute, Robbe-Grillet, and Butor do with the specific things and feelings they describe in their novels. Both groups have a scruple for probity (with the possible exception of Buffet) and are preoccupied with the style and quality of their work. They seem to reflect the desire of certain French youths to avoid assuming poses and insincere emotions as a means of "cheating" in the game of life. With these writers and painters French art enters a new period of seriousness

151

and loses its frills, its facile wit, and, according to many people, its humanity.

In Buffet's still lifes the physical objects—chairs, stoves, bottles, an egg in a skillet—have a dead but concrete reality of their own, which is heightened by the boldness of his colors and the thickness of his lines. When he paints people, they too are unmistakably real, but devoid of human warmth. François Mauriac says of him:

> His universe is ours, the one that he contemplated as a child under the occupation and as an adolescent during the liberation. . . . "The horrors of war," is an uninterrupted story across the centuries, on which painters have reflected from generation to generation. But this somber stream crosses other epochs without inundating them completely. The work of Bernard Buffet, on the other hand, spreads out like a dead sea over a world that is spiritually dead.

The fact that some *avant-garde* painters have adopted a figurative style does not mean that they are expressing the same things as earlier artists. Buffet's canvases may recall German Expressionism, a Minaux may look like a Cézanne, and Lorjou may remind us of Van Gogh, but in each case the resemblance is only on the surface. The vital import of these newer works is as impersonal as their creators can make it. Lorjou's "Canard de Barbare au Crochet" (1949) shows us a plucked fowl, a chair, and a stand, all of which seem to exist in a world unrelated to man (though someone presumably shot the duck). Minaux's "Paysage" (1950) and "Île de France" (1955) are exterior scenes in which houses, roads, trees, and telephone poles—far from being abstract forms, as in Cézanne —are concrete objects. They are devoid of ornamentation, symbolism, or sentiment, and their colors (grays, beiges, green-browns, shaded whites) convey a feeling of bright drabness.

In music the trend that parallels "objectivism" in painting and literature is *musique concrète*, which tries to create an expressive language out of naturally created sounds. The men who invented this technique—Pierre Schaeffer, Pierre Henry (and John Cage in America)—began by producing evocative sound effects. They recorded various combinations of noises made by musical instruments, human voices, bird calls, boat motors, or things hitting against other things. By varying the dynamic levels and speeds (and therefore the pitch), they were able to filter, modulate, and transpose these in an unlimited number of ways, thus adding to the resources of the conventional composer—especially one writing for radio or motion pictures.

Some men and women who are sensitive to sound hear *musique concrète* as a meaningful, expressive form of contemporary culture. Pierre Henry's "Music without a Title" moves from an ultramodern atmosphere of exterior din to one of interior anxiety and primitive terrors. In his dramatic cantata "The Veil of Orpheus," Henry attempts to fashion a definite synthesis from a few carefully chosen sources like voices, the tearing of a cloth, and a "concrete orchestra." The voice of Fate is particularly striking, since it is first heard in an affirmative, articulate way, and is then broken down, made to contradict itself, and caught in the immense disarray of the world the composer creates.

Although electronic music is put together in a different way than *musique concrète*, the two forms often produce similar effects. The goal of both is to contribute new means of producing sounds as a form of musical expression. One chooses artificial, electronic tones as its starting point; the other begins with natural ones. Yet the person who listens to these two types of composition over and over again begins to hear the same things in two closely related languages. The difference becomes smaller in the later works than it was originally, as can be observed by comparing the electronic pieces of Pierre Boulez or Edgar Varèse with the *musique concrète* of Schaeffer and his school after 1956.

All these works express patterns, tensions, speeds, and rhythms that are strange to modern Western man. They seem impersonal—whether one calls them abstract or concrete—mechanical, harsh, and weird. Like the *avant-garde* novels and paintings, they evoke a world in which the individual personality has no place, a world that is spiritually dead. Only concrete objects and disconnected, elemental feelings remain. Is this music for sophisticated robots? Or does it indicate the infinite possibilities of sonorous expression that can be achieved by eliminating the presence of mere performers and exploiting the marvels of electronics?

Most French composers writing for conventional instruments continue to produce works in the prewar modern style (for example, Milhaud, Poulenc, Françaix, Pierre Capedeville, Jean Rivier, Henri Dutilleux; Honegger died in 1956); but by 1940 Olivier Messiaen was already reaching beyond the boundaries of his own time and country for sound sources. He found these in the complex rhythms and scales of India, the percussive sonorities of Chinese and Balinese music, modes and instruments from antiquity, and stylizations of bird songs. He has worked all of them into a traditional musical fabric (as in his Turangalila Symphony) to give it color. His *Vingt regards sur l'enfant Jésus* creates remarkable effects with a piano alone. Here is music of religious exaltation. Some passages are Wagnerian in their soaring emotional quality, though they are simpler in form and thoroughly modern in feeling. Messiaen has created a language of mystical love, which is varied, powerful, tender, sometimes brutal, and many-colored.

While Messiaen introduced the postwar generation of *avant-garde* composers to all kinds of non-conventional music, René Leibowitz became the main champion of the twelve-tone serial system of Schönberg and Webern in France. Pierre Boulez is the outstanding product of these two diverse influences. His instrumental and vocal works are basically of the twelve-tone type, but they are more melodic and luminous, conveying feelings similar to those of a Hartung or Soulages painting. *Le Marteau sans maître* (a cycle of chamber pieces inspired by a René Char poem) combines abstraction and lyricism in a haunting way without completely decomposing human emotion into the elemental chaos of the early *musique concrète*. Like Minaux and the later Sarraute, Boulez seems to be showing that today's *avant-garde* may be abandoning yesterday's ultramodern styles mainly because the effectiveness of these has been exhausted, and not out of despair with the world around them. (We wear out everything so fast in the twentieth century.)

There is no denying that the traditional values of European culture seem to have lost their impressiveness for the young *avant-garde* artists in France. These men and women are not disillusioned (like the "lost generation" of the twenties—one has to have a home before he can be lost) or bitter (like the current "beat generations" of France and the United States or Britain's "Angry Young Men," who feel that society overlooks them by not giving them status or a sense of direction). They accept the world as they find it and try to understand what happens in it rather than explain its ultimate meaning. Neither the intellectual dogmas nor the extremist attitudes of the thirties and forties (especially communism and Existentialism) stir them. Although they lack enthusiasm, humor, and a sense of tragedy, they are not antihumanist monsters. They simply cannot see man as the measure of all things anymore.

Composers like Boulez, writers like Sarraute, and painters like Minaux believe that the creative artist should play the game with the most rational dice and according to the strictest rules he can imagine. They reject all previous theories, just as scientists have abandoned theories of nature that did not explain what actually happens. The works of these creative young Frenchmen are based upon preconceived systems, but, because they operate intuitively, these may change from one work to the next. In most cases, however, they have put aside the anguish of their predecessors and tried to describe the details of the world around them with the objectivity of an atomic physicist.

From Folk Culture
to Mass Culture

France's artistic and intellectual *avant-garde* has had virtually no influence on the bulk of the population. For centuries the rural masses knew little beyond their local folk cultures. Even in the cities the different social classes had their own distinctive styles of life. The mass media of communication gradually broke down some of these social and cultural barriers, but they still expressed a predominantly bourgeois outlook before the middle of the twentieth century. In its fully developed form, mass culture consists of those themes, values, and products that can be shared by all members of a society with no class distinctions.

Although the ideals of social democracy and mass culture date back to the French Revolution, the attempt to make them prevail at that time was premature. They can thrive only in a country where the dominant view of the world is based upon economic progress and an advanced stage of technological development, neither of which existed in France during the 1790's. Government-

8

sponsored festivals attracted enthusiastic participants among the budding urban proletariat, for whom the guilds and the church had ceased to provide cultural norms. But trees of liberty, temples of reason, and the new-fangled calendar meant little to the majority of people, who were mainly interested in burying "feudalism," safeguarding their property, and defending their national independence.

Any regime or movement that tried to enforce more drastic changes in the country's traditional civilization was bound to fail. Robespierre's ill-starred Republic of Virtue was followed by the Thermidorean Reaction. Napoleon codified the law, founded institutions like the Bank of France and the University of France, created the Legion of Honor, and tried to make public careers open to all men of talent; he did not alter France's social or economic structure. Throughout the nineteenth century the rich grew richer, the gap between the educated and the unlettered sections of the population became wider, and different groups of Frenchmen clung to their own styles of life.

The rural masses preserved their traditional folk cultures. These contained elements from prehistoric times, from Christianity, and from the different ethnic groups—Ligurian, Celtic, Roman, Burgundian, Frankish, Basque, Norman, Flemish, Alsatian—that had invaded or occupied various parts of the country. Torchlight and bonfire festivals were associated with saints' days, but they retained their primitive meanings of warding off the evil spirits that brought diseases to cattle and grain and of stimulating fertility and fecundity. They also had the social function of bringing young people together to find marriage partners. Ceremonies like these expressed all the beliefs of a particular community, so that everyone was concerned with their good effects. They were spontaneous and obligatory gatherings of a whole village for the purpose of taking part in a collective act.

A series of folk ceremonies found throughout France until the early twentieth century was Carnival—the festivities of the week preceding Lent. The church had tried to give it Christian meanings, but its main themes came from pagan times. One aspect of Carnival was the visit to this world by the spirits of the dead, whose role was played by young men wearing masks. The general license they enjoyed was justified by their useful function of bringing purification and driving out demons and sorcerers. Belief in the "fertilizing" character of the dead in renewing life was a typically "illogical" archaic notion. Today the revelers throw confetti at the tourists during the commercialized Mardi Gras festival in Nice. In earlier times masked village youths flung flour or white clay at their neighbors in order to purify them. They also went from one farmhouse to another demanding choice pieces of cooked meat (in a kind of medieval "trick or treat").

Carnival preserved other themes from the remote past. It marked the end of the season of saints' festivals, when young men and women had been able to meet and get acquainted. During these last few days they were expected to announce their betrothals. At the same time, married couples were supposed to patch up their quarrels and restore domestic peace. Those who did not had to submit to a charivari, which was an uproar made in front of their house by masked youths banging tin kettles together.

Several connotations were attached to the ceremony of burning a giant effigy on Ash Wednesday. The figure looked like a bloated Gargantua from folk legend. He could also be viewed as a symbol of the spirit of Carnival and of all the revelers who had gorged themselves on the perishable food and drink of this world. Thus, he became a scapegoat full of the vices and sickness of the community. By setting fire to him its inhabitants sent him back to the realm of the dead to renew himself, while they renounced the fat of this world for forty days.

All true traditions "engage" the very personalities of the individuals who transmit them. Their acquisition does not rest on a simple appeal to memory or habit (which is the case with many modern forms of knowledge). One does not copy models for traditional behavior, one must relive them. The members of a traditional community live through a synthesis of logically unrelated ideas and acts in common. Their style of life—constantly refurbished by a kind of empirical common sense shared by the group—gives them the implicit wisdom they need in order to get along in their circumscribed little world.

In a traditional culture the everyday world of work is ordered by prescriptions expressed in sayings, proverbs, and homilies. Under ordinary circumstances they permit one to bring about a favorable course of events and avoid accidents. If an unfavorable event or an accident occurs, it is because one has not fulfilled the appropriate prescription to the letter, or because some occult power or outside influence has interfered to change the order of things. As recently as the 1940's you could still observe this attitude in remote rural areas. You drove past a peasant leading a cart pulled by two oxen; they pulled off the road and overturned the cart. When you stopped and approached him, he said to you: "It's your fault, since I was in front of my animals" (where I belong). If you tried to reason with him or insisted that he might have altered his course in some way, he became indignant and got angry, and all the local people supported him.

A traditional style of life is made up of chains of operations.

Once one has taken the first step, one must go on to the finish. This notion is expressed in folk sayings like: "The wine has been opened, we have to drink it." Yet, there are no laws governing the world, for the folk mind does not see any interrelationship between two different chains of events. There are only stories and anecdotes, where the particular accounts for the particular. In the oral literature of a traditional culture imagination elaborates permanent themes. It knows a circumscribed universe of special personages, each of whom is characterized by a certain number of adventures and traits peculiar to him. In order to explain the "forces" it cannot grasp, the archaic imagination invents myths and legends personifying them.

Folk lore gets along without logically systematized thought, especially scientific thought. It is traditional, as opposed to logical or scientific. In France neither political revolutions, growing indifference to the church, universal military training, nor compulsory primary schooling obliterated it completely in those areas where the old economic pattern and style of life remained unchanged.

Although public school teachers taught their pupils the Mother Goose stories of Charles Perrault and the fables of La Fontaine, these did not take root in the more remote villages. The people there—whether peasants, artisans, or tradesmen—continued to speak their local *patois* and to preserve their earlier oral versions of these tales. Peddlers and itinerant craftsmen brought a few novelties to the natives without really changing their basic style of life. (The various crafts represented by the Compagnons de la Tour de France had their own subcultures, but their influence in spreading the national culture was restricted mainly to the larger towns.) Family remedies were preferred to patent medicines, traditional forms of dress to city clothes, and home-made alcoholic beverages to "imported" ones. Rural Frenchmen differed in their attitudes on politics and religion from one province to the next. Still, as long as they spent the bulk of their lifetimes within the sight of the parish church tower and the sound of its bells, they identified themselves with the community it served and viewed people from other communities as "foreigners."

Until less than a century ago the content of most Frenchmen's social and cultural activities was usually derived from the functional groups in which they lived and worked. Christianity united them all to some extent, but each profession, each class, and each locality gave it the stamp of their specific outlook. Peasants, artisans, soldiers, and priests each shared in a separate subculture, with its own forms of action, thought, and expression. (Even the men of letters had their traditional culture, which was essentially rhetorical, and which they expressed orally in frequent Latin phrases culled from the classical authors they had read in school. The *Petit dictionnaire Larousse* still contains a section of such phrases printed on pink paper.) They looked upon these forms as an immutable framework for their behavior. Sometimes they gave them new meanings, as in the case of northern coal-miners who used the feast-day honoring the patron saint of their town as a means of compensating for their dreary lives through drunken revels. But the "occasion" still reinforced their feeling of belonging to a separate social group.

In the big cities different social groups became increasingly isolated from each other. Until the mid-nineteenth century it was common to find some of them living on separate floors of the same building—with the rich at the street level and the poor in the garrets. But industrialization (and the renovation of Paris by Baron Haussmann) brought a change in the housing pattern that created whole districts in which one particular class set the standards. In the new factory-suburbs of the capital there were people who rarely saw the Champs Élysées and whose daily speech was far different from that of the aristocrats in the Faubourg Saint-Germain or the intellectuals of the Quartier Latin. The workers had their own forms of pronunciation and syntax and they borrowed many words from the *argot* of the underworld. They became increasingly conscious of being mistreated, despised, and segregated. Perhaps this was why they felt a special need for their own language, especially since the public schools tried to teach them the official language of a society that made no place for them.

For the dominant themes, values, and products of France's nascent mass culture were self-consciously bourgeois. During the nineteenth century popular and academic artists relied increasingly on routine mannerisms and hackneyed sentiment as the means of reaching a growing public. Romanticism, which had been a fresh and original style at first, was watered down and sweetened to attract the tired businessman and his bored wife. In this process the borderline between authentic art and high-class trash was overstepped more and more. Eugène Sue reduced the heroic proportions of Victor Hugo's *Les Misérables* to pathos in his own serial novels. Saint-Saëns outdid Berlioz in bombast without approaching him in grandeur. In painting, Ernest Meissonier's meticulously constructed scenes of past glories and tragedies were lifeless compared with those of Delacroix.

The historical novel, the operetta, and the bedroom farce became the principal vehicles of contrived adventure and artificial romance in the second half of the nineteenth century. Alexandre Dumas, *père*, with the assistance of a half-dozen hack writers, repeated the formulas of *The Three Musketeers* in a manner that presaged the novel-writing factory described in George Orwell's *1984*. Jacques Offenbach's *Orphée aux enfers* and *La Belle Hélène* delighted boulevardiers who wanted satire, tears, and excitement in small but sparkling doses. City-bred Frenchmen could experience at second hand the *furia francese* of D'Artagnan and the cancan dancers, or the forbidden delights of adultery as performed in the plays of Georges Feydeau. Even such present-day genres as "science-fiction" and "horror comics" were already being anticipated by Jules Verne and the *Grand Guignol*.

In general, however, the urban bourgeoisie in France resembled its contemporaries in other Western countries in wanting to retain the outward appearances of a preindustrial society. The French did not go as far as the English and the Germans in making railroad stations look like Gothic cathedrals or Hellenistic temples. Except for the Grands Magasins du Printemps in Paris they did not build their department stores in the form of Venetian palaces or medieval fortresses, like some American specimens of the 1890's. Garnier's opera house and a few structures left over from various international expositions were deliberately ostentatious, but most public buildings in the capital and the other major cities were given official, "classical" façades well into the twentieth century. A few pioneering engineers developed the use of steel and reinforced concrete for structural purposes. Although for them the Eiffel Tower was the supreme monument of naked industrial power and the herald of a new era, millions of other Frenchmen viewed it as a monstrosity.

Natural and functional forms of all kinds were padded, embellished, and extended in the late nineteenth century. Whenever possible, past styles were copied with an egregious eclecticism. Skilful and not-so-skilful *ébénistes* manufactured antiques in ever increasing quantities for petit- and grand-bourgeois collectors. These urban apartment dwellers cluttered their rooms with furniture and bric-a-brac in every style from Gothic to Louis XVI. Paris designers in search of variations in exaggerated ornamentation replaced the hoop-skirt with the bustle. The men grew beards.

While up-to-date people in the provinces copied the changing fashions of the capital, millions of others were devoted to a sentimental popular literature and imagery that was old-fashioned without being true folklore. In 1790 a man named Pellerin had founded a factory in the town of Épinal, which turned out colored pictures showing episodes from history (of the Saint-Joan-crowning-the-Dauphin variety) and scenes of rustic and domestic bliss. The style of these *images d'Épinal* was a combination of Grandma Moses and cigar-box art. They had a far wider circulation than the woodcuts portraying the ideals of the Revolution, and they survived them for over a hundred years. There was also a store of French-language tales, homilies, proverbs, and songs, which were transmitted orally to those provincial communities near the national highways that had been built in the late eighteenth century.

Another national public for early forms of mass culture comprised the faithful followers of *le bon Dieu*. Shops in the Place Saint Sulpice and peddlers throughout the country sold them sentimental paintings, miniature statues, and devotional tracts, which the impious called *bondieuseries*. Unlike the iconography of Eastern Europe and Latin America, these were not products of a traditional folk society. A company that manufactured kewpie dolls for carnivals would have had no difficulty in "converting" for the church-art market. The Catholic church itself preserved the medieval dignity and exotic texture of its formal ritual. It sponsored no revival meetings, boxing matches, or guitar-playing priests. But it did sanction religious calendar-art, hackneyed biographies of the saints, and routine piety as harmless substitutes for true belief.

France's folk cultures were able to incorporate *images d'Épinal* and *bondieuseries* into their age-old traditions and to survive as long as the basic framework of their action and thought remained unchanged. They began to disappear only when the traditional outlooks that supported them were destroyed by the intellectual, technological, and organizational forms of industrial civilization. Harvest ceremonies involving the symbolic use of bundles of grain cut with a scythe lost their meaning as modern tools replaced this ancient one. The railroad turned formerly self-sufficient peasants into producers for distant markets and consumers of factory-made goods and cultural themes elaborated in urban editorial offices. These people ceased to transmit their own non-intellectual traditions to their children when their style of life no longer imposed the necessity of "living" them as a daily experience.

Technological progress and the disruptive effects of modern warfare gradually destroyed the traditional cultures of the French masses after 1870 and especially after 1919. The first uprooted section of society to be swept into the mainstream of the dominant national culture was the white-collar employees. Neither their jobs nor their social milieu provided them with meaningful cultural themes—as was still the case for millions of artisans, farmers, and shopkeepers before the First World War—and they lacked the feeling of class solidarity shared by many industrial workers. Office clerks and shopgirls came into contact with real bourgeois in their daily work and in public places. The quality and size of their wardrobes were inferior, but the men wore black coats and ties, and the women wore high heels. Though their occupation required these forms of dress—plus a modicum of refinement in their speech—it also conditioned them to adopt other kinds of middle-class behavior and attitudes. Then, with the advent of the movies, radio, illustrated magazines, and paid vacations, the majority of Frenchmen began to imitate them.

For the normal person the products of mass culture wear a "cap of invisibility." He reads the labels on them and troubles no further. Only when he can relate them to his own immediate experience do they take on any meaning for him at all. And then this meaning may be personal, private, and even secret. Frequently something or someone in a motion picture, a comic strip, a vaudeville act, or a radio program helps the spectator to relieve his tensions, displace his illicit impulses, or express his hostility to or identification with the authorities, criminals, and pranksters, without his being aware of what is happening. The creations of the mass media of communication are not necessarily viewed as their creators wish. They can mean different things to different people. The same is true for the literary, artistic, and musical forms a person knows. But unconsciously his attitudes and feelings are molded by the stereotyped images, phrases, and sounds he sees and hears every day. These condition his responses, along with the language that shaped his thought in infancy and the social and cultural norms that he learned at home, in school or church, in the army, and at work.

Guillaume Apollinaire once said that "the energy of art imposes itself on men and becomes for them the plastic standard of the period," though there is usually a time lag of at least a generation between popular and advanced taste. In the 1920's most Frenchmen found no meaning in the works of the cosmopolitan Stravinsky or the sophisticated cave man Picasso. If they had any interest at all in serious art or music, they preferred traditional and academic styles to "modern"—Rosa Bonheur and Massenet to Léger and Honegger. A strident saxophone, a factory chimney, or a used package of corn flakes may have been objects of poetic significance to distressed aesthetes, but the common man looked for sentimental fictions and hackneyed splendor in his art.

The most striking example of the widespread devotion to old artistic forms was in architecture and public monuments. Not only was the average building in France over one hundred and fifty years old; most of those that had been destroyed during the First World War were replaced by exact replicas, with no effort to introduce contemporary design or conveniences. The majority of Frenchmen were therefore conditioned to an earlier culture by the buildings they saw every day. As children they were also shown Versailles, the Hôtel des Invalides, the great cathedrals, and the chateaux of the Loire, which reminded them of their country's past glory and made them resist the simple, functional style of architects like Le Corbusier. The bigwigs of the École des Beaux Arts also frowned on modern architecture and put pressure on the government to commission second-rate academic designers for its new edifices.

This school was one of the five branches of the venerable Institut de France; the others were the Académie des Inscriptions et Belles Lettres, Adadémie des Sciences Morales et Politiques, Académie des Sciences, and Académie Française. Almost everyone recognized these institutions as the custodians of France's traditional literary, artistic, and intellectual values. Membership in one of them brought immense prestige. (Even Jean Cocteau—who had once suggested burning down the Louvre Museum—was delighted when he was ultimately elected as one of the "forty immortals" of the Académie Française.) As government consultants, compilers of dictionaries and official bulletins, critics, and bestowers of coveted prizes, the academicians exerted a conservative influence in French cultural life, which was unparalleled in any modern country.

While traditional and academic styles continued to predominate in the 1930's, the energy of contemporary art began to impose itself on the products of mass culture in a watered-down version. Film producers, billboard advertisers, and furniture designers borrowed forms and techniques from Léger, Matisse, Mondrian, and Miro, emptied them of their original emotive import, and used them as a modern backdrop for a preindustrial style of life. Eventually this new décor was to have an effect in conditioning the average Frenchman to the twentieth century, but the "modernistic" furniture of the Galérie Barbès, like the new neon-and-chromium movie palaces and cafés, won out slowly over Louis XV and Second Empire.

In addition to his physical surroundings, a person's daily routine conditions his feelings and responses. Until the past decade or so millions of French women still cooked on wood or coal stoves, shopped every day because they had no refrigerators, and did their household chores without vacuum cleaners or automatic washers. The French had to spend a great deal of time doing things like bathing (without bathtubs), walking or bicycling to work or to the market, and getting fuel. Single people living alone could buy various personal services, but most adults were married and performed these services themselves. Urban bourgeois families and well-do-do farmers usually had maids, though the average housewife—with or without a maid—had little time for bridge and church bazaars. She spent her leisure moments sewing or gossiping with her neighbors. The "man of the house" usually stopped at a café for a drink on his way to and from work and stayed in at night. When he and his wife did go out, they took the children with them.

Poor people drank more a century ago than they do today; in the early days of industrialization, drunkenness was the only effective release from an otherwise brutalizing existence. Although a glass of wine is still considered necessary as a ritual social accompaniment to eating and conversation, "serious drinking" has lost its working-class connotation. In the mid-1950's the government of Pierre Mendès-France began trying to discourage the French from consuming more alcoholic beverages per capita than any nation in the world. Since then the governments of the Fourth and Fifth Republics have used posters and billboards to point out the menace of alcohol to health and safety. But, as recently as 1958, half of the respondents in a survey said that they believed in giving diluted wine to infants.

Although the French are as sports-minded as most modern nations today, they spent relatively little of their leisure time exercising their muscles or watching athletic events before the 1930's. France's noblemen and rich bourgeois hunted, rode horseback, fenced, and began to play tennis, while the rest of the population tended to view such activities as signs of conspicuous leisure and class distinctions. (*Le Chasseur français* was the most widely read sports periodical until the Second World War. Today *L'Équipe* —which covers mass spectator-sports—has a larger and more plebeian audience than this hunter's magazine.) Only gradually did the urban masses adopt physical exercise as a form of relaxation. In the nineteenth century young workers had learned the techniques of *savate* (a kind of boxing with one's feet as well as one's fists), but this was more a means of self-defense than an idle pastime. The first truly national sport in the early twentieth century was bicycling.

The degree of interest shown by different French social groups in sports reflected their corresponding acceptance of or resistance to contemporary civilization. Sport-mindedness was traditional with the nobility; otherwise, it seemed to be directly correlated with the degree of mechanization in people's work and in their daily lives. Peasants did not play tennis, and they rarely watched football matches or auto races, even when these were held in nearby towns. In the cities, on the other hand, industrial and clerical workers began to find a common interest with the upper classes in horse-racing, boxing, and football, and they provided the bulk of the spectators at all of the big events. Professional men and self-employed proprietors resisted these forms of mass culture longer than other sections of the urban bourgeoisie, but their sons were beginning to break away from such conservative attitudes toward "modern" social behavior by the mid-thirties.

Like so many other activities in France, athletics was viewed more as a cult than a pastime. Leftist politicians associated it with militarism and clericalism, while some conservative nationalists favored it for its ascetic and character-building possibilities. Snobs and antisnobs also gave it "American" overtones. During the interwar years France produced outstanding individual champions like the boxer Georges Carpentier, the tennis star Suzanne Lenglen, and the runner Jules Ladoumègue, but no self-respecting intellectual dared show any enthusiasm for such "vulgar" idols. Neither the state, the church, the schools, nor the communes provided adequate large-scale facilities for mass participation in sports, so that French children were deprived of the kind of conditioning for co-operative effort that teamwork offers. It was the Vichy regime that organized physical-training programs for all school-boys, and even today they tend to view these as another form of educational regimentation.

The home-and-family orientation of most Frenchmen prevented them from being very much concerned with the outside world until the end of the Second World War. The very construction of their dwellings—with their thick walls, locked gates, and metal shutters —closed them in and kept strangers out. Some factories, offices, and large stores had facilities and décors that differed radically from those of the home, but the majority of people did not work in such surroundings. Before the late thirties, few Frenchmen saw unfamiliar places as tourists or had much contact with different social groups. (And under the German occupation most of them—except for a minority of émigrés and Resistance fighters—again withdrew into their familiar shells.) The mass media of communication gave them their main images of outsiders, whose ways of behaving were viewed as amusing curiosities or contemptible deviations from the right way, the only way, the French way.

During the interwar years Parisian newspapers and magazines had a large national circulation, and inexpensive, paper-bound books were sold at kiosks, railroad stations, and bookstores in small towns throughout France. The French had pioneered the mass dissemination of the printed word in the late eighteenth century, and millions of them continued to spend a good deal of their leisure time reading. Cheap editions of the classics were especially popular. They reinforced the presence of the past that was felt in so many other ways. But most periodicals gradually adopted a more modern format. The best-selling weeklies, fortnightlies, and monthlies included fifteen fashion and woman's journals, twelve humorous magazines (some of which specialized in racy forms of Gallic wit), ten literary reviews, ten devoted to politics and satire (including the iconoclastic *Canard enchaîné*), five to popular science and radio, three to the movies, and three to sports.

The images and themes presented in the influential *L'Illustration* suggested the slowness with which the dominant French outlook changed between the First and Second World Wars. This illustrated weekly was for the non-intellectual bourgeoisie of that period what Diderot's *Encyclopédie* had been for the educated classes a century and a half earlier—an informative guide to the latest developments in all fields—as well as a news magazine. Its numerous picture-stories about foreign royalty seemed to appeal to a stubborn nostalgia for France's glorious past under her own kings, even among avowed republicans. This theme was also expressed in almost every issue with photographs of old castles, old furniture, and the unchanging aspects of Paris and the provinces.

By the late 1930's *L'Illustration* had increased the proportion of its images showing modern housing, furniture, and gadgets, both in its text and in its advertisements. One article stressed the need to clean up the unsanitary districts of the capital; another showed the new garden-cities in the industrial suburbs. Yet, just as the academic art of the official salons was given more space than contemporary styles, traditional examples of man's utilitarian handiwork continued to predominate. Sports were usually presented as upper-class, non-competitive pastimes—mainly skiing, boating, and horsemanship—with little attention given to plebeian spectator-events like soccer (called football in Europe) and bicycle-racing. The heroes and heroines of *L'Illustration* were national ones, especially generals, Joan of Arc, and an occasional airplane pilot who had broken a world record for speed or endurance. Its readers were led to believe that technological progress consisted of spectacular individual exploits and inventions, and that their country could hold its own in this respect without giving up its traditional cultural pattern.

Because the government subsidized several musical organizations and theaters, more lower-class Frenchmen heard and saw the classics performed than Americans and Englishmen, but most of them preferred vaudeville to opera and Tom Mix to Racine. Some of the less-educated bourgeois, in turn, were abandoning the saccharine strains of operetta and the *bals musettes* for American jazz. Commercialized "primitives" like Josephine Baker and Duke Ellington were almost as popular with the middle-brows as African masks were with the highbrows.

Although few rural Frenchmen listened to radio broadcasts before the late thirties, city-dwellers rapidly became conditioned to the themes of industrial society as presented by this new mass medium of communication. In addition to news and commentary on current topics, the French stations offered numerous educational and service programs: reviews of books, English lessons, advice to women on the care of children and the home, setting-up exercises in the morning, and hourly time signals from the Paris observatory (to remind easygoing Frenchmen of the importance of punctuality in modern living). Most of the national networks were state-controlled, and the musical and dramatic fare they presented was of a higher caliber than that of commercial broadcasting. But French listeners could get all the jazz and unsophisticated comedy they wanted from the privately operated transmitters in France or by tuning in broadcasts beamed to their country from Luxembourg, Andorra, and England. These stations advertised the advantages of the latest factory-made products and gadgets along with their free entertainment.

One-half to three-fourths of the films shown in France during the interwar years were foreign productions that depicted environments, styles of life, and physical types that were strange to the French viewer. Images of Emil Jannings, Pola Negri, and Douglas Fairbanks silently cavorting in exotic and historical settings were as remote from the French way of life as the Arabian Nights. The problem of talking pictures from other countries was solved by dubbing in native voices, a technique that produced Wyoming cattle-rustlers and Chicago gangsters expressing themselves in the *argot* of the Faubourg Saint-Antoine. Even so, the movies made Frenchmen familiar with the sights, sounds, and daily routine of industrial civilization in America, while the products they saw advertised on the screen during intermissions showed them what modern living could be like in their own country.

One foreign film star with whom millions of Frenchmen could identify themselves was Charlie Chaplin. Both the intellectuals and the masses saw in him the personification of the marginal man who suffers as a result of technological change and its organizational consequences. Affectionately known to the French as Charlot, the little tramp expressed the responses of what Karl Mannheim called the "hand-cart mind" in the machine age. In his bowler hat, cane, and black coat—which were obvious symbols of petit-bourgeois status to Europeans—Chaplin played the role of the clown. In other words, he gave his audience an image of a character who was marginal socially as well as economically (though of course many people simply thought he was funny without giving his behavior any sociological implications).

Marginal types appeared frequently on the stage and screen in France during the interwar years. They asserted the human value of the "little man," despite his growing alienation from a complicated and regimented world that seemed to be run for the benefit of the privileged few. In the 1930's vaudeville entertainers like Bach, Noël-Noël, and Fernandel portrayed the lovable clown and "fall-guy," while in the movies Arletty habitually played the sympathetic prostitute, and Jean Gabin the misunderstood worker or gangster. René Clair's *Sous les toits de Paris* and *À nous la liberté* also presented inept and humble people in a favorable light and made fun of "stuffed shirts."

Indeed, the most beloved characters in French mass culture before 1940 were marginal with regard to modern industrial society. Many people secretly envied fictional *clochards* ("hoboes" who were "jacks-of-all-trades-but-masters-of-none"), whether they were called Laurel and Hardy or "Deux Nigauds." American comic-strip personalities like Moon Mullins, Mutt and Jeff, Tilda (in "The Gumps"), and the Katzenjammer Kids had their French counter-parts in "Les Pieds Nickelés" (a "gang" of three idlers who spent their time outwitting the authorities, but who had their own code of loyalty to people like themselves), "Bibi Fricotin" (a traditional *gavroche* type of street urchin), and "Bécassine" (a nineteen-year-old servant-girl—in a Breton costume—who traveled as a lady's maid; she was kind but stupid, and always doing the wrong thing; her name became a household word for her kind of behavior). Ordinary Frenchmen liked to ridicule the antics of these characters, but they often identified themselves unconsciously with them in their protest against impersonal authority, regimentation, mechanization, and the ruling classes. By the late thirties, however, some little boys were becoming attached to more up-to-date heroes like Tarzan, Luc Bradefer, and Nick Carter.

The movies were the most popular form of mass entertainment and they provided both the reflections and sources of many daydreams and popular myths in France. Daydreams represent an imaginary working-over of emotional problems and conflicts, which, in different cultures, are given a variety of solutions. People who share a common culture—whose private worlds overlap—are likely to have certain typical daydreams, and the movies provide these ready-made. They allow the viewer to project himself into roles that he would hesitate to assume himself, because of either guilt-feelings or lack of imagination. Such roles sometimes involve attitudes toward different ethnic, social, and occupational groups, as well as the army, religion, and the state—attitudes that reflect group myths more openly and more articulately than the language and action of ordinary social intercourse.

French film-makers were the first to represent the lives of the masses in a realistic fashion, and *Le Crime de Monsieur Lange*, released in January, 1936, was the earliest example of this new style. Unlike directors such as D. W. Griffith, Serge Eisenstein, and René Clair, Jean Renoir achieved an effect of realism in this production without resorting to history or fantasy. The setting of *Le Crime de Monsieur Lange* is a working-class suburb of Paris. Produced just before the Popular Front electoral victory, this film is a remarkable documentary on the depression years. It reflects the hopes of the artisans, shopkeepers, and little people of Paris, the development of the trade union and co-operative movements, and the desire for social legislation. *Le Crime de Monsieur Lange* is also one of the few prewar French moving pictures to give its humble setting a tone of optimism. Almost all of its successors showed the sordid and hopeless side of lower-class life. For, like the myth of the Popular Front itself, this optimism was a flash in the pan.

The story of *Le Crime de Monsieur Lange* illustrates the moral that good, simple people, working together, can triumph over the selfishness of individual employers. It begins when the head of a small printing firm, a crafty businessman—played by Jules Berry, the stock French "heavy"—withdraws the company's capital from the bank and disappears. In order to keep the enterprise running the employees band together and, with what money they are able to raise among themselves, undertake to print the popular novelettes of their neighbor, Monsieur Lange—played by the star of *Le Million*, René Lefèvre. With the honest workmen in control of the business, the printing concern prospers. Hearing of this success, the unworthy proprietor tries to take it over again. When this happens, the indignant Monsieur Lange kills him. The alliance between the workers and the intellectuals who champion their cause is also suggested here.

La Belle Équipe, another film released in 1936, portrayed the virtues of the ordinary man in the street, with his "hand-cart mind." Like *Le Crime de Monsieur Lange*, it showed that a little group of men with the right spirit could find the cure for the ills of modern society by working together with common sense and naïve honesty. Although the story, like that of René Clair's *Le Million*, begins when several poor people win a large sum of money in a sweepstakes, the characters in *La Belle Équipe* are unemployed workers rather than impoverished gentlefolk. The winners use their prize to buy a broken-down music-hall and work together to get it running again. In this film Jean Gabin won international acclaim for his fine, sympathetic portrayal of the French worker. He showed that under the muffler and the cloth cap there were human feelings of weakness and strength, courage, a quick understanding, tenderness, a temper easily aroused, a sense of humor, and a strain of brutality.

If Gabin was the symbol of the French workingman in the late 1930's, then the fatalism and cynicism of his succeeding roles could be interpreted as illustrating the quick disillusionment of the workers with the optimism of the Popular Front episode. He portrayed this later mood of despair in *Le Jour se lève* (*Daybreak*) in 1939. This film, directed by Marcel Carné and also starring Jules Berry, Jacqueline Laurent, and Arletty, was the crowning achievement of the prewar realistic style.

Le Jour se lève takes place in a cheap hotel room in a working-class neighborhood. Gabin plays the role of a quiet, unassuming foundry worker who has just killed a disreputable circus performer (Jules Berry) for allegedly having seduced his sweetheart. The police come to arrest him, but he barricades himself in his room. Until daybreak, when he finally commits suicide, Gabin recalls in a series of flashbacks the unhappy love affair that led him to his present hopeless situation. He is a poor bachelor, past thirty-five, who has fallen in love with a young shopgirl (Jacqueline Laurent) in whom he mistakenly sees the incarnation of purity. The mistress (Arletty) of the circus performer is obviously a loose woman, but she is capable of loving Gabin and understanding him. He rejects her, however, and finds himself completely alone, the victim of his vain hopes.

Gabin played the same bitter individualist against a hostile society in *Quai des brumes* (*Port of Shadows*), *Pepé le Moko,* and *La Bête humaine,* all of which pointed out the meanness and weakness of human beings, the irony of missed opportunities and fortuitous events, and the stupidity of many social conventions. These themes had appeared frequently in drama and literature from Molière to Courteline and from Balzac to Zola. But the films of the immediate prewar years expressed a despair that was different from the usual "that's-life-so-make-the-best-of-it" attitude of the French. Though not typical of the average commercial production, they were numerous enough to suggest a real fatalism in the daydreams of many Frenchmen and in the national outlook.

Cynical and fatalistic attitudes were especially evident in *Un Carnet de bal.* In this film a widow discovers an old dance program and decides to look for the men who signed it twenty years earlier. She finds them all, except one who has died, and they are all failures. The heroine, beautifully played by Marie Bell, seems to personify the mood of the French nation itself on the eve of the Second World War. In trying to recapture a brilliant ball in the past she learns that men are destined to failure, all striving is vain, and only old age, degeneration, and death are certain. One famous scene with Pierre Blanchar is photographed at a thirty-degree angle to intensify the crookedness of the world in which the widow finds herself.

In contrast to this trend toward fatalism and sordid realism, the majority of French commercial films in the 1930's were "canned" dreams of a rosy, exotic, and glamorous existence—in which men were men and natives were natives. One of dozens of its type, *La Route impériale* threw together banal elements of adventure and romance and starred Pierre-Richard Wilm in his standard role. He was a combination of Rudolph Valentino and Kirk Douglas, and in this film he plays a dashing, tempestuous, colonial army officer who lets himself be accused of treason to protect the woman he loves. Then he goes through a series of exciting adventures to free himself from the charges against him. With throbbing temples, passionate embraces, and daredevil feats of courage he gains his prize. Almost all his other vehicles had similar exotic settings and, like most motion pictures everywhere, they offered an escape from the real world of depression and the threat of war to one of sentimental fantasy.

The alleged contradiction between French cynicism and French sentimentality disappears in those cases where the former applies to society and the state, and the latter to interpersonal relations. In the 1930's this compartmentalization of attitudes persisted in fictional portrayals of ordinary citizens who still lived in relatively self-contained social groups, but it was becoming less clear with respect to men and women who moved in the competitive world of the modern-minded bourgeoisie. Marcel Pagnol illustrates these two points in his plays and films. He gives a romanticized picture of the lives of simple *méridionales* in the Marseille dock area in his *Marius-César-Fanny* series. Millions of Frenchmen have seen the film versions of these stories again and again. They consider their alternation between broad comedy and tearful moralizing as true to life. The characters involved—the sentimental manual laborer, the noble-spirited bistro-keeper, the good-hearted merchant, the sensitive, coquettish, honest girl of the people—became popular stereotypes.

On the other hand, Pagnol's *Topaze* is an Aristophanes-like satire on politics corrupted by "finance." The hero—Professor Topaze—is a teacher of moral principles in a private boys' school. His classroom is decorated with sayings like: "It is better to *suffer* evil than to inflict it" and "Money doesn't bring happiness." He is honest and naïve until the age of thirty, when he is dramatically confronted with the facts of the "real world." First he loses his job when he refuses to give a good grade to the son of a rich woman. Then he becomes involved with a shady politician and his mistress in a scheme to overcharge the city for a fleet of street-cleaning machines. Not only does he accept the credit for having invented these machines, but he ultimately goes into business for himself as a bogus contractor—thus stealing the thunder (and mistress) of the politician for whom he had posed as a front-man.

Although the main message of this play—and its more widely seen film version—is the corruption of politics, journalism, and even education, by money, it also expresses a nostalgia for a pre-industrial society, in which honest people with "hand-cart minds" could live virtuously. The unscrupulous, worldly characters move in an American-style office setting, which is shown unsympathetically. By becoming successful in this environment, Topaze adopts a cynical outlook toward everyone. In the last scene he tells his former colleague Tamise that, if he were able to return to his teaching post, he would say to his pupils: "My children, once, perhaps, the proverbs you see on the wall of this classroom were related to a reality that has disappeared. Today one could say that they only serve to send the crowd on a false path, while the clever people divide the prize; so much so, that in our time contempt for such proverbs is the beginning of making a fortune."

Sacha Guitry was another writer-producer who expressed satire and cynicism in his plays and films. His *Faisons un rêve, Le Roman d'un tricheur* (*The Story of a Cheat*), *Les Perles de la couronne* (*Pearls of the Crown*), and *Remontons les Champs-Élysées* were slick, clever, and basically repetitious. They ridiculed social values and institutions in both contemporary and historical settings. Guitry himself usually played the leading role, in which he personified the fast-talking man-about-town and sly operator. His moral was that the good people are "suckers," and that the bad ones have all the fun. Happiness is not to be found through patriotism, social justice, honesty, and loyalty. The group is a pious hoax; long live the man who looks out for himself!

The petit-bourgeois and working-class audiences of Guitry's films were introduced to themes like adultery and cynicism in watered-down versions of pre-1914 boulevard comedies. But their own lives lacked the framework of social stability and material comfort that had allowed the characters in *La Dame de chez Maxim's, La Vie parisienne*, and *Madame Sans-Gêne* to poke fun at the existing order without really threatening it. In the late

1930's cynicism was no longer an innocent way of projecting one's daydreams into the fantasy-world of the stage. Millions of Frenchmen became dependent on it as an escape mechanism that helped them to forget their own poverty and their country's diplomatic weakness. On the eve of the First World War, the national mood as expressed in vaudeville, the press, and popular songs had been one of patriotism and eagerness to fight. At the time of the Munich Agreement everyone was singing "Tout va très bien, Madame La Marquise."

French city-dwellers had many forms of cheap entertainment—cafés, public dances, café-concerts, circuses, races, popular-priced theaters, and puppet shows—but the most authentic exponent of their popular culture was the *chansonnier*. Sophisticated practitioners of this vocal art worked in fashionable night clubs or intimate theaters. In the tradition of the medieval tellers of *fabliaux* they delighted their bourgeois listeners with songs that combined gaiety and keen perception, mockery and racy sensuality, irreverence and political satire. The urban masses also had their *chansonniers*, whom they heard in neighborhood vaudeville houses, working-class cabarets (*caboulots*), or the street. In such places Edith Piaf (before she became famous) and other singers like her evoked the personal sorrows and joys of the proletariat.

No major industrial country has produced and sustained a proletarian genre comparable to the French "blues." In the United States the Negro "blues" was comparable to it in some ways, but it was not as self-consciously proletarian. The nineteenth-century rural proletariat—mainly cowboys and southern share-croppers—sang of loneliness, lost love, hard work, and poverty. But American urban workers did not create their own cultural genre. This was so partly because so many of them were recent immigrants from different European countries, and partly because they never developed a class feeling as intense as that of their French counterparts.

The French "blues" dates back to the late nineteenth century. Sung by a woman in a hard-boiled, husky tone of voice, it sometimes suggests the lot of a working girl out of a Zola novel, sometimes that of a prostitute or gangster's "moll" like Arletty. Its main theme is: Life is hard, so be grateful for any kind of love, no matter how bad the man is. A classic example of this type of song is "Mon Homme" (which was made famous in this country as "My Man" by Fanny Brice during the 1920's). Like the "Apache" dance, it seemed to express the sado-masochistic quality of lower-class and underworld *amour*.

Even if the average worker did not beat his wife or girl friend, he showed little trace of aristocratic or bourgeois "chivalry" toward her. The French woman of the people worked hard, got little consideration from men, and had none of the Cinderella dreams of shopgirls and young women in the middle and upper classes. She was tough and fatalistic, she had few feminine adornments, and she often settled for a common-law marriage.

Many workers began to lose their interest in older proletarian genres as these ceased to express their life-experience and social milieu in the 1930's and 1940's. By that time sentimental ballads about love and Paris were the most favored variety of musical fare for the lower as well as the middle classes. Tino Rossi was the outstanding example of the new type of singer in France's mass culture. His message was no longer a real experience or emotion, but the sensuousness and forced romanticism of his public personality. Jean Sablon was another *chanteur de charme*, though he also revived "Le Fiacre," a boulevard favorite of the 1890's. (The form of bourgeois adultery described in "Le Fiacre" was not related to the lives of workers and clerks, who could not usually afford extramarital relations and who would have had considerable difficulty in concealing their illicit promenades on a bicycle or in the subway.) Maurice Chevalier and Charles Trenet relied more on whimsy and wholesome optimism in helping people to forget the unpleasantness of industrial society and war. In 1945 "La Vie en Rose" may have been an expression of whistling in the dark, but, along with "Un petit vin blanc," it was the most popular song in France during the Liberation period. Meanwhile, the "Apache" dance and songs of the "Mon Homme" variety were relegated to the realm of "folklore," where—along with examples from real folklore—they became objects of curiosity for bourgeois tourists.

In Paris and the larger industrial centers American influences on popular taste became increasingly noticeable after 1919. Films from

Hollywood and songs from Tin Pan Alley often had more fans than native productions. The bulk of the motion-picture public comprised young people from working-class and petit-bourgeois backgrounds, for whom the more traditional forms of entertainment were losing their appeal. A cheap literature preoccupied with the pathos of urban life also had a large following in these social groups. The daily soap opera never appeared on the state-controlled radio in France, although the big newspapers and the "True-Romance" type of magazine offered essentially the same sort of endless sentimentality by running serial novels in their columns.

But much of what conservative writers lamented as the Americanization of French tastes was the inevitable result of industrialization. Although the United States provided models and names for activities that began to flourish in the bigger cities, all of these were obviously not American in origin. After all, it was a Frenchman, Louis Lumière, who had created motion pictures, along with Edison, while Charles Cros had developed a phonograph before the wizard of Menlo Park. Another Frenchman, Georges Claude, had invented the neon lamp, and Hippolyte Mège-Mouries had introduced oleomargarine to the modern housewife. Many other products that old-fashioned people considered abominations could not be legitimately attributed to America alone. They simply preferred to do so rather than to admit that French culture could change.

It was changing, though. By the mid-twentieth century modern technology and new forms of economic organization had produced a synthetic mass culture whose themes, values, and products the majority of Frenchmen shared in varying degrees. Their participation in it grew as the older ways of transmitting habits and taste by "rubbing off" in comparatively static groups lost their force. More money for more people made more choices available, and the mass media of communication served increasingly as guides to the attitudes that determined the style of life most people chose.

9

Mass Culture and the New Levels of Conformity

If you were to ask any Frenchman what his status was, he would probably tell you that he was a worker, farmer, teacher, shop-keeper, priest, *rentier*, lawyer, industrialist—or he might simply identify himself with the bourgeoisie or the common people. To-day, however, these social and occupational groups no longer have distinctive styles of life. Members of any one of them may own a car, read the daily *France Soir*, watch a television program, spend a vacation at a seaside resort, or drink a name-brand vermouth before dinner. There is still social stratification in France, but the traditional criteria for it are breaking down.

As birth, breeding, profession, and inherited wealth lose their importance, Frenchmen adopt new ways of distinguishing them-selves from one another. Formerly one's social role determined one's style of life. Now the relationship between them is complex

181

and full of ambiguities. France is not yet a land of occupational and residential nomads (like the United States), where socially functional groups no longer set the basic norms for behavior and where the organization of social relations becomes a cultural goal rather than a fixed framework. She is approaching the point where status in the community is something to be achieved and not merely taken for granted. Hence, more and more of her citizens are seeking new standards of conformity at various levels.

The stratum to which one belongs tends to determine one's degree of active participation in the themes and products of a technical civilization that is superseding all other forms of culture. At the same time, the "destratification" of leisure-time activities and their growing homogeneity have been accompanied by a compartmentalization of the forms in which they are practiced socially. Some people try to preserve the ties between membership in a given group and certain kinds of activity by setting up private clubs, friendly societies, youth movements, and trade-union auxiliaries. In a manufacturing city in eastern France the factory workers have their soccer league, and the office clerks have theirs. Elsewhere the Communist party sponsors one film-subscription club, the employers another. But none of these activities expresses the cultural values of a specific social or occupational group. They cut across all traditional class barriers, and any special prestige ascribed to them is purely artificial.

In France mass culture has even begun to standardize formerly contrasting temperaments. Under its influence the inhabitants of Toulouse are losing much of their traditional gaiety and impulsiveness, while those in Rouen are becoming less solemn and restrained. Frenchmen can still observe differences in regional accents, and they want to know which part of the country a celebrity or a quiz-show contestant comes from. Even so, jokes about provincial stereotypes like Marius or the Norman bumpkin are less common than they used to be. There is now no greater cultural difference between Marseille and Lyon than there is between New Orleans and Chicago, or Munich and Berlin.

As mass culture replaces the subcultures of different regions and social groups in France, her way of life seems to lose some of its national uniqueness as well and to take on the characteristics of a general Euro-American civilization. But in such things as clothes, grooming, housing, automobiles, resorts, and the decorative arts France has produced its own styles for the well-to-do to adopt and for the aspiring masses to imitate. While the wives of Parisian executives buy refrigerators with built-in radios (the ads say that "not even in America do they have this yet"), young *midinettes* try to rearrange themselves to look like carbon copies of Brigitte Bardot. Even some of the natives in France's former overseas territories wear double-breasted suits and comb their hair like her male film stars. In Dakar the Europeans stopped wearing sunglasses when the Africans started to wear them. They have not yet taken to going barefoot—a practice that was the rage on the Riviera in 1958—but they may be driven to it eventually.

Until recently Frenchmen in the provinces were less affected by mass culture than their city cousins, although Flaubert's *Madame Bovary* illustrated two types produced by the mass culture of over a hundred years ago: the bored, frustrated housewife, and the know-it-all pseudo-intellectual. A small-town druggist like Monsieur Homais was able to master a little medical jargon from semi-popular technical magazines, while a village girl like Emma could batten herself on superficial romantic novels. (In addition to sentimental "classics," the mid-nineteenth-century reader could choose such contemporary trash as *Amélie de Mansfield* and *Les Aventures d'une grande dame*.) Once she became the victim of their illusory values, she was not content merely to dream of adultery and perhaps flirt a little. Instead, she acted out her wishes with Léon and Rodolphe and found her illusions shattered. After having disposed of his unfortunate heroine, Flaubert ironically raised Monsieur Homais to a position of public honor. This pompous quack not only hoodwinked his neighbors into believing that he could serve them as well as a real doctor, he also received a government decoration.

Today the mass media cater to millions of would-be Madame Bovarys. Adultery is a frequent theme in the popular woman's magazine *Elle*. Unlike Flaubert, *Elle* presents this topic in an allegedly neutral way, based on interviews and opinion polls. On December 11, 1959, for example, it reported that one married woman out of three found conjugal love disappointing. A week later it published an article entitled "Why Does She Deceive Her Husband?" While concluding that adulterous wives are lonely and unhappy, its author seems to be blaming imperfect men for making them that way. The women he interviewed chastised their spouses for not being models of devotion and tenderness and for not giving up such bachelor habits as going out for a drink with the boys. *Elle*'s readers want their men to be glamorous, good providers, and home-centered—very much like the American female's ideal of a husband who is handsome, attentive, and a good dish-washer.

The conflict between a longing for glamor and a desire for respectability is the curse of the housewife with too much time on her hands. It is not peculiarly French (or even restricted to women), but it has been an especially frequent theme in French fiction of all forms since the Middle Ages. Traditionally it was a problem only for aristocratic and wealthy bourgeois ladies, who accepted their lot as long as appearances were preserved. Today the products and themes of mass culture have brought about two important changes. The proportion of latent Madame Bovarys has been increased by labor-saving appliances, and the notion of female emancipation as expressed in magazines like *Elle* has emphasized the injustice of not being able to have one's cake and eat it.

Respectability—which requires conformity to the norms of the dominant majority—has apparently become an important goal for nearly all Frenchmen. Few of them want to be "marginal" any more. Their new outlook is reflected in the mass media, where the *clochards*, "fall guys" (even Fernandel has acquired some *savoir-faire* in his recent films), and clumsy underdogs who were so popular before the war have virtually disappeared. Nonconformists and lawbreakers are also presented less sympathetically than they used to be. People still resent laws that threaten their political and economic rights, but there is less questioning of the authority of the state itself than in the past. Although policemen are not glorified to the same extent as in American television, they no longer appear as dunces or sadists.

There are many reasons for this apparent readiness of most Frenchmen to accept the validity of the national norms for behavior. Growing indifference toward political and ideological issues is one; the recent decline in class antagonisms is another. But the desire to participate in the themes and products of the dominant culture is particularly important in explaining this new attraction of conformity. In 1939 the film *Le Jour se lève* (see p. 174) showed the hopelessness of the effort of a foundry worker to attain either glamor or respectability. Two decades later another "quality" film, *Les Amants* (*The Lovers*)—in which Jeanne Moreau plays the thirty-year-old wife of a prosperous newspaper publisher in Dijon—gave its heroine a choice. Assuming that in each case the working-class members of the audience identify themselves with the "stars," we can see how their attitudes have changed in twenty years. Not only would they like to have illicit romance, but they want it in a setting of bourgeois luxury.

In *Les Amants* the heroine is a twentieth-century Emma Bovary who lives on an eighteenth-century estate with all the modern conveniences. She has three servants to run the house and take care of her little daughter, and her husband is absorbed in his work. In order to overcome her boredom and loneliness she makes frequent trips to Paris, where she moves in the fashionable world and takes on a rich polo player as a lover. But she is still bored and lonely. Then an attractive young archeologist (from a good family) comes into the picture, and in a one-night courtship that is both glamorous and sizzling they become lovers. All of this happens in the heroine's own house and garden while her husband, daughter, guests, and servants are asleep. The following morning the dewy-eyed pair drives off in a baby Citroën to the astonishment of the whole household, which is gathered in the courtyard. Our 1959 Emma does not die full of remorse. She has to give up a certain amount of her respectability and luxury and she begins to wonder if she is not a bit too old for her new partner. But she has obviously found happiness.

Although many French men and women may secretly envy the hero and heroine in *Les Amants*, a larger number seems to look to the royal family of Monaco as the ideal model of glamor and respectability. People on both sides of the Atlantic have seen photographs of Prince Rainier, Princess Grace, and their children, but these are most popular in France, where they appear regularly in the big picture magazines. What meanings do these images convey, and what attitudes do they evoke? An inquiry conducted by the weekly *L'Express* in the summer of 1958 produced thousands of answers whose explicit and implicit content reveals much about the current outlook of the French masses.

All the respondents explicitly stated that, to them, Grace and Rainier symbolized happy married life. They and their children are attractive and healthy, and they have no financial worries. The fact that a successful movie star voluntarily gave up her career to become a mother sanctifies motherhood; the fact that a royal prince married a commoner reinforces the status of the middle classes. (Until his marriage Prince Rainier was a notorious playboy whose liaisons with certain French actresses were common gossip. Now that he is a "family man," the typical French response seems to be to forgive—if not forget—these earlier escapades.) Several people described this couple as "the sublime example of bourgeois happiness"! (Surely Monsieur and Madame Dupont never "had it so good"!) All of the conventional virtues were read into the image of the Monacan royal family: marital fidelity, procreation, common sense, simplicity, love of children, and that traditional middle-class ideal—*le bonheur raisonnable*.

Another appeal of this happy household is its apparent immunity from outside disturbances. Rainier and Grace live in a sunny seaside resort which everyone associates with carefree vacations and no taxes to pay. Monaco has no overbearing allies and no rebellious colonies. It is unaffected by events like the Hungarian Revolution, the Suez Crisis, and the Algerian War. One woman said that Princess Caroline was a delightful alternative to General Massu. Because Monaco does not threaten anybody, the French can devote their attention to its sovereigns without betraying their own patriotism—especially since this little principality is practically a tributary of France.

The admiration of millions of Frenchmen for Grace and Rainier also reflects certain implicit attitudes. It shows that the masses now

186

believe in their own right to happiness, and that they would prefer to achieve this through socially approved means like marriage, wealth, and family life. Far from disapproving of a man who, at the age of thirty-seven, lives in luxury and idleness, they willingly imagine themselves in a similar situation. Curiously enough, some of the same people criticize the large incomes of Françoise Sagan and Brigitte Bardot, even though these girls work for their living. The average Frenchman is supposed to be egalitarian, but he seems to judge others on the basis of their rank and riches rather than their abilities or their services to the community. The popularity of frequent picture stories about members of the French Pretender's family supports this observation.

It would be unjust to attribute the narrow, lukewarm ideal personified by the Monacan royal couple to the whole French nation. Many of its citizens devote their lives to other people's welfare, to science and the arts, to the national interest. But the majority of them apparently prefer to be let alone to concentrate on improving their standard of living. They would like to belong to a great, civilized country without international responsibilities. In other words, they want to have the best of France and Monaco. They find it really too unjust that Arabs and Africans should threaten the peaceful Sunday afternoons of good Frenchmen who do not wish any harm to anyone. (But in matters of complacency and self-righteousness an American has no right to cast the first stone!)

It is ironical that the mass media—which are technically so advanced—tend to perpetuate models, values, and attitudes that are no longer related to the products and situations created by an industrial society in a nuclear age. They distribute old wine in new bottles to a public that has become isolated through the loss of its traditional subcultures and that is eager to share in the central themes of the community as a whole. What this public often gets instead are modern versions of the defunct oral literature of folklore. While real scientists struggle to control such impersonal processes as nuclear fusion and electronic feedback, advertising represents the achievements of science as a new form of magic—a mysterious hocus-pocus performed by wizards in white coats for the purpose of making individual persons look prettier and smell better. Many newspaper, radio, and television reporters explain the complex problems of the contemporary world as a tissue of anecdotes. They delight the modern mass audience with their mixture of the true and the marvelous in much the same way that the storytellers of earlier times captivated simple peasants on long winter evenings in front of the fire. Most movies and popular fiction also appeal to prescientific (if not prelogical) forms of imagination.

Since the French no longer believe in fairies and ogres, and since love cannot be carried on in a two-room apartment as it allegedly was in a medieval castle, certain modifications have been made in their traditional tales. Even in their folk versions, these were less fantastic, less gory, and more easily related to ordinary experience than those of other lands. In France *Bluebeard* was a straight horror melodrama in which a frighteningly human villain almost adds his new bride to his list of earlier victims. To many little girls Bluebeard resembled *loup-garou* (also called *croque-mitaine*), a sinister male bogey who was given to excessive violence and destructive sexuality and who unconsciously symbolized threatened incest from their fathers. *Donkey-skin* also dramatized the theme of the menacing father-figure. Modern French parents do not transmit such terrifying images to their children. Even *Little Red Riding Hood* is toned down in the puppet shows, where a policeman arrives on the scene just as the heroine is about to be eaten by the wolf. But the most popular tale of all, *Cinderella*, has a happy ending in all its versions. (There are over five hundred in Europe alone, and others all over the world.) It still pervades all forms of fiction—including the public image of Prince Rainier and Princess Grace—for mass consumption in France.

Thirty years ago teen-age French girls absorbed the Cinderella–Prince Charming theme from the novels of Delly (between 1928 and 1945 the twenty-five books by this author sold around three million copies); today they and their older sisters find it in the mass-circulation magazines of the *Presse du coeur*. The leading ones are *Confidences, Nous deux, Intimités,* and *Festival.* Their message is familiar to anyone who has seen a soap opera on American television or read *True Romance*. They present it in a sequence of still photographs accompanied by bits of printed dialogue. Cinderella is usually a shopgirl or office clerk; Prince Charming often wears a tuxedo, but he may also appear in bathing trunks or in the outfit of a sports-car driver. The technique of the *Presse du coeur* is to create romantic situations in a modern décor. In this way its stories make what is near and familiar seem glamorous. Unlike the original fairy tales, they camouflage the gap between reality and fantasy. The *Presse du coeur* has been called conservative because it implicitly suggests conformity to the norms of the ruling classes. It is also reactionary, but in quite another sense, since its themes are the fantasies of a preindustrial age.

Many current songs also express a desire to escape from the tribulations of modern life through old-fashioned romance. Here again, the manner of presentation is deceptive, with its synthetic smiles, slinkily dressed females, and tuxedoed, groaning males. In the late 1950's the most popular singer in France was an American expatriate named Eddie Constantine. His appeal is that of a twentieth-century "tough guy" with the sentimentality of a Rousseauian noble savage. In "Les Amoureux du Havre" he tells his sweetheart that they don't have to worry about the world around them because their love alone will sustain them. (Compare this song to the earlier American hit proclaiming that "Love Is Here To Stay," even though ". . . the Rockies may crumble / Gibraltar may tumble," and "The radio and the telephone and the movies that we know / May just be passing fancies and in time may go.") Dalida, a sexy Italian import, created a sensation in 1958 by combining the themes of traditional love songs with the style of an ultra-modern glamor girl.

In the movies too, a modern Cinderella—Brigitte Bardot—is the main attraction, and carefree romance is the most popular theme. The following titles of typical commercial films released in the past decade speak for themselves: *Deux amours, Je n'aime que toi, Ma Femme est formidable, Paris chante toujours, Mademoiselle Striptease, Une Femme par jour, Une Nuit de noces, La Valse de Paris, M'amzelle Pigalle, Mimi Pinson*. There are, of course, other themes in both the movies and popular songs. Yves Montand,

Patachou, and many talented singers interpret a wide variety of human feelings, and all styles from "beat" jazz and whimsical ditties about animals to Calypso and the urbane satire of Les Frères Jacques are represented. And sweet romanticism is self-consciously banished by the brutal realism of "New Wave" films like *Le Dos au mur* (*Back to the Wall*) and *Les Cousins*, which show the piteousness of man.

While romance makes what is near seem glamorous, adventure makes what is far away seem near. In the United States its main genre in the mass media is the "Western"; in France it is the detective story. (Each month French publishers sell around two million books of this type—almost a third of the total literary production.) Despite the formal realism of the average gangster film, Montmartre night clubs and police courts are as remote for most Frenchmen as the Dodge City of the 1870's is for Americans today. The spectator can enjoy the violence and amorality portrayed because he knows that the characters and situations are make-believe. But the gap between reality and fantasy becomes narrower in the novels of Georges Simenon and the films of H. G. Clouzot— for example, *Le Salaire de la peur* (*The Wages of Fear*) and *Les Diaboliques*.

In contrast to most detective novels and gangster films, *The Adventures of Tintin* take place in remote and exotic settings. Superficially this comic-strip series resembles the Tom Swift stories of the early twentieth century, although Tintin relies more on reason and imagination than his American forerunner. He is a boy-reporter who has his own apartment in Paris and who leads a completely independent existence consisting of one adventure after another. Everywhere he goes he is the intrepid, wholesome hero— a juvenile d'Artagnan with the brains of an Inspector Maigret.

Like the stories of the Comtesse de Ségur (see pp. 42–44, above) Tintin's adventures convey a code of behavior and an image of an ordered society on an unconscious level. Since Tintin usually operates in places like North Africa, India, the comic-opera kingdom of Syldavia, and even outer space, both his friends and his enemies are foreigners. He has no visible racial or national prejudices, but in every situation he takes the side of the authorities.

190

All the characters he meets have a specific profession and status whose standards make their behavior completely predictable (like the personages of folklore). Every one of them is a traditional stereotype—the testy sea captain, the bearded professor, the slick-haired jewel thief, the square-jawed airplane pilot. The order of each setting in which Tintin finds himself is clearly defined, and those people who try to upset it are the villains. He sees every state as ruled by wise leaders and threatened only by wild-eyed anarchists and spies.

Tintin is impatient with people who put on airs instead of keeping their proper place. An eleven-year-old boy who saves whole nations from sabotage and revolution, who outsmarts and brings to justice thieves, smugglers, and enemy agents, and who is rewarded by kings and secret-service chiefs is pretty pompous himself. But he personifies the dreams of his readers who are socially marginal. Although Françoise Sagan and King Baudouin are Tintin fans too (and, like millions of other people, read *Tintin* for sheer pleasure), the bulk of them are children, white-collar employees, skilled workers, and other people who look forward to becoming fully integrated members of society. They want to be independent and mobile (both socially and geographically), but they want the rest of the world to stay put so that they will know where they are when they get there.

The more opaque and complicated modern life becomes, the more people are tempted to cling to clichés that bring some order into it. Yet even the cyberneticists admit that human behavior cannot be predicted and manipulated with complete certainty. They compare human processes to games with incompletely defined rules, which are themselves functions of a particular time. The variation of the rules depends upon the situations engendered by the game itself and upon the psychological changes in the players caused by the continuous feedback of the results of their performance. This theory is one of the major themes produced by contemporary science. It is also mirrored in the arts, philosophy (in his *Philosophical Investigations* the logical empiricist Ludwig Wittgenstein called language itself a game), and in a number of motion pictures. In general, however, the mass media in France appeal to two themes from her traditional cultures: everything should be domesticated, and everything is understandable.

The most completely domesticated and understandable form of mass entertainment is professional wrestling. Known in France as "Catch" (from catch-as-catch-can), it is as popular there as it is in the United States, both in live performances and on television. In every match the triumph of Justice over Evil is total (even more so than in American wrestling). This dramatization appeals to the popular and ancestral notion that anything real is perfectly intelligible. As actors the wrestlers transport their audience out of the ambiguous daily situations in which it lives and into an unequivocal, panoramic vision of Nature, where every gesture and every sign corresponds to an immediately understandable reality.

Not only do the French masses want every kind of public performance they watch to be completely understandable, they insist on knowing what goes on "inside." Consequently, in their presentation of athletic contests the mass media emphasize the feelings of the performers. Frenchmen certainly admire the physical prowess of these men, but the press and newsreels also stress their home life, their "secret" strategy, their recriminations, and their preferences in bottled drinks. The public especially enjoys the dramatic interplay among the bicycle-racers during and after each lap of the Tour de France. In July, 1958, the daily *L'Équipe* and the monthly *Sport et vie* published "Les Confidences" of Charly Gaul (that year's winner), in which he told how he had tried to give a former champion, Louis Bobet, a helping hand. They also showed pictures of Raphaël Geminiani crying when he lost the yellow polo shirt (symbol of the first place at a particular stage in this grueling cross-country marathon) and claiming that he had been "betrayed by Judases." No one could figure out what he meant by this mysterious charge, but it illustrated the kinds of emotions the fans were invited to share.

The French are especially responsive to the "you-are-there" feeling offered by television. (Perhaps they will lose this responsiveness after the novelty wears off. French television has reached a mass audience only since the late 1950's.) A program that purports to bring the viewer into intimate contact with someone else's private life is "Au gros plan" ("Close-up"), on which some well-known film star is interviewed in his or her home each Saturday night. One week Danielle Delorme—without makeup and wearing a loose-fitting sweater—explained her secret reasons for having chosen an acting career. Another time Françoise Rosay told about her stay in the United States and concluded with a confession of the anxiety she experienced in switching from the movies to the legitimate stage.

A welcome novelty to *blasé* French viewers is the technique of replacing actors with "real people" on popular quiz shows like "Télé-Match." In the early summer of 1958 one of the contestants on this program became a minor national hero after five successive appearances. Louis Maury was a forty-six-year-old high-school teacher from Evreux. He was a little man who had been in a con-centration camp during the war and who had rehabilitated himself physically by becoming an accomplished bicycle-rider. This last fact is important, since on "Télé-Match" the contestant must excel with his legs as well as his mind. (The show's subtitle is "Tête et jambes.")

Monsieur Maury taught geography and history, so he was ques-tioned about these subjects. The questions were presented in the form of skits, riddles, and movies of places in various parts of the world. On one occasion he solved a problem of comparative dis-tances between several cities by drawing a series of overlapping circles around them on a map he improvised at the blackboard. Another time he had to name the native countries of a number of exotic birds that were brought onto the stage. When he made a mistake he had to make up for it by getting on a racing bike and riding around a one-hundred-meter track six times in forty-five seconds or less. Although a "little man" both physically and socially, Louis Maury was respectable—unlike Charlie Chaplin— and clever, as well as hardy and persevering. He personified the image of the versatile amateur so widely admired in France. (The American television show "Brains and Brawn" was copied from "Tête et jambes," but in this land of specialists the two different roles were performed by scholars and professional athletes. As a result, there was no plebeian hero with whom the audience could identify itself spontaneously and enthusiastically, as the French were able to do with Monsieur Maury.)

The programs mentioned so far are all broadcast by the state-controlled Radiodiffusion-Télévision Française, but there are also commercial radio and television channels beamed to French audiences from Luxembourg and Monte Carlo. These are more responsive to the average taste than the RTF, which caters mainly to the modern-minded "happy few" and to those people who would like to belong to this group. Many Parisians prefer Radio-Luxembourg to their own stations. Its signal is just as clear, and its major programs are prerecorded in Paris. In addition to soap operas and disk jockeys, it has a quiz show that is far different from the sophisticated "Télé-Match." "Cent francs par seconde" ("A Hundred Francs a Second") is an obvious imitation of the American program "Truth or Consequences." While the studio audience laughs, the contestants get dumped into a tank of water after having missed the answers to relatively simple questions. The show is sponsored by Verigoud soft drinks, which come in five delicious flavors and large family-size bottles.

Some Frenchmen see mass culture as an instrument of domination in the hands of the ruling classes—a new opium of the people. One could argue that the fairy tale of Cinderella and Prince Charming emphasizes the gulf between the lower and upper classes by showing the exceptional nature of the heroine's success in bridging it. (In Perrault's tale she is the daughter of a gentleman, but in the traditional oral versions of French folklore she is a peasant girl.) Still, by using the same basic plot, the fiction in today's slick-paper women's magazines leads all its readers to look for rich, handsome, well-dressed husbands from good families. The skilled worker who dreams of buying an automobile may be trying to "increase his standing," as the advertisements suggest. It is more likely that he simply wants what everyone else wants. These examples illustrate the ambiguous and contradictory role of the mass media in contemporary France.

Other opponents of mass culture view it as a terrible leveler, which makes everybody and everything equal to everybody and everything else. Compared to this bulldozer, they say, nationalism, socialism, and love are like hammers, sickles, and arrows. The bishop of Beauvais complains that young Catholics weaned on the *Presse du coeur* lose their capacity for religious experience as they become increasingly unable to distinguish between real and false feelings. A professor at the University of Grenoble cringes at the thought of half-educated people talking about science and philosophy in catch phrases picked up from *Sélection du Readers' Digest*. Some representatives of high and folk cultures take refuge in out-of-the-way places with their art treasures and their bagpipes. They dread being "discovered" and put into a picture weekly or on a television show.

Yet, far from lowering tastes to one common level, the mass media tend to reinforce existing taste patterns at all levels. With typical French "logic" the RTF broadcasts different types of programs on its three radio networks: France I (general), France II (light), and France III (serious—roughly equivalent to the Third Program of the BBC). Unfortunately, both its radio and television producers have failed to find the formula for being educational without being boring. Their interviews, panels, and documentaries are sometimes endless streams of talk. As long as they remain so, they will not reduce the intellectual and social distances among Frenchmen. There is a public for horoscopes (which are advertised in magazines like *Elle* and the picture weekly *Jours de France*) and one for the *Que sais-je?* series of popularizations of contemporary knowledge written by distinguished scholars. As in the United States different forms of mass culture in France appeal to "lowbrows" and "highbrows," "lower-middle-brows" and "upper Bohemians."

While the bulk of the motion-picture public still wants pure entertainment, there is a growing minority that judges films on their artistic merit. A trend toward art films that were viewed as such by their audience was set in the early 1940's by *Les Visiteurs du soir*, *L'Éternel retour*, and *Les Enfants du paradis*. Since then young people from almost all social classes have developed a high level of taste and discrimination and have become devotees of specific directors—both French and foreign. This pattern has become so widespread that it has made a number of "serious" films big commercial successes (like Robert Bresson's *Le Journal d'un curé de Campagne* and *Un Condamné à mort s'est échappé* and H. G. Clouzot's *Le Salaire de la peur*). Today's "New Wave" is as much a new category of spectators as a new generation of directors like François Truffaut (*Les 400 coups*), Claude Chabrol (*Le beau serge* and *Les Cousins*), Louis Malle (*Les Amants*), and Alain Resnais (*Hiroshima, mon amour*).

The most popular personality in French broadcasting, Jean Nohain, is a man who tries to please a wider cross-section of the population. He is Steve Allen, Dave Garroway, and Arthur Godfrey all in one person. For years millions of boys and girls knew him as "Jaboune" on the radio, and in the late 1950's he became the master of ceremonies on the television variety show "Les 36 chandelles" ("Seeing Stars"). He always begins this program with a masquerade of well-known entertainers, but from there on he "rejuvenates the formula" (these are his own words) periodically. At first he brought members of the audience onto the stage to tell about some personal experience in exchange for a prize. (One coalminer won a trip to the United States.) Later he switched to vaudeville acts. More recently he has dedicated each show to different occupational groups (postmen, merchant seamen, railroad workers, airplane pilots) and activities (vacationing in France, the advantages of keeping clean, how to carve a turkey). In his present role Jean Nohain is probably France's best salesman of modern living.

Another entertainer, Jacques Tati, expresses many Frenchmen's nostalgia for a more lackadaisical, traditional style of life. Tati is a king-size Charlie Chaplin who plays the role of Monsieur Hulot, the last of the lovable misfits in a machine-age environment. His recent film *Mon Oncle* pokes fun at both old and modern ways, though it obviously favors the former. *Mon Oncle* is mainly a sequence of gags in two contrasting backgrounds: a run-down, urban neighborhood, and the ultra-modern ranch house and factory of Hulot's brother-in-law. A series of shots in the former setting shows a street-cleaner who takes all day to sweep a pile of rubbish into

196

the sewer because he is constantly gossiping with passers-by. Another one concentrates on a man staggering into the local bar with an overcoat over his pajamas. When his wife calls to him from her window, he does not hear her. Then she calls his dog, who leads him back home. In this world everyone is easygoing. Human relations are warm and spontaneous; people fight, have a drink, and make up.

In the modern setting of *Mon Oncle* everything is mechanical, artificial, and disturbingly sanitary. Monsieur Hulot's sister is a slave to her push-button home and her compulsion to keep it and her little boy spotless. Her husband is a super-efficient business executive who makes everyone around him behave like a machine. His secretary, for example, is always running to him with some paper to sign; her difficulty in doing this in a tight skirt is one of Tati's many symbols for the inhuman rhythm of contemporary life. The husband and wife rarely talk to each other, and their main joy consists in acquiring a garage door with an electronic eye.

Although Jacques Tati expresses in an extreme form the ambivalent feelings of many Frenchmen toward industrial civilization, the "modernists" seem to be winning out. (A line from a current popular song says: "Adieu Paris accordéon; bonjour Paris néon.") The magazine *Elle* presents itself as a combination of reporter, judge, confessor, tutor, and director of modern taste and opinion. The following "counsels" from its 1959 Christmas issue indicate the themes it purveys to the ambitious career girls and up-to-date housewives who read it:

Look for new decorating ideas for your Christmas dinner table.
Buy food whose prices have been lowered (by government decree).
See the exhibition of paintings by an American (female of course) impressionist artist.
Use "Satin Velvet" furniture polish.
Try "Polyroll" plastic wrapping paper.
Give blood to the blood bank.
Keep your voting registration up to date.
Give your free time to the care of orphans.
Join a parachute club.

Those Frenchmen who share most weakly in the values and products of their democratic technical civilization submit most passively to the mass media and are socially the most isolated. Television brings the northern coal-miner or farmer into an attenuated kind of contact with the whole world. But since his own traditional subculture has disappeared, he has little else to orient his life outside of his home and family. Many young employees and workers (except those who are highly skilled) no longer have to go through a professional and social apprenticeship before they can get the best that their place in society affords. They start doing the kind of work they will do for the rest of their active lives at an early age and they often achieve a degree of efficiency—and a wage —that they will be unable to maintain as they grow older. These youths are extremely susceptible to the mass media and strongly committed to their informal group ties. Some of them have even formed "gangs" and taken to wearing black leather jackets and racing through the streets with their girl friends on motor scooters.

While reinforcing the cultural isolation of a large segment of the population, mass culture has, at the same time, turned France into a nation of individual and group activists. Since the late 1940's, for example, the number of amateur theatrical groups has grown to over ten thousand. In 1959 two million out of a total of eight million people between the ages of fifteen and twenty-five declared themselves to be amateur athletes, and six hundred thousand of these belonged to soccer teams. Almost half the urban workers and the majority of the middle classes now take vacation trips, in France and in neighboring countries. In fact French tourists now outnumber German ones in Italy and Spain. All these activities are definitely new cultural themes elaborated by a technical civilization.

On the other hand, the "do-it-yourself" craze seems more like a form of escape from industrial society and a return to traditional forms. The most popular of these today are gardening, camping, and all kinds of amateur craftsmanship and puttering (*bricolage*). Like many aspects of French mass culture these activities express ambiguous and contradictory attitudes. Some people adopt them in order to compensate for the mechanization in their work; others do so out of snobbery. They mean different things to different social groups and to different individuals.

This freedom of interpretation regarding many of the themes

198

and products of mass culture is the counterpart of their amoral and asocial character. They are viewed increasingly as goals or objects rather than as models. Rather than defining norms of conduct, they deal with such non-normative activities as scientific discoveries, the world-wide dissemination of on-the-spot news reports, and the spectacular performances of instruments, machines, and the human body. All of these are cultural themes organized around the notions of progress, and the domination and control of natural conditions, yet they impose no rule of social behavior. Neither do garden tools, "do-it-yourself" kits, or camping equipment bought in department stores. When one goes to the movies or watches a television program he is a member of an anonymous audience, free to "project" or "identify" himself with what he sees without any fixed rules about how he should respond.

A similar freedom of response has occurred in the history of the dance. A folk dance was usually a group affair in which the situation and feeling of each participant were prescribed for any given moment. As the individual couple became the main unit, the definition of social roles was effaced, and the importance of personal interpretation increased. While a waltz or a tango still imposed certain conventional responses on the dancers, "jitterbugging" and its current derivatives do not express the feelings of the partners. These dance forms are almost exclusively a matter of technique, shorn of all social and moral conventions. In Lille or in Akron, Ohio, the couples who perform them may give their movements a secret personal significance, but the blank looks on their faces suggest no objective meaning.

For many people even religion has undergone the transformation from a socially and morally prescribed mode of conduct (with its rites and obligations) to a form of behavior freely oriented toward objects or values that have a more purely personal meaning. Catholicism has resisted this change successfully for the most part, but the activities of the French worker-priests express it—and for this reason they have often been taken to task by the Vatican. The worker-priest does not look different from his fellow factory workers, though he must now live in a church-run residence. While he is on the assembly line he is not protected by a mass of explicit rules of conduct; he simply gives his life a different meaning. With few exceptions, French Catholics no longer live in a different social and moral world from non-Catholics; they only live through different experiences.

The mass media today rarely show people with financial worries or housing difficulties and they tend to bypass controversial and unpleasant subjects. Some critics say that the general policy of avoiding the new situations and problems posed by industrial society is a conspiracy on the part of the ruling classes to prevent the masses from understanding them. But the real reason may be a desire not to shock any section of public opinion. The masses are still too passive and socially isolated to understand the new cultural goals of a technical civilization, and even the more enlightened classes are not certain what these are.

Actually, mass culture supports the status quo and reinforces conventional social norms in all societies, whether these are democratic or totalitarian. Regardless of the system of ownership and control, radio, television, movies, and the popular press rarely give expression to controversial and revolutionary issues and proposals. In France, as elsewhere, they confine themselves largely to peripheral social concerns. Only a minority of the public reads Leftist weeklies like *L'Express*, and *France-Observateur*, and Rightist ones like *Aspects de la France* (formerly *L'Action Française*) and *Rivarol*. The majority gets its news and commentary from allegedly apolitical mass-circulation dailies like *France-Soir* and *Le Parisien*, the weekly picture magazine *Paris-Match*, or the radio. None of these challenges the basic organization and functioning of the existing society.

It is true, however, that the mass media in France are conservative largely because the people who control them want them to be so. As in prewar days, the commercial press is owned by big capitalists who seek to preserve the present social and economic systems. The Agence France Presse (one of the world's five largest news services, along with Reuters, Associated Press, United Press, and Tass) and the RTF are directly dependent upon the government, though the former gets part of its funds from its subscribers.

Except at election time, extremist parties like the Communists and Poujadists have no access to the state-controlled broadcasting facilities, and their activities are rarely reported in the newspapers.

The position of the RTF has been especially crucial, since many people have considered its news and commentaries to be politically neutral. Until 1958 it was theoretically a separate administration and not subject to control by members of the cabinet. In practice, though, the minister of information sometimes interfered with its presentation of events like the wars in Indo-China and Algeria and parliamentary debates that put the current regime in an unfavorable light. Jacques Soustelle, who held this post briefly in the summer of 1958, openly strengthened the government's hold on the national radio and television system by putting Gaullists in its key administrative positions. His excuse for this action was that the Communists had "colonized" certain branches of the RTF (though my own sampling of pre-Soustelle news broadcasts failed to reveal the heavy hand of Moscow) and that he was trying to assure its "objectivity" by rooting them out. Meanwhile, he used its networks to propagate official views and gave no voice to any opposition groups.

Even when the RTF news broadcasts try to be impartial—which has often been the case—they do not give Frenchmen a true picture of the realities they represent. Like other forms of reporting, they are the products of selection and editing. The image the viewer or listener gets is incomplete, because it stresses domestic over foreign events. It is also distorted, for the regular news programs fill in the same period of time each day with insignificant items when there are no important ones to report. In this way the latter are given the same status as the former; sometimes a minor personal misfortune is transformed into a major occurrence. Finally, the presentation of happenings in alien cultures is falsified by the use of familiar but inaccurate stereotypes—especially of the natives in France's overseas territories (until these became independent).

Like modern man everywhere, the average Frenchman has a passion for news of any sort, as long as it purports to be *so*. He seeks to be reassured that things he can understand continue to happen, but his superficial familiarity with a host of current events often cloaks an underlying apathy toward the real problems of society. In any case, the mass media give him what he wants. They devote more time and space to Gina Lollobrigida's or Brigitte Bardot's first baby than to the discovery that the human body's neuro-vegetal system combats noxious viruses. During an international crisis they play up the travels of Messieurs "H" (Hammarskjøld) or "K" (Khrushchev), rather than the complexities of power politics.

By giving important and trivial topics equal coverage the mass media threaten to undermine people's sense of proportion about what is important and what is not. In late 1957, for example, *Paris-Match* presented two series of "at home" picture stories—one on Premier Félix Gaillard, the other on the Mexican bombshell Maria Félix. Several issues later it gave much more space to Jayne Mansfield's arrival in Paris than to that of John Foster Dulles. Between mid-June and mid-July, 1958, the press, radio, and television covered the Tour de France as fully as the activities of the new De Gaulle regime. Millions of Frenchmen seemed to be as emotionally involved with the bicycle-racer Charly Gaul as they were with Premier Charles de Gaulle. Nevertheless, they are not deluded into thinking that France is in the same class as the United States and the Soviet Union, despite all the newsreel shots of her military parades, new jet fighter planes, and the explosion of her first atomic bomb. They see these two giants as the main contestants in the world power struggle and tend to view themselves as interested spectators.

The 1959 film *Les 400 coups* is a notable exception to the general tendency of the mass media to confine themselves to peripheral social concerns. It shows the development of a thirteen-year-old Parisian boy into a juvenile delinquent because his family and society as a whole failed to give him love, guidance, and emotional security. His mother and father are both office clerks who are preoccupied with acquiring the prestige products of mass culture—smart clothes for her, a car for him—but who are basically ignorant. They are rootless and socially isolated, and, to make matters worse, they show no warmth or consideration for each other. The boy sleeps on a cot in the hallway of their cramped apartment and hears the sordid details of their quarrels. He learns that his mother is a slut and he loses respect for his father for the cowardly way in which he accepts her behavior. The other "blows" he receives come from an unsympathetic teacher in an overcrowded school, from the police, and from the authorities in the reformatory where he is ultimately sent.

One of the most striking features in this film is the contrast between the boy's inward longing for security and affection and his outward *sang-froid*. (The only time he cries is when he is being taken away in a police van and is looking for the last time at the neon signs of his beloved Paris, which had been a substitute for the real love he lacked.) In a way, he symbolizes the whole current generation of young Frenchmen. Like him they have subconsciously accepted the need to protect their deepest feelings from hard blows. They seem to be striving for insensitiveness, but they also want to "belong." As adolescents they cling to their friendships and their informal group ties; as adults they look upon marriage and family life as an anchor. In the long run, however, they are earnestly seeking meaningful norms to guide them. Like much of the youth in the Western world they want to conform to, rather than rebel against, the dominant culture. Through concrete action in a limited frame they hope to achieve a modest form of happiness.

A Nation in Search of a Mission

Frenchmen have sharp minds and lively spirits. Neither mass culture nor the nation's declining power has destroyed their ability to take life as they find it and to appreciate its ironical aspects. When confronted with a problem, they quickly see an abstract principle or human motive involved. Then they delight in improvising plausible—though sometimes superficial—explanations and solutions. Except for national honor, nothing is so sacred that it cannot be ridiculed by some malicious wit. The French can be devastatingly critical or extravagantly polite, but they are seldom merely "nice." If they seem touchy, it is because they want to be proud of their way of life and resent having its virtues questioned by outsiders.

For the French people still believe that their country has a mission in the world. Although different groups of them have long disagreed about what this might be, most of them have reasoned from the same set of assumptions. In each case they have based their arguments on the special qualities of the civilization, geog-

10

raphy, and racial composition of the French nation. These assumptions find expression in scholarly works, official oratory, public school textbooks, the illustrated press, and all forms of mass entertainment from football to vaudeville. Contradictory interpretations regarding any one of them have not shaken the belief that France has a world mission. The substance of the claim is the belief itself.

The racial argument is based on diversity rather than purity. Every French school child learns that he is descended from the Gauls, Romans, and Franks. Different writers have tried to prove that one or another of these "races" gave France her national character and institutions, but the general view has been that she combines the best qualities of all three. In the twentieth century several million immigrants from Eastern and Southern Europe also made their home in France and were absorbed into the population through intermarriage. Hence, the French people see themselves as the most balanced and universal of all nations because they are the most varied and complete examples of all human types.

France's geographical attributes have prompted two lines of argument to prove her uniqueness and universality. One concerns the variety of climate and topography within the beautiful hexagon formed by her borders. In what other single country, the Frenchman asks, can one find snow-capped mountains, rolling plains, vine-covered hills, foggy seacoasts, thick forests, and semitropical gardens? (An outsider could answer that Italy, Spain, Russia, and the United States have all of these and that they too have been invaded and occupied by peoples of diverse cultures and races. His interlocutor would still cling to what he had been taught since childhood.) The second argument is based on an image of France as the crossroads of the Continental, Mediterranean, and Atlantic worlds. According to it, her culture is a mixture of elements from all three of these areas, and her political and economic interests are dictated by her continuing contacts with them. A corollary of the "crossroads-of-the-world" argument is the reputation of Paris as the undisputed center for the arts, high fashion, and international conferences.

These racial and geographical arguments have also served as supports for the claim that France's civilization is the highest and most universal expression of humanity. For centuries the French have used this belief to justify their "civilizing mission" in the world, and it is the one they have been most reluctant to abandon. They have found it difficult to exchange the role of teacher for that of learner. Partly because of their unwillingness to do so, France was surpassed in political, technological, and military achievements by countries that had changed their roles the other way around. For the United States, Russia, and even Germany were all learners until less than a hundred years ago. Outside of Asia only England has a national culture as old as France's. But the English did not become one of the world's teachers until the eighteenth century, while the French had held this position since the Middle Ages.

Actually, France had become the cultural, intellectual, and religious leader of Western civilization by the end of the twelfth century. French was the language of the English court for over two hundred years and the *lingua franca* of many Continental merchants. The religious revival that brought the papacy to its zenith began in the monastery at Cluny and was nurtured by Saint Bernard of Clairvaux. In addition, the cult of chivalry was based upon the *Chanson de Geste*, which depicted the successful Frankish resistance to the complete conquest of the West by the Arabs in the eighth century. This cult was further developed several hundred years later when Norman knights led the offensive against the Moslem world in the war known as the Crusades. Finally, French music, the architecture of the great cathedrals, and the learning of the scholars who came to the University of Paris were among the supreme expressions of the medieval genius.

Although the modern phase of European civilization originated in Italy, the upper classes stopped copying the Italian style of living and began following the fashions of France in social manners, clothes, furniture, architecture, and cooking in the age of Louis XIV. They even adopted her language, which became truly international in aristocratic and educated circles in the eighteenth century. Foreign monarchs like Catherine of Russia and Frederick of Prussia called themselves enlightened disciples of Voltaire and tried their own hand at writing plays and treatises in French. Having thus set the standards for European high culture in a cosmopolitan era, Frenchmen developed the following line of reasoning:

> What is good is good for all peoples;
> What is French is good;
> Therefore, what is French is good for all peoples.

But France never monopolized a world culture as Greece had once done. Even during their most creative period her philosophers and scientists had to vie with men like Newton, Leibniz, and Kant. And her artistic products could rarely be sufficiently cheapened to reach a mass audience, like the hackneyed copies of Hellenistic painting, sculpture, and comedy that were once marketed throughout the Roman Empire. (When Hollywood made the movie *Carmen Jones*, the French authorities called it a sacrilege against Bizet's opera and banned it in their country.) France's cultural themes have been meaningful only to a small elite of connoisseurs, while the Greeks provided popular religions and games for the masses of the entire Mediterranean world. The French language was never adopted by whole nations, as Greek, Latin, Arabic, and Spanish had been.

The French were not alone in believing that their civilization was the best one available for export. Many foreigners outside of Western Europe continued to prefer France's cultural models to those of any other modern country well into the twentieth century. As recently as thirty years ago anybody who was anybody in Bucharest or Buenos Aires conversed in French and made a conscious effort to live like a cultivated Parisian. Even more "lowly" types believed that the language, fashions, and products of France conferred prestige on those people who adopted them. Night-club proprietors from Constantinople to Singapore hired French-speaking *chanteuses* and *croupiers* and printed their menus in French to impress the tourists; Armenian moneylenders cluttered their homes with Louis XV bric-a-brac; South American gigolos posed as the bastard sons of French noblemen.

Since the Second World War American cultural models have supplanted French ones, and English with a midwestern accent is replacing French as the second language in the Near East and Latin America. The leisure class that valued gracious living has disappeared in Eastern Europe and has lost its role as the arbiter of taste and manners in the Atlantic world. New-rich businessmen and their wives no longer imitate it as slavishly as they once did, and most prosperous managers and technicians prefer the informality of California to the elegance of Versailles.

Aside from their cultural leadership the French acquired the most important mission in their history as a unified nation—revolution—in 1789. Everything they did during the next few years served as a model for the attainment of modern man's dream of freedom and equality. They carried to extremes the eighteenth-century belief that good laws can alter the character of a society, and "constitution" became a magic word for democrats everywhere. It was the French who identified democracy with republicanism in the Old World. They also sanctified the bourgeoisie and its political, civil, and economic rights. France became the land where talent and enterprise triumphed over privilege, where religious and racial minorities were treated as equals—the true home of *humanité*.

Having created this image of themselves, the French set out to spread the benefits of their revolution to the rest of Europe. At first they were welcomed as liberators by "fifth columns" of local democrats in many ramshackle kingdoms and principalities on the Continent. But it eventually became clear that the conquerors, though cosmopolitan in their talk, were nationalistic in their acts. What was good for the French may have been good for all peoples, but under Napoleon this notion was used as an excuse for political domination. After his final defeat the ideals of 1789 went underground and soon reappeared in native dress in those countries that had freed themselves from France's physical presence.

For over a hundred years democrats and patriots in Europe and Latin America adopted the slogans of the French Revolution as their program and the "Marseillaise" as their battle hymn. In the early twentieth century idealistic intellectuals who were soon to lead Communist and colonial revolts throughout the world studied in France—though *liberté, égalité,* and *fraternité* came to mean something different from a bourgeois republic for them. The French revolutionary tradition remained a source of symbols to be exploited by protest movements everywhere until the Comintern proclaimed itself the official spokesman for all victims of capitalism and imperialism. In June, 1958, when he was De Gaulle's minister of information, André Malraux said that the French people became unhappy and aimless after they had lost the role of signifying justice to the Soviet Union and that of signifying power to the United States. According to him, they still need a mission of some kind, even today.

France's claims to having a world mission have not rested primarily on her political and economic strength, but they have been affected by her military victories and defeats. Until 1940 France had been a great power for a longer time than any other country. After a relative decline in the mid-eighteenth century she dominated Europe from 1793 until 1815 as no state had done since ancient

Rome. Unfortunately, she succumbed to what Denis Brogan calls "the greatest overdose of glory a nation ever fed on" under Napoleon. She overextended herself and was defeated by the peripheral European powers—Great Britain and Russia—after the new Caesar had brought about the birth of modern nationalism in Germany and Italy.

The defeat of 1815 brought a temporary end to thoughts of French national expansion through force of arms and a return to the older mission of civilizing other peoples by peaceful means. In his *Soirées de Saint-Pétersbourg* Joseph de Maistre said that the disposition, the need, the mania for trying to influence others was the most prominent feature of France's character and that she lived only to satisfy it. De Maistre was a clerical-authoritarian philosopher, but "liberals" like the historian-statesman François Guizot also had their version of their country's *mission civilisatrice*. According to this pillar of the July Monarchy, France was the vanguard of modern civilization. By the 1840's, however, a renewed craving for Napoleonic military glory became widespread among young Romantics who were "bored" with the safe-and-sane foreign policy of Louis Philippe.

Owing to England's voluntary isolation and the gradual decline of tsarist Russia, France had recovered a position of strength during the half-century after 1815. In the 1850's Napoleon III again accumulated a series of victories that were to serve later as the names of streets and subway stations. But Sebastopol, Magenta, and Solferino were cheap replicas of Austerlitz, Jena, and Friedland. The nephew of the great Bonaparte could not control the states of Europe by diplomacy as his uncle had done by military force. His dreams of glory and empire were already being shattered in Mexico City and at Sadowa by 1866. Nevertheless, when he went to war with Prussia four years later, his deluded subjects still thought they would win.

By 1870 it was no longer France that gave Europe a cold when she sneezed, it was Germany. Prussia, with her Rhenish industrial provinces, was already as populous as France and better organized politically and militarily. All that Bismarck needed to make his country supreme on the Continent was to lead the remaining German states in a forced alliance against the Second Empire. His victory was decisive. By annexing Alsace-Lorraine he deprived France of valuable mineral resources as well as the strategic advantages of the Rhine frontier. Finally united, Germany now surpassed her western neighbor in population, industrial potential, and political power.

France—and especially Paris—acquired renewed prestige as the standard-setter in the arts in the late nineteenth century, but the defeat of 1870 sparked a determination to restore her national power. This mission was expressed by patriotic writers of the Left, like Victor Hugo and Ernest Renan, and the Right, like Maurice Barrès and Charles Maurras. The republican government instituted universal military training, bought modern weapons, and raised the status of the army in the public mind. Within a generation France acquired a new colonial empire and alliances with Russia and Great Britain. It was clear that the French were again in training for a contest of power.

In 1914 the French people were confident in their strength. Anarchist, Syndicalist, and Socialist manifestations of pacifism were based on moral grounds, not on fear of defeat. "Radical" teachers in the primary schools trained their pupils to abhor war, but they also stressed love of *la patrie* and its way of life. The raising of the period of compulsory military service to three years in 1913 aroused much opposition on the Left, though all Socialists were not pacifists. Jean Jaurès proposed a national militia as a more democratic alternative to the existing army, not as a means of limiting France's armed might. Few Frenchmen were ready to fight for Morocco or Serbia, but fewer still doubted the seriousness of the German menace. As the diplomatic tension mounted after Sarajevo, expressions of patriotism increased in the press, popular songs, and public demonstrations throughout France. Even *bienpensants* who had prophesied her inevitable decadence under the Republic and all it stood for admitted that she was herself again.

During the First World War the French people showed that they could adapt themselves to the requirements of the twentieth-century power struggle. The politicians buried their differences for the duration and rarely questioned the actions of the generals and ministers. Despite the loss of the coal, iron, and factories in the northeast, government planners and industrialists developed France's munitions industries to the point where they produced more guns and aircraft than Great Britain or the United States. They introduced mass-production techniques in their armament plants on an unprecedented scale. In the early years of hostilities their equipment was inferior to that of the Germans. Eventually, however, they manufactured and used large quantities of heavy artillery, tanks, planes, poison gas, and all the other technological marvels of modern warfare. France could not have held out for four years without allies, but she would have collapsed in six weeks without the extraordinary courage and determination of her soldiers and civilians.

Although they felt that their allies had cheated them out of some of the fruits of victory at the Paris Peace Conference, millions of Frenchmen believed that their country had at last resumed its dominant role in the world. Few doubted that Germany alone had caused the war and would pay for the damage she had done, that France would be able to interfere in German affairs indefinitely, and that the cost of reconstructing the devastated areas would keep the former enemy economically weak. In 1919 Germany and Russia were not great powers, the United States was already returning to her traditional isolation, Italy was experiencing an internal crisis, and Japan was fully occupied in the affairs of the Far East. Great Britain appeared to be France's only rival for world power and control of the newly formed League of Nations. France had increased the size of her colonial empire, and her predominance on the European Continent seemed assured.

Yet France's long-term decline was accelerated more by her Pyrrhic victory than by her defeats in 1815 and 1870. Her manpower losses were larger in proportion to her total population than those of any other major belligerent. Almost all Frenchmen felt that they had put forth their last great burst of energy to preserve their country and their way of life and that this effort had exhausted their moral and physical reserves. To them the First World War was "The War"—the final reckoning. They had hoped to see the last judgment written into the peace treaties, in which the

212

wicked would be condemned to eternal damnation and the righteous would be relieved of further military trials. In the United States and Great Britain many people also wanted to believe that they had fought the "last war" and achieved "normalcy." But the Americans did not feel that they had debilitated their reserves. The British were not as defensive in their attitudes as the French, although they too were weary—profoundly weary.

In the postwar period there was a split between those Frenchmen who still saw their country's civilizing mission as creative and progressive and those who came to view it as a defense against new forms of barbarism. Many government leaders and liberal writers vaunted the victory of 1918 as the triumph of French civilization over German "technicism." They tied France's political hegemony in Europe to her intellectual superiority. According to them the rest of the world would still look to France for spiritual values and lofty ideals, no matter how materialistic and mechanized it might become. On the other hand, gloomy conservatives were already predicting that the western tip of the European continent—far from being the crossroads of three worlds—would one day be the scene of a last-ditch stand against the hordes of Asia and the economic mass of Russia and the United States.

The history of France's conception of her mission in the 1930's can be understood as a series of attempts to linger in the eighteenth-century City of Man. Though some Frenchmen allowed themselves to be charmed by demagogues who wanted to substitute race, class, war, and the state for this, a larger group continued to put what little faith it had left in Left-wing humanists like Édouard Herriot and Léon Blum. The fact that these men failed their followers was frustrating, but the French were like people disillusioned by their own fathers, who spend their lives looking for other fathers. Disappointment in an object—hero, lover, or institution—may transform love into hate without eliminating the search for the ideal symbolized by the rejected object. The French were seeking leaders and policies that would maintain their nation as a great power while at the same time preserving the cultural values of an earlier age.

In the face of a resurgent Germany and the threat of another bloodletting many Frenchmen became increasingly demoralized. The following quotation from an article written by Antoine de Saint-Exupéry for the two million readers of *Paris-Soir* expressed this demoralization on October 1, 1938, the day after the Munich Agreement.

> We chose to save the Peace. But in saving the peace we have mutilated our friends. And there were undoubtedly many among us who were ready to risk our lives for the duties of friendship. These people now experience a sort of shame. But if they had sacrificed the peace they would be just as much ashamed. For they would have sacrificed man; they would have accepted the irreparable destruction of Europe's libraries, cathedrals, and laboratories. They would have accepted the ruination of its traditions; they would have been willing to transform the world into a cloud of ashes. And this is why we have wavered from one view to the other. When we thought the peace was menaced we discovered the shame of war. When we seemed to be spared from war we felt the shame of the Peace.

Jean Giraudoux expressed a "peace-at-any-price" outlook that began as pacifism and ended as defeatism. In 1936 his play *La Guerre de Troie n'aura pas lieu* (*The Trojan War Will Not Take Place*—more recently called *Tiger at the Gates*) had already pointed out the folly of war. When he was Daladier's minister of information in 1939, Giraudoux said that it was no longer France's right to pass judgment on life abroad. Her mission was simply to keep herself worthy of her own traditional civilization, in which human relations were regulated by happy self-moderation and polite gentility, rather than Faustian drives. Like many of his country's leaders in all fields Giraudoux was living in the past, while the Nazis were launching a modern war.

Germany's superior military strategy was the main cause of the French defeat in 1940, but the sudden impact of this catastrophe was so stupefying that most people ceased to think about France's future as an independent nation and a world power for the next four years. A number of intellectuals searched for the "consciousness of the native French essential," and the Vichy regime put on pathetic displays of military pomp. The masses, however, lived through this humiliating period in silent submission.

While France's right to a voice in the councils of the major powers was merely a pious hope for most Frenchmen in the Liberation period, General de Gaulle had never ceased to assert it. He had been trying to strengthen his country's diplomatic and military position throughout the Second World War, not only as a nationalist, but also as an imperialist. In every part of the empire where Allied troops were stationed—from New Caledonia to Syria —he insisted on maintaining "French presence." As a haughty *émigré* and as head of a government that depended upon American and British support, he constantly demanded being treated as the leader of a great nation. Pétain had been willing to be the reigning prince of a tributary state within a larger power bloc; De Gaulle refused to reign unless he also ruled. These two men stood for the minimum and maximum views of France's role in world affairs.

Since 1945 French foreign policy has been guided primarily by the maximum view: France must be recognized as a great power and she must retain her independence within any larger power bloc. At first General de Gaulle tried to give his country the role of mediator between the United States and the Soviet Union, but the beginning of the Cold War and the need for American economic assistance ended this approach by late 1947. For the next two years the French took the lead in "building Europe" as a Third Force through schemes for political and economic co-operation. Washington viewed these projects as useful reinforcements to the NATO alliance and gave them its blessing. As long as Marshall Plan aid was indispensable to French economic recovery, and as long as West Germany remained weak and divided, most Frenchmen accepted this blessing without committing themselves to its implications. By 1950, however, the United States government began talking about the necessity of German rearmament. With a large part of the French army bogged down in Indo-China, this suggestion seemed to threaten France's position as the dominant power in continental Western Europe.

Communist expansion in the Far East led the American government to adopt a sympathetic attitude toward French colonialism in Southeast Asia, but large numbers of Frenchmen resented the "little wars" in Korea and Indo-China. Their alarm over the possibility of a world conflagration led many of them to make the

United States their whipping boy and to accuse her of provoking the catastrophe they feared. The French mistook bellicose pronouncements by American generals and magazine articles advocating preventive war for official policy. They overlooked the fact that the Korean conflict was almost as unpopular with most Americans as the Indo-Chinese campaign was in France. Instead, they began to feel that their country was becoming an American military satellite and that the various plans for European integration would make them junior partners in a Western Europe dominated by the Germans.

In the early 1950's the Federal Republic of West Germany was not only catching up with France economically, it was acquiring a diplomatic importance that few Frenchmen had been prepared to foresee. Both the ruling Christian Democrats and the opposition Socialists were talking about reunification with the Soviet Zone and the restoration of the territories beyond the Oder-Neisse line. Except for the Communists, few Frenchmen expressed hatred for the Germans as a nation. What they feared was that a dynamic Germany would dominate them in a European economic community and drag her partners into a new *Drang nach Osten*. Such a prospect seemed like Hitler's "New Order" under "democratic" auspices.

Thus, the real hostility toward the EDC in France was not merely the result of opposition to German rearmament; it was based on a fear of losing her national independence. Though many people supported the EDC, few of them *liked* it. Within all the political parties—except the MRP and, of course, the Communists—it had its advocates and its opponents. Finally, in the summer of 1954 Premier Mendès-France put it before parliament for ratification, but without recommending it himself.

The debate on the EDC seemed to involve France's status as a world power. She was already losing her hold on her colonial empire, as the defeat at Dien Bien Phu had dramatically shown. Now she was being asked to submerge herself in a European superstate. The national assembly said no. This decision was very disappointing to France's allies. Prime Minister Churchill threatened her with being treated as an "empty chair" in world diplomacy, and

Secretary of State Dulles spoke of America's "agonizing reappraisal" of the policy that had made France the mainstay of Western European defense.

Faced with these threats of diplomatic and military isolation, Mendès-France felt obliged to accept Anthony Eden's plan for rearming Germany within NATO. He also prepared the way for the early transfer of the Saar to the Federal Republic. This territory might have been "Europeanized," if the French assembly had ratified the EDC. By 1955 the Coal and Steel Community was all that remained of the various "Europes" that France's leaders had proposed and that her people rejected.

In 1955 and 1956 political "immobilism" at home and frustration as a world power led to a brief wave of nationalist neutralism. If the rest of the world did not recognize France's mission, then she would have to "go it alone." The various factions that expressed this feeling showed little agreement over which way France should "go." Some wanted her to lead the Western powers in a program of aid to underdeveloped countries as an alternative to preparing for a war against the Soviet Union. Others tried to prevent the revival of Germany under American sponsorship and to hang on to the last shreds of the French Empire. Still others contented themselves with asserting France's cultural and ethical superiority over the United States. The crowning humiliation came when outside diplomatic pressure obliged an Anglo-French expeditionary force to abandon its occupation of the Suez Canal Zone just after it had routed the Egyptian army.

Since the end of 1956 the leaders of the Fourth and Fifth Republics have returned to the policy of co-operation with France's Continental neighbors—especially West Germany—as the basis for accomplishing her mission in the world. Businessmen who had balked at lowering economic barriers changed their minds when oil stopped coming from the Middle East during the Suez crisis. They knew that they needed partners in finding more reliable sources of energy to keep their machines going. The government saw German capital as a useful supplement to its own efforts to develop the resources of French territories in Africa. There was also reason to hope that the welding-together of a Continental bloc could increase France's bargaining power in her dealings with the United States and Great Britain. The French decided to take the plunge. They signed treaties with West Germany, Italy, Belgium, the Netherlands, and Luxembourg, which set up the Common Market and Euratom (a joint program of atomic research).

President de Gaulle has continued the efforts of his immediate predecessors to make France stronger through a close alliance with West Germany. Indeed, he has made this partnership the keystone of French foreign policy and he has dissipated the qualms of his countrymen toward their traditional enemy. When one looks at a map one is struck by the fact that the Europe of "The Six" practically coincides with the old empire of Charlemagne. The new Charles the Great wants each part of this realm to preserve its national sovereignty, but he has taken the most decisive step in eleven hundred years toward making Western Europe a community of peoples with a common destiny.

The French have never been lucky with their empires. From the time of Napoleon I, they have been faced with native nationalists who did not want to be Frenchmen. Spaniards and Russians in 1812 set the precedent for guerrilla attacks against the occupying power, which Vietnamese and Arabs were to revive in the 1950's. Today even the most "backward" peoples want immediate independence. Ferhat Abbas and Leopold Senghor—who are representative leaders of the Algerian and African nationalist movements—each went to school in France, graced her literary salons and her political assemblies, and married one of her daughters. But they do not want to be Frenchmen either. Every colonial motherland experienced this kind of response after the Second World War, but the French were less willing to adjust themselves to it than most of the others.

France joined the other modern industrial states in the race for territories in Africa and Asia about eighty years ago. She grafted her *mission civilisatrice* onto her imperialism, but her real mission was to maintain her status as a world power. One of the main motives of the French empire-builders was to compensate for the loss of their country's hegemony in Europe after 1870. Many na-

218

tionalists disapproved of this policy, arguing that it diverted France's energies and resources from the task of *revanche*. After the First World War, however, they came to view the overseas territories as symbols of power and prestige.

Aside from the remnants of the eighteenth-century holdings in the Western Hemisphere and India, the French Empire until 1945 consisted of Indo-China, West Africa, Equatorial Africa, Madagascar, Tunisia, Algeria, Morocco, Syria, the Lebanon, and some islands in the Pacific and Indian oceans. Algeria was technically a part of France and, hence, not a colony; Tunisia and Morocco were protectorates under the nominal rule of native princes; Syria and the Lebanon were League of Nations mandates. Although the goal of assimilation—or, at least, "association," which Marshal Lyautey had advocated before the war in Morocco—was not abandoned as an ideal, the possibility of transforming all the Congo Negroes, Moslem North Africans, and Annamese peasants into one hundred million Frenchmen was patently unrealizable by the 1920's. The colonial office in Paris concentrated on Gallicizing the native elites as a first step in this direction, but it made no serious effort to train these people for self-rule. Most Frenchmen at home were apathetic toward their empire, while a few hundred thousand settlers came to regard it as frontier country to be developed for their benefit. They exploited the colonies with little regard for native rights and demands for independence. By doing so, they often hampered the constructive work of many dedicated civil servants, army officers, and missionaries.

In 1946 the post-Liberation government decided to show the colonies its gratitude for their wartime help to the Free French forces and its desire to keep up with the times. It "abolished" the empire and established the French Union, which was supposed to resemble the British Commonwealth. Unfortunately, West Africa was not Canada, and Madagascar was not New Zealand. All of France's overseas territories were inhabited by an overwhelming majority of non-Europeans at various levels of underdevelopment. This very fact served as a justification for treating them like adopted children who needed to be shaped in the image of their foster parents before being given mass representation in the great family councils—the National Assembly and the Assembly of the French Union in Paris. In other words, not until these people were really Frenchmen could they claim the privileges of free adults.

The French Union was an abstraction. It did not change any of the existing realities in the areas concerned, any more than the various schemes for a united "Europe" produced a reality corresponding to this name. In the postwar period French designers in all fields—from women's fashions to political constitutions—created a "new look" every few years. But a dress was not transformed into a pair of pants by lowering or raising its hemline two inches. A colony was still a colony, whether it was called a territory, a protectorate, or an overseas department; and a Tunisian or a Cambodian did not become a Frenchman by an act of parliament.

From Saigon to Casablanca the French (like Europeans and Americans elsewhere) have lived apart from the natives in what they themselves call "colonies." Therefore, this word has two meanings: the entire territory under their control, and the smaller settlements within it which they reserve entirely for their own use. In some cases these last are merely clubs and beaches; in others, they include as much as half of a major city. Except for a handful of idealistic administrators, the majority of Frenchmen in the overseas territories never took the myths of assimilation and association seriously. For them, East was East, and West was West, and never the twain would meet. But their "West" was not France; it was their colony within a colony.

Small worlds breed small minds. When a handful of "us" is surrounded by masses of "them," it is difficult to think of letting down the barriers. As long as they are docile, we can treat them with paternalistic kindness and admire some of their quaint, though "childish," ways. After all, they do all the manual labor—even if they are incorrigibly "lazy." Their presence, at the proper distance, also reassures us of our own superiority, which no one in our own little group is likely to challenge. We consider this corner of the earth as ours, and then one day we learn that some of them are claiming that it is theirs. That's the thanks we get for giving them clinics and teaching them to read!

This type of colonial "mind" hindered the Paris governments

from adjusting their policies to native nationalism, but it did not express itself in the same way everywhere. Until the natives in a particular territory actually threatened the privileged status of the colonists, the latter usually discriminated against the former on a social rather than on a racial basis. They viewed them the way European landlords viewed their serfs in earlier times—as an inferior caste. (It can be argued that this was also the view of many whites in the American South before 1860. The real racial hatred there developed during and after the Reconstruction period.) In Indo-China and North Africa this was the case until the early 1950's and in Black Africa until the late 1950's. Only in Madagascar, Morocco, and Algeria did racial antagonism lead to mob violence.

Many of the big capitalists in South Vietnam, Morocco, and Tunisia have adjusted themselves to their new status as foreigners, but in Algeria they and the one million other European settlers consider themselves in their own country. The rich wine-producers have been especially concerned, since they would lose their subsidies and markets if separated from France (which "imports" one-fourth of its wine from Algeria). As the nationalist rebellion that began in late 1954 continued, they gave increased backing to the politicians, newspaper editors, and local vigilantes who were determined to maintain French predominance in Algeria. Actually, the wealthy landowners and big businessmen are less race-conscious than the small farmers, shopkeepers, and employees, who comprise the majority of the European population. Many of these people fear losing their privileged status vis-à-vis the nine million Moslems, and they have become increasingly hostile to the home government. They believe that it might "sell them out," as it "sold out" the settlers in Morocco and Tunisia by granting these countries their independence in 1956. (By 1959, 60,000 of the 320,000 French citizens in Morocco and 90,000 of the 180,000 in Tunisia had left these countries and moved to France. Many of these "*émigrés* in reverse" have found it difficult to adjust themselves to their new lives as ordinary Frenchmen.)

In France itself the majority of the people slowly began to write off its country's colonial mission elsewhere, and a growing minority expressed its alarm lest some of the methods used to combat the Algerian rebels compromise France's reputation as a land of humanity and justice. In the past the Foreign Legion used punitive raids, torture, and occasional acts of paternalism as the means for keeping the natives in line throughout North Africa. The exploits of the Legionnaires were glorified in the movies for decades, so that no one could claim ignorance about them. But when the regular army and the local police adopted their tactics in the Algerian war, men of conscience at home deplored this behavior and said that it was unworthy of France.

Writers representing many shades of opinion condemned a policy of "pacification" that relied on torture—for example, Henri Alleg (Communist), François Mauriac and Pierre-Henri Simon (Liberal Catholics), and independent liberals like Albert Camus and Roger Martin du Gard. Even André Malraux (Gaullist) protested against the suppression of Alleg's book *La Question*. In July, 1957, an International Commission against Concentration Camp Tactics made an objective study of the way in which captured rebels were treated in Algeria. It was composed of a Belgian, a Dutchman, and a Norwegian. In their report they stated that most prisoners seemed to receive humane treatment; that the main problem was the denial of civil liberties; that torture was used in some cases to get information, but that it was not a general policy (text cited in *Le Monde Hébdomadaire*, July 25–31, 1957).

The last government of the Fourth Republic lost control over what went on in Algeria, as the military authorities and civilians there took matters increasingly into their own hands. Soldiers and settlers met rebel terrorism with counter-terrorism—including the bombing of Sakhiet Sidi Youssef in February, 1958, in reprisal for an ambush of a French patrol by Algerian rebels who used this Tunisian market town as their base of operations. Then they broke completely with Paris in May and set up their own Committee of Public Safety to keep Algeria French. They even began "fraternizing" with the Moslems in order to show that they were not colonialists any longer. Convinced of their mission of "integration," they were ready to impose it on the motherland itself. Although General de Gaulle was criticized at the time for accepting the premiership without repudiating the backing of these insurrectionists, it is difficult to see how he could have "saved the Republic" in any other way. For only his command—six days before he actually took office—stopped the "Resurrection" plan for the occupation of Paris by paratroopers.

After his return to power on June 1, 1958, De Gaulle was handicapped for two and a half years in his efforts to solve the Algerian problem by the army and the European settlers. Little by little he tried to dispel the myth that "Algeria is a part of France" by fostering the notion of an "Algerian personality" in his public pronouncements. At the same time, he committed the French economy to a costly development program for that troubled territory, with the obvious hope of winning the non-Europeans away from the rebels. As another means of putting pressure on the Moslems he even hinted at the possibility of partition. If this plan were carried through, it would force several million of them to become refugees in a new land-locked Jordan, while grouping the Europeans into a new Israel along the coast. De Gaulle would have preferred to make Algeria's relationship to France similar to that of Puerto Rico to the United States—a free Commonwealth closely associated with the "mother country." Neither the European nor the Moslem extremists would be satisfied with this arrangement, although the bulk of the population might be better off under it than they are now (while the war still goes on) or than they would be in a weak and defenseless Algerian Republic.

But since late 1960, events on both sides of the Mediterranean have increased the likelihood of an independent Algeria. The Moslem majority has shown that this is its goal, regardless of the consequences. In France itself, 75 per cent of the voters supported their president's policy of self-determination. If he chooses to do so, De Gaulle can now negotiate with the rebel leaders with little to fear from the small minority of colonialists and military extremists. France's mission in Algeria may eventually be the protection of her nationals who remain there, rather than the Gallicization of the natives.

Undoubtedly President de Gaulle would like to maintain his country's status as a Eurafrican power through its economic, cultural, and strategic ties with its former dependencies south of the Sahara, but he has abandoned the old arguments of assimilation and association as excuses for keeping them as wards of France. By the late 1950's the relationship between France—the Metropole —and her territories in Black Africa had already evolved to the point where the old distinction between Frenchmen and natives was losing its meaning. The following question put to two French travelers by a Senegalese student in Dakar illustrated the naïve self-assurance of the new Negro elite: "Since you have been in Arkansas, can you tell me the exact proportion of metropolitans and Africans in Little Rock?"

Today "The Community" no longer has the word "French" in front of it, and the new republics in what was formerly French West Africa, French Equatorial Africa, and Madagascar are all independent. Their relations with France are cordial, and they continue to welcome her public investments and technical experts. French cultural influence—especially her language and her traditional educational pattern—persists even in those areas that have severed all ties with the former colonial power. A Berber, a Vietnamese, a Syrian, and a Guinean leader communicate with each other in the language of the country against which they are passing some sort of resolution in the United Nations.

Charles de Gaulle has said repeatedly that France cannot be herself without greatness, and through his words and his manner he has made himself the symbol of this mission of grandeur. He openly admits in his memoirs that he had to behave in this way in order to strengthen the international position of his battered motherland between 1940 and 1946. While France has recovered remarkably since then, she does not have the military, economic, and political assets of a world power today. For this reason De Gaulle can hardly hope to get what he wants by speaking softly and carrying a big stick (though it is amazing what the explosion of three junior atomic bombs will do for a country's reputation when combined with shrewd diplomacy and strong leadership at home).

The price of grandeur is high. Less temperate nationalists than De Gaulle could compromise France's claim to be a land of freedom and justice by a desperate fight to keep Algeria French. Large expenditures on modern weapons and ambitious development programs overseas impinge on domestic needs such as schools, lodgings, capital investments, and new jobs for a growing population. Farmers, workers, and pensioners are already grumbling about the material sacrifices they are being forced to make in order to balance the national budget, control inflation, and allow their country to compete in the international market. A recent survey showed that the majority of today's youth has no "will to power" for their country. They want France's world mission to be an intellectual and moral one rather than a political and military one, which they consider unrealistic.

Whatever mission they ascribe to their country, most Frenchmen now want it to fit the requirements of the modern world. The minority that hopes to keep French clocks running on different time is fighting a losing battle against economic and technological development. It could still cause trouble in a political crisis—especially if President de Gaulle should suddenly disappear from the scene. But the French people are not likely to give up their democratic liberties and their present leadership in Europe for the sake of a few die-hard colonialists and chauvinists. The groundwork for a new kind of greatness has been too well laid. In addition to its other commitments, the government is providing special funds for large-scale scientific research projects that will co-ordinate the activities of different disciplines. This program is without precedent in France. The scientists themselves see it as a means of making French civilization excel in action as well as in knowledge. As long as a nation is capable of such creative adaptations of the best of the old to the best of the new, it has a mission.

Notes on Sources

The "material" for this book was gathered from what I have read, seen, and heard over the course of nearly twenty years. My primary sources are the behavior of the French people and the products of their serious and popular culture as I have studied and observed them. I have relied upon other people's studies and observations, as well as my own, for both concrete data and abstract opinions. But I could not hope (even if space permitted) to compile a list of all the secondary sources I have consulted at one time or another. The following bibliography is merely a selection of those books and articles that I found most useful.

CHAPTER 1. FRANCE 1960

Until the past decade or so, most political scientists interested in France focused their attention on parliament, the electoral process, and the constitution. Robert de Jouvenel's *La République des camarades* (Paris: Grasset, 1914) remains the classic description of the "you-scratch-my-back-I'll-scratch-yours" outlook of the deputies toward one another under the Third Republic. Roger Soltau's *French Parties and Politics* (New York: Oxford University Press, 1930) explains how certain parties worked together to get one another's candidates elected on run-off ballots and then went their own way until the next election—how their platforms were designed to run on, not to stand on. The first major analysis of the growth of extraconstitutional agencies was Maxime Leroy's *Les Tendances du pouvoir et de la liberté en France au XXe siècle* (Paris: Sirey, 1937). Maurice Duverger and François Goguel have a long chapter on the function of the electoral system in French politics in their comparative study *L'Influence des systèmes électoraux sur la vie politique* (Paris: A. Colin, 1950). G.-E. Lavau shows the unreality of party activities in his *Partis politiques et réalités sociales* (Paris: A. Colin, 1953). My information on French "joining" behavior comes partly from the *Journal officiel de la République Française, avis et decrets* (1926–36 and 1948–56), in which lists of the names and purposes of every new organization in France are published. For works on the political *history* of the Third and Fourth Republics, see the sources for chapter 6.

There have been a number of recent studies on the bureaucratization of politics, the power of the high civil service, and pressure-group activities. Christiane Marcilhacy describes these first two trends beginning in the eighteenth century in her "De la conception française de la politique," *Politique*, Vol. XX (1946), and Raymond Aron brings the story up to date in his *Immuable et changeante* (Paris: Calmann-Lévy, 1959). A convenient summary of the role of France's permanent administration may be found in Alfred Diamant's "The French Administrative System: The Republic Passes but the Administration Remains," in William Siffin (ed.), *Toward the Comparative Study of Public Administration* (Bloomington, Ind.: Department of Government, Indiana University, 1957). On political centralization see Brian Chapman's *Prefects and Provincial France* (London: Allen & Unwin, 1955). The growth of pressure groups—especially since 1946—is discussed in Philip Williams' *Politics in Postwar France* (London: Longmans, Green, 1958), Henry W. Ehrmann's *Organized Business in France* (Princeton, N.J.: Princeton University Press, 1957), and Jean Meynaud's *Les Groupes de pression* (Paris: A. Colin, 1958).

The following works deal with the transition from the Fourth to the Fifth Republics and the prospective development of the new regime: André Siegfried's preface to *L'Année politique*, 1958 (Paris: Presses Universitaires de France, 1959); Otto Kirchheimer's "France from the Fourth to the Fifth Republic," *Social Research*, Vol. XXII, No. 4 (Winter, 1959); Maurice Duverger's *La Ve République* (Paris: Presses Universitaires de France, 1959); Vol. IX, No. 1 (March 1959) of the *Revue française de la science politique*, which is devoted entirely to the constitution of the Fifth Republic; Dorothy Pickles' *The Fifth French Republic* (New York: Frederick A. Praeger, 1960); and Philip M. Williams' and Martin Harrison's *De Gaulle's Republic* (New York: Longmans, Green, 1960), which is the best and most recent analysis in English.

My main general sources on the French economy in the 1950's are two books by Jean-Marcel Jeanneney: *Forces et faiblesses de l'économie française: 1945–1956* (Paris: A. Colin, 1956) and the companion volume of tables, *Tableaux statistiques relatifs à l'économie française et l'économie mondiale* (Paris: A. Colin, 1957). I also took material on occupational distribution, the decentralization and concentration of industry, instalment buying, and advertising from the following periodicals published by the French government: *Institut National de la Statistique des Études Économiques: Bulletin mensuel de statistique* and *Les Informations du Conseil Économique*. Some of my comparisons between France and other Continental countries come from the *Rapport sur la situation des pays de la Communauté* (Brussels, September, 1958).

I learned much about France's long-term economic growth from Arthur Dunham's *The Industrial Revolution in France, 1815–1848* (New York: Exposition Press, 1955), Louis Girard's *La Politique des travaux publics du Second Empire* (Paris: A. Colin, 1952), Paul Combe's *Niveau de vie et progrès technique en France depuis 1860* (Paris: A. Colin, 1955), and Maurice Lauré's *Révolution: Dernière chance de la France* (Paris: Presses Universitaires de France, 1954). The paragraph about the construction of pipelines comes from Lauré.

Urbanization and other demographic developments are discussed in Louis Chevalier's *La Formation de la population parisienne au XIXe siècle* (Paris: Presses Universitaires de France, 1950) and in Georges Friedmann's collection of papers by a number of social scientists, *Villes et campagnes* (Paris: A. Colin, 1953).

I relied heavily on *Villes et campagnes* for information concerning other aspects of French economic and social life, especially the transformation of rural France. *Consommation, numéros 2 et 3 de 1960* (Paris: Dunod, 1960) gives results of a study (by the Centre de Recherches et de Documentation sur la Consommation) of consumer expenditures by occupation and region. My figures on salaries and wages come from Jeanneney and from the *Institut National de la Statistique des Études Économiques: Bulletin mensuel de statistique* for November, 1959.

In the past ten or fifteen years public opinion research in France has become as skilled and as accurate as it is in the United States, thanks to the work of Jean Stoetzel and his associates in the French Public Opinion Institute. The official journal of this organization is *Sondages: Revue française de l'opinion publique*. Unless otherwise indicated, all the surveys mentioned in this book were published in *Sondages*. The one on working-class attitudes appeared in Volume XVIII (1956) and confirms my own impressions. I have also observed the kind of behavior of white-collar employees described in Michel Crozier's "L'Ambiguité de la conscience de classe chez les employés et les petits fonctionnaires," *Cahiers internationaux de la sociologie*, Vol. XVIII (1955).

My main general sources on historical trends in the French population are the numerous books and articles by the dean of French demographers, Alfred Sauvy. The quarterly journal *Population* and Gérard Duplessis-Le Guélinel's *Les Mariages en France* (Paris: A. Colin, 1954) were also useful.

A good popular description of how French men and women "go modern" is Jean Fourastié's and André Laleuf's *Révolution à l'Ouest* (Paris: Presses Universitaires de France, 1957).

CHAPTER 2. CHILDREN OF THE PAST

Although the idea of national character is as controversial as it is old, today's cultural anthropologists have tried to refine it into a working concept with some scientific usefulness. Clyde Kluckhohn equates it with a type of personality structure in his "Culture and Behavior," *Handbook of Social Psychology*, ed. Gardner Lindzey (2 vols.; Cambridge, Mass.: Addison-Wesley, 1954), II, 921–76 (see also Alex Inkeles and Daniel J. Levinson, "National Character: The Study of Modal Personality and Sociocultural Systems," *ibid.*, pp. 977–1021), while Margaret Mead uses it to indicate a cluster of culture traits in her "National Character," *Anthropology Today*, ed. A. L. Kroeber and others (Chicago: University of Chicago Press, 1953), pp. 642–67 (see also A. Irving Hallowell, "Culture, Personality, and Society," *ibid.*, pp. 597–620). The culture into which a person is born provides him with certain distinctive norms and patterns of behavior. It also teaches him how to justify and rationalize specific ways of behaving—so that an outside observer must take into account both what he does and what he says he does. Finally, it gives him a few broad, general principles of selectivity and ordering with which he tends to see and respond to the world around him.

Culture is the precipitate, not the precipitator, of history. It molds both personalities and social systems, but it does not determine in advance the actions of persons and groups. Individuals tend to alter their habits, and societies ultimately transform their institutions when these cease to safeguard the values inherited from the past. (See H. G. Barnett's *Innovation: The Basis of Cultural Change* [New York: McGraw-Hill, 1953].) Still, most people resist changing their way of life as long as they can. In doing so they sometimes cling to culture traits that are no longer functional in preserving their cherished values. Such behavior on the part of millions of Frenchmen made it difficult for them to adjust themselves to the twentieth century. (The best of numerous books on this point is Ernst Robert Curtius' *The Civilization of France* [New York: Macmillan Co., 1932].)

Only that part of culture that a person has "got inside himself" shapes his personality. He shares a common way of life with his neighbors to the extent that their "private worlds" overlap. In a complex,

230

stratified, and segmented society like that of modern France these "private worlds" have overlapped for the majority of the total population only on the broadest issues. Furthermore, the generalized national culture has had a varying impact on diverse social, economic, political, and religious groups. At times specific classes or cliques have tried to carry the leitmotiv of historical development, but all the voices must be heard in each period if one wants to grasp the whole contrapuntal pattern.

My observations about child-training in France are largely my own. Useful works on this subject include Claude Lévi-Strauss's *Les Structures élémentaires de la parenté* (Paris: Presses Universitaires de France, 1949) and guidebooks such as *Le Guide de la jeune mère* (8th ed.; Paris: Les Éditions Sociales Françaises, 1947). In *Themes in French Culture* (Stanford, Calif.: Stanford University Press, 1954) Rhoda Métraux and Margaret Mead discuss the child in the home on the basis of information gathered from a battery of interviews and tests given to a group of French adults living in the United States. (The French edition of this work—*Thèmes de "Culture" de France* [Collection de l'Institut Havrais de sociologie économique et de psychologie des peuples, 1958]—includes criticisms of it by leading French social scientists.) Laurence Wylie, in his masterly study, *Village in the Vaucluse* (Cambridge, Mass.: Harvard University Press, 1957), gives the best description that I have seen of how children grow up in small rural towns. Case studies and generalizations concerning children in the families of workers, farmers, and intellectuals in the Parisian region can be found in Juliette Favez-Boutonnier, Jenny Aubry, and Irène Lézime, "Child Development Patterns in France" and "French Case Studies" in Kenneth Soddy (ed.), *Mental Health and Infant Development* (2 vols.; New York: Basic Books, 1956). This work is the product of an international congress of child psychologists.

The most recent general description in English of the French educational system is "French Education: Why Jeannot *Can* Read," *Yale French Studies*, No. 22 (Winter–Spring, 1958–59). Analytical articles on various aspects of this topic may also be found in Volume XV (*Éducation et instruction*) of the *Encyclopédie française*. On the influence of laicism in the schools see Célestin Bouglé's *L'Éducation laïque* (Paris: Rieder, 1921) and his *The French Conception of "Culture Générale" and Its Influence upon Instruction* (New York: Teachers College, Columbia University, Bureau of Publications, 1938). American and French schools are compared in Roger Thabault's "Les Institutions scolaires aux États-Unis et en France," *Annales*, Vol. X, No. 1 (1955). The following articles are examples of the numerous discussions of reforms in the French system during the late 1950's: J. Guilhem, "Pourquoi il faut réformer l'enseignement," *Cahiers français d'information*, June, 1957, and "La Réforme devant l'Assemblée," *Le Monde*, July 24 and 27, 1957, which describe the proposals of the National Teachers' Congress.

On the laic and religious traditions in France see Georges Weill's *Histoire de l'idée laïque en France au XIXᵉ siècle* (Paris: Alcan, 1925); Adrien Dansette's *Histoire religieuse de la France contemporaine* (2 vols.; Paris: Flammarion, 1952)—which covers the nineteenth and early twentieth centuries—and his *Destin du catholicisme français, 1926–1956* (Paris: Flammarion, 1956); and Mildred J. Headings' *French Freemasonry under the Third Republic* (Baltimore: Johns Hopkins Press, 1949). My main source for information about French religious practices is Gabriel Le Bras's *Études de sociologie religieuse* (2 vols.; Paris: Presses Universitaires de France, 1956), which is a collection of his major studies on this subject. For a criticism of M. Le Bras's methodology see Père Chombard de Lauwe's "La Sociologie religieuse: Effort de vérité," *La Nef*, Vol. XI, No. 5 (1954). This issue of *La Nef* contains other articles on religion and the church, including Daniel Rops's "L'Église de France en marche." Another prominent Catholic writer, Georges Hourdin, discusses such topics as the controversial worker-priest movement and the reorganization of the French episcopate in a series of articles entitled "La Situation actuelle de l'Église Catholique en France," *Le Monde*, May–July, 1957.

In addition to my own readings in the Comtesse de Ségur, I am indebted to my colleague Micheline W. Herz for her observations in her unpublished manuscript "L'Angélisme chez Madame de Ségur."

CHAPTER 3. MALTHUS AND THE BOURGEOISIE

Economics is not called the dismal science for nothing. Until about twenty years ago *scarcity* was the key concept of almost all economists and economic historians. Since then the idea of development—or *growth* —has begun to replace it. Two pioneering works explaining this new approach are Colin Clark's *The Conditions of Economic Progress* (London: Macmillan & Co., 1940 and 1957 eds.) and Jean Fourastié's *Esquisse d'une théorie générale de l'évolution économique* (Paris: Presses Universitaires de France, 1947). The gloomy outlook of Malthus, Ricardo, and Marx seemed so well justified by the French economy during much of the first half of the twentieth century that even the champions of the development school have had difficulty in seeing the brighter side of that period. Maurice Lauré and Paul Combe (in their books cited for chapter 1) started to do so in the early 1950's, and Jean-Marcel Jeanneney has carried this revision further. His two books (see chapter 1) give a considerably different picture of French economic growth before 1945 than Charles Bettelheim's pessimistic *Bilan de l'économie française, 1919–1946* (Paris: Presses Universitaires de France,

232

1947), though these two authors agree on many specific points about French economic behavior.

The retardative factors in French economic growth in the past have been analyzed by many writers. On the protectionist role of the government see Shepard B. Clough's *France: A History of National Economics* (New York: Scribner, 1939) and on more general topics see his "Retardative Factors in French Economic Development in the 19th and 20th Centuries," *Journal of Economic History*, Supplement VI (1946), and Rondo Cameron's "Economic Growth and Stagnation in France, 1815–1914," *Journal of Modern History*, Vol. XXX, No. 1 (March, 1958). The story of the relationship between the state and the economy in the 1950's is described by Warren C. Baum in his *The French Economy and the State* (Princeton, N.J.: Princeton University Press, 1958). On government policies toward agriculture see Michel Augé-Laribé's *La Politique agricole de la France* (Paris: Presses Universitaires de France, 1950). David S. Landes has written two excellent articles on the conservatism of French businessmen: "French Entrepreneurship and Industrial Growth in the Nineteenth Century," *Journal of Economic History*, Vol. IX (May, 1949) and "French Business and the Businessman: A Social and Cultural Analysis," in *Modern France*, ed. Edward Mead Earle (Princeton, N.J.: Princeton University Press, 1950).

Many aspects of the French economy during the interwar years are described in a collection of studies edited by Charles Rist and Gaeton Pirou: *De la France d'avant-guerre à la France d'aujourd'hui: Vingt-cinq ans d'évolution de la structure économique et sociale française* (Paris: Sirey, 1939). On monetary problems see Martin Wolfe's *The French Franc between the Wars, 1919–1939* (New York: Columbia University Press, 1950).

My information on economic developments since 1956 comes mainly from the government publications cited for chapter 1, from *Le Monde* and other newspapers, and from conversations with Jean Fourastié and Jean Gottmann.

The history of the middle and upper classes in France since the early 1700's has undergone considerable revision in recent years. Philippe Sagnac's *La Formation de la société française moderne*, Vol. II: *La Révolution des idées et des moeurs et le déclin de l'ancien régime* (Paris: Presses Universitaires de France, 1946) is a good general work on the breakdown of France's traditional social structure in the eighteenth century. Franklin L. Ford shows how the aristocracy strengthened its position by adding fresh talent to its ranks from the high magistrature until around 1750 in his *Robe and Sword: The Regrouping of the French Aristocracy after Louis XIV* (Cambridge, Mass.: Harvard University Press, 1953). After that date, however, there occurred what Georges

Lefebvre called a feudal reaction, which included the barring of non-nobles from the *noblesse de la robe* and the officer corps of the army. Robert R. Palmer's *The Age of Democratic Revolution*, Vol. I: *The Challenge* (Princeton, N.J.: Princeton University Press, 1959) is a brilliant and original synthesis on political and social developments in Europe and North America during the last third of the eighteenth century. Palmer's thesis is that the key issue of that period was aristocratic versus democratic forms of community.

Using the sociological methodology of Talcott Parsons and Robert K. Merton, Elinor Barber has challenged the traditional notion of a united bourgeois class with common aspirations in her *The Bourgeoisie in 18th Century France* (Princeton, N.J.: Princeton University Press, 1955). Mrs. Barber explains how the eighteenth-century bourgeois was the victim of the prevalent ambivalence regarding social mobility and how those who had the necessary qualifications and attitudes for moving upward shared the prevailing disapproval of this kind of "climbing." She also maintains that different sections of the so-called bourgeoisie—wealthy landowners, merchants, lawyers, etc.—often had opposing goals.

French historians and sociologists show no signs of abandoning the concept of the bourgeoisie—which some American scholars find a bit fuzzy. Maurice Halbwachs used it in his posthumous *Esquisse d'une psychologie des classes sociales* (Paris: Rivière, 1955—see also the English edition: *The Psychology of Social Class* [Glencoe, Ill.: Free Press, 1958]). In this work Professor Halbwachs tries to analyze the "collective representations" (a key concept in the Durkheim school of sociology) of all social classes as they have evolved historically. He maintains that in France the middle-class outlook set the tone for the whole country after 1789. Charles Morazé shows how the bourgeoisie "arrived" and then tried to close its own ranks to outsiders in *La France bourgeoise* (Paris: A. Colin, 1946) and *Les bourgeois conquérants* (Paris: A. Colin, 1958). Emmanuel Beau de Loménie's *Les Responsabilités des dynasties bourgeoises* (3 vols.; Paris: Denoël, 1943–54) is sometimes biased and ill informed, but its basic thesis—that nineteenth- and early twentieth-century France was controlled by a few bourgeois dynasties—is provocative and worth considering.

From Flaubert to Sartre "bourgeois" has been a dirty word in much of French fiction and drama, and politicians and popular historians have blamed the bourgeoisie for everything that went wrong in France since the First World War. Scholars try to be more objective, but they, too, paint a pretty dismal picture of bourgeois selfishness and resistance to change. This topic is discussed in John E. Sawyer's "Strains in the Social Structure of Modern France," John B. Wolf's "The Elan Vital of France: A Problem in Historical Perspective," and David Landes'

"French Business and the Businessman" (all in Earle's *Modern France*); in Harry M. Johnson's "The Fall of France: An Essay on the Social Structure of France between the Wars" (unpublished Ph.D. thesis, Harvard University, 1949); in Jesse Pitts' "The Bourgeois Family and French Economic Retardation" (unpublished Ph.D. thesis, Harvard University, 1958); and in Georges Gurvitch's "The Social Structure of Pre-War France," *American Journal of Sociology*, Vol. XLVIII (May, 1943). Thomas Bottomore describes the continuing hold of the upper bourgeoisie on the high ranks of the civil service in his "La Mobilité sociale dans la haute administration française," *Cahiers internationaux de la sociologie*, Vol. XII (1952). The effect on this class of the post-Liberation nationalization of certain big enterprises is explained by Mario Einaudi, Maurice Byé, and Ernesto Rossi in their *Nationalization in France and Italy* (Ithaca, N.Y.: Cornell University Press, 1955).

In addition to the writings of Alfred Sauvy, the following works provided me with much information on what might be called demographic Malthusianism in France: Adolphe Landry's *Traité de démographie* (Paris: Payot, 1949), Joseph J. Spengler's *France Faces Depopulation* (Durham, N.C.: Duke University Press, 1938), and Wesley Camp's "Marriage and the Family in France since the Revolution: An Essay in the History of Population" (unpublished Ph.D. thesis, Columbia University, 1957). The startling figures on abortion rates given at the end of this chapter come from David V. Glass's *Population Policies and Movements in Europe* (Oxford: Clarendon Press, 1940). Glass cites a number of French demographers, some of whom say that there were more abortions of all types than live births in that period. The depression may have made matters worse, but it was not the main factor.

CHAPTER 4. LA FONTAINE VERSUS EINSTEIN

In this chapter I have relied mainly on my own interpretations of the examples of literature, philosophy, art, and music that I discuss, but the following works on literary history and criticism were helpful: Marcel Braunschvig, *Notre Littérature étudiée dans les textes* (2 vols.; Paris: A. Colin, 1946); René Jasinski, *Histoire de la littérature française* (2 vols.; Paris: Boivin, 1947); Henri Peyre, *Les Générations littéraires* (Paris: Boivin, 1948); Jacques Barzun, *The Energies of Art* (New York: Harper, 1956); Selden Rodman (ed.), *One Hundred Modern Poems* (New York: New American Library of World Literature, 1951)—especially the introduction; Wallace Fowlie (ed.), *Mid-Century French Poets* (New York: Grove Press, 1955)—especially the introduction.

On art and music I used the following works: Georges Duby and R. Mandrou, *Histoire de la civilisation française* (2 vols.; Paris: A. Colin, 1958)—which is the best survey of its kind available; Susanne K. Langer, *Philosophy in a New Key* (Cambridge, Mass.: Harvard University Press,

1942); André Malraux, *Psychologie de l'art* (2 vols.; Geneva: Skira, 1947–48); Herbert Read, *Art Now* (London: Pitman, 1948); Guillaume Apollinaire, *Méditations esthétiques; les peintres cubistes* (Paris: Eugène Figuière, 1913); Aaron Copland, *Music and Imagination* (Cambridge, Mass.: Harvard University Press, 1952); Wilfred Mellers, "Music," in *The New Outline of Modern Knowledge*, ed. Alan Pryce-Jones (New York: Simon & Schuster, 1956); Roger Fry, *Vision and Design* (London: Chatto & Windus, 1925); and Martin Cooper, *French Music* (London: Oxford University Press, 1951).

On science and philosophy the following works were suggestive: James B. Conant, *Modern Science and Modern Man* (New York: Columbia University Press, 1952); *Encyclopédie française*, Vol. I: *L'Outillage mental*, and Vol. XIX: *Philosophie, Religion;* Émile Bréhier, *La Philosophie et son passé* (Paris: Presses Universitaires de France, 1940); Abel Rey, "Une Opposition de tendances dans la science de 'temps modernes,'" *Revue de Synthèse*, Vol. I (October, 1931); Gaston Bachelard, *La Formation de l'esprit scientifique* (Paris: Vrin, 1957); Henry A. Guerlac, "Science and French National Strength," in Earle's *Modern France; La Nef*, Vol. XI (1954), No. 6—entire issue devoted to problems of French science; Léon Daudet, *Souvenirs des milieux littéraires, politiques, artistiques, et médicaux* (2 vols.; Paris: G. Crès, 1920)—Daudet expresses the typical reactionary attitude of hostility toward science; and Jean Perrin, *La Science et l'espérance* (Paris: Presses Universitaires de France, 1948).

Chapter 5. Humanists in a Wasteland

As in the preceding chapter, the interpretations expressed here are mostly my own, though the following works of literary history and criticism were helpful: Gaeton Picon, *Panorama de la littérature française* (Paris: Gallimard, 1951); Pierre-Henri Simon, *Histoire de la littérature française au XXᵉ siècle* (2 vols.; Paris: A. Colin, 1956); *Procès du héros* (Paris: Éditions du Seuil, 1950) and *L'Homme en procès* (Paris: Baconnière, 1949); Edmund Wilson, *Axel's Castle: A Study in the Imaginative Literature of 1870–1930* (New York: Scribner, 1931); Henri Peyre, *Hommes et oeuvres du XXᵉ siècle* (Paris: Corrêa, 1938) and *The Contemporary French Novel* (New York: Oxford University Press, 1955); Germaine Brée, *Marcel Proust and Deliverance from Time* (New Brunswick, N.J.: Rutgers University Press, 1955); André Maurois, *À la recherche de Marcel Proust* (Paris: Hachette, 1949); Klaus Mann, *André Gide and the Crisis of Modern Thought* (New York: Creative Age Press, 1943); Harold March, *Gide and the Hound of Heaven* (Philadelphia: University of Pennsylvania Press, 1952); Justin O'Brien, *Portrait of André Gide* (New York: Alfred A. Knopf, 1953); André Gide, Supplement to his *Journal* (Paris: Gallimard, 1949); Elaine Marks, *Colette*

(New Brunswick, N.J.: Rutgers University Press, 1960); Wilbur Merrill Frohock, *André Malraux and the Tragic Imagination* (Stanford, Calif.: Stanford University Press, 1952).

The following works express typical intellectual attitudes of the 1920's and 1930's: Julien Benda, *La Trahison des clercs* (Paris: Grasset, 1927); Henri Barbusse, *Manifeste aux intellectuels* (Paris, 1927); Louis-Ferdinand Céline, *Bagatelles pour un massacre* (Paris: Denoël, 1937); and Georges Bernanos, *Scandale de la vérité* (Paris: Gallimard, 1939).

CHAPTER 6. THE FAILURE OF THE "ISMS"

Of the countless books on modern French political history the following standard works were especially helpful to me for the theme of this chapter: Denis W. Brogan's *France under the Republic* (New York: Harper, 1940), François Goguel's *La Politique des partis sous la Troisième République* (2 vols.; Paris: Éditions du Seuil, 1946), and David Thomson's *Democracy in France* (London: Oxford University Press, 1952). Raoul Girardet's *La Société militaire dans la France contemporaine* (Paris: Plon, 1953) and René Rémond's *La Droite en France de 1815 à nos jours* (Paris: Aubier, 1954) are two excellent historical essays on the Rightist forces. André Siegfried's *Tableau politique de la France de l'ouest sous la Troisième République* (Paris: A. Colin, 1913) is a classic regional study. A good summary of the Boulangist episode is Adrien Dansette's *Le Boulangisme et la révolution dreyfusienne*, Vol. I: *Le Boulangisme, 1886–1890* (Paris: Perrin, 1938). Guy Chapman's *The Dreyfus Case: A Reassessment* (New York: Reynal & Co., 1955) offers no new information on France's most notorious *Affaire*, but it has a good bibliography. John A. Scott's *Republican Ideas and the Liberal Tradition in France, 1870–1914* (New York: Columbia University Press, 1951) and Eugen Weber's *The Nationalist Revival in France, 1905–1914* (Berkeley, Calif.: University of California Press, 1959) are good monographs on specific ideological movements before the First World War.

On the crises of the 1930's and their background, the following books were useful: François La Rocque, *Service Public* (Paris: Grasset, 1934); Alexander Werth, *France in Ferment* (London: Jarrolds, 1934); Henry W. Ehrmann, *French Labor from Popular Front to Liberation* (New York: Oxford University Press, 1947); Maurice Thorez, *France Today and the People's Front* (London: Gollancz, 1936); Léon Jouhaux, *La C.G.T.: Ce qu'elle est, ce qu'elle veut* (Paris: Gallimard, 1937); Léon Blum, *For All Mankind* (New York: Viking, 1946); Jean Galtier-Boissière, *Le Bourrage de crânes* (Paris: Crapouillot, 1937); Charles A. Micaud, *The French Right and Nazi Germany, 1933–1939* (Durham, N.C.: Duke University Press, 1943); Édouard Dolléans, *Histoire du mouvement ouvrier* (3 vols.; Paris: A. Colin, 1936–53); Val Lorwin, *The French Labor Movement*

(Cambridge, Mass.: Harvard University Press, 1954); Gérard Walter, *Histoire du parti communiste français* (Paris: Éditions Self, 1948); and Adolf Sturmthal, *The Tragedy of European Labor, 1919–1939* (New York: Columbia University Press, 1943).

The literature on the Fall of France in 1940 and on the ensuing four years is enormous and mostly partisan in character. (Even the publication of documents continues to stimulate controversy and the compilation of counter documents by scholars who dislike the tone of the most recent collection.) Marc Bloch's *L'étrange défaite* (Paris: Société des Éditions Franc-Tireur, 1946) is an especially perceptive analysis of France's weaknesses at the beginning of the Second World War. The best summary of the Vichy regime is Alfred Cobban's "Vichy," in *Survey of International Affairs, 1939–1946,* ed. Arnold and Veronica Toynbee, Vol. IV: *Hitler's Europe* (London: Oxford University Press, 1954). Other general works on this period include Paul Farmer's *Vichy: Political Dilemma* (New York: Columbia University Press, 1955)—which mistakenly sees the continuation of the prewar conflicts between the Right and the Left in the disputes between Pétain and the Paris fascists; Robert Aron's *Histoire de Vichy* (Paris: A. Fayard, 1954)—which tries to be objective and to patch up old quarrels; and Dorothy M. Pickles' *France between the Republics* (London: Contact, 1946). Louis R. Franck's "The Forces of Collaboration," *Foreign Affairs*, Vol. XXI (October, 1942) is especially severe with the high ranks of the civil service. Henri Michel's *Histoire de la Résistance* (Paris: Presses Universitaires de France, 1950) and A. J. Liebling's *The Republic of Silence* (New York: Harcourt Brace, 1947) are lively accounts of the Resistance movements. Of the many memoirs of the Second World War, Maurice Weygand's *Rappelé au service* (Paris: Flammarion, 1950) and Charles de Gaulle's *Call to Honor, 1940–1942* (New York: Viking, 1955) and *Unity, 1942–1944* (New York: Simon & Schuster, 1959) were the most helpful to me. The reports on the trials of well-known collaborators were also revealing, particularly *Le Procès du Maréchal Pétain: Compte rendu sténographique* (2 vols.; Paris: A. Michel, 1945).

On the Liberation period and the Fourth Republic the following works provided much information. Gordon Wright's *The Reshaping of French Democracy* (New York: Reynal & Hitchcock, 1948) shows the ideological confusion in the framing of the constitution of the Fourth Republic. Two good histories of this ill-fated regime are François Goguel's *France under the Fourth Republic* (Ithaca, N.Y.: Cornell University Press, 1952) and Jacques Fauvet's *La IVe République* (Paris: A. Fayard, 1959)—the quotation of Bidault is from Fauvet. On communism and the Cold War see M. Einaudi, J.-M. Domenach, and A. Garosci, *Communism in Western Europe* (Ithaca, N.Y.: Cornell University Press,

1954); Gabriel Almond, *The Appeals of Communism* (Princeton, N.J.: Princeton University Press, 1954); Raymond Aron, *Le grand schisme* (Paris: Gallimard, 1948); and Laurent Casanova, *Le Parti communiste, les intellectuels, et la nation* (Paris: Éditions Sociales, 1949)—which was written by the party's hatchet man for unsubmissive intellectuals.

On the "Fall" of the Fourth Republic see Alexander Werth, *Lost Statesman: The Strange Story of Pierre Mendès-France* (New York: Abelard-Schuman, 1958); *Les Élections du 2 janvier 1956*, ed. Maurice Duverger, François Goguel, and Jean Touchard (Paris: A. Colin, 1957); Stanley Hoffmann, *Le Mouvement Poujade* (Paris: A. Colin, 1956); Jean Planchais, *La Malaise de l'armée* (Paris: Plon, 1958); Edward L. Katzenbach, Jr., "The French Army," *Yale Review* (Summer, 1956); Merry and Serge Bromberger, *Les 13 complots du 13 mai* (Paris: A. Fayard, 1959); and Jean Touchard, "La Fin de la Quatrième République," *Revue française de science politique*, Vol. VIII, No. 4 (December, 1958)—which is a review article by an eminent political scientist of a dozen books on this subject. I found Eugen Weber's "The Right in France: A Working Hypothesis," *American Historical Review*, Vol. LXV, No. 3 (April, 1960), most provocative, especially his contention that Gaullism and Poujadism did not fit into the traditional category of the Right. The representatives of these movements sat on the right side of the national assembly, but their ideological confusion prevented them from agreeing among themselves. I still feel, however, that their goals and their temperaments are obviously different from those of the Communists and what remains of the traditional Left.

Chapter 7. From Anguish to Atomization

As in chapters 4 and 5, the interpretations here are mostly my own, but, in addition to the surveys of contemporary French literature already cited, the following sources were helpful: Marjorie Grene, *Dreadful Freedom: A Critique of Existentialism* (Chicago: University of Chicago Press, 1948); Jean Wahl, *Petite histoire de "l'existentialisme"* (Paris: Club Maintenant, 1947); Simone de Beauvoir, *Pour une morale de l'ambiguité* (Paris: Gallimard, 1947) and *Les Mandarins* (Paris: Gallimard, 1954); Germaine Brée and Marguérite Guiton, *An Age of Fiction: The French Novel from Gide to Camus* (New Brunswick, N.J.: Rutgers University Press, 1957); Maurice Nadeau, *Littérature présente* (Paris: Corrêa, 1952); Everett W. Knight, *Literature Considered as Philosophy: The French Example* (New York: Macmillan Co., 1958); Germaine Brée, *Camus* (New Brunswick, N.J.: Rutgers University Press, 1958); Claude Mauriac, *La Littérature contemporaine* (Paris: A. Michel, 1958); and *Esprit*, No. 7–8 (July–August, 1958)—entire issue devoted to articles on "Le nouveau roman."

CHAPTER 8. FROM FOLK CULTURE TO MASS CULTURE

I first got the idea that the Revolution of 1789 occurred too early to transform French culture from Denis W. Brogan's "Was the French Revolution a Mistake?" *Cambridge Journal*, Vol. I, No. 1 (October, 1947), though the inferences I draw from it are my own.

My main sources on French folklore were André Varagnac's *Civilisation traditionnelle et genres de vie* (Paris: A. Michel, 1948) and Arnold Van Gennep's *Manuel de folklore français contemporain* (6 vols.; Paris: Picard, 1937–46). Varagnac stresses the transformation of folk cultures through time and disagrees with Van Gennep's contention that customs that have survived into the twentieth century are the same as they always were. My analytical observations about the nature of traditional culture come largely from Varagnac. Other works that proved helpful on specific points were Lucien Febvre's *La Terre et l'évolution humaine* (Paris: A. Michel, 1922), Marc Bloch's *Les Caractères originaux de l'histoire rurale française* (new ed.; 2 vols.; Paris: A. Colin, 1956), Louis Chevalier's *Les Paysans: Étude d'histoire et d'économie rurale* (Paris: Denoël, 1947), Paul Delarue's *Le Conte populaire français* (Paris: Éditions Érasme, 1957), and Duby and Mandrou's *Histoire de la civilisation française* (see notes to chap. 4).

I have observed some of the language patterns mentioned in this chapter. For their history I used the following books: Charles Bruneau, *Petite histoire de la langue française* (2 vols.; Paris: A. Colin, 1955); Albert Dauzat, *Précis d'histoire de la langue et du vocabulaire française* (Paris: Larousse, 1949); and Henri Bauche, *Le Langage populaire* (Paris: Payot, 1946).

On rural and urban cultural patterns in the nineteenth and twentieth centuries I found many ideas in these sources: Georges Friedmann (ed.), *Villes et campagnes* (see notes to chap. 1), Charles Morazé's *Le Bourgeois conquérants* (see notes to chap. 6), and *Population*—the quarterly review of the Institut National d'Études Démographiques—for opinion surveys and specialized studies. But much of what I say is based on my own observations of people and my own examination of the cultural products —buildings, magazines, operettas, *images d'Épinal*, etc.—mentioned in the text.

The following analytical and historical works were helpful guides to my own study of the examples of twentieth-century mass culture discussed in this chapter (for other works on mass culture see chap. 9): Susanne K. Langer, *Feeling and Form* (New York: Scribner, 1953); Nathan Leites and Martha Wolfenstein, *Movies: A Psychological Study* (Glencoe, Ill.: Free Press, 1950); and Georges Sadoul, *Histoire de l'art du cinéma* (Paris: Flammarion, 1953).

CHAPTER 9. MASS CULTURE AND THE NEW LEVELS OF CONFORMITY

This chapter is based almost entirely on my own observations of the examples of mass culture mentioned in the text and of the behavior of the French people. The following works helped me to formulate some of the sociological implications of mass culture: Jean Fourastié and others, *Migrations professionelles: Données statistiques sur leur évolution en divers pays de 1900 à 1955* (Paris: Éditions de l'Institut National d'Études Démographiques, 1957); Georges Friedmann, *Le Travail en miettes: Spécialisation et loisirs* (Paris: Gallimard, 1956); Père H. Chombart de Lauwe, *La Vie quotidienne des familles ouvrières* (Paris: Éditions du Centre National de Recherche Scientifique, 1956); Paul Delarue, *Le Conte populaire français* (see notes to chap. 8); Jacques Durand, *Le Cinéma et son public* (Paris: Sirey, 1958); E. Morin, *Le Cinéma ou l'homme imaginaire* (Paris: Éditions de Minuit, 1958); Johan Huizinga, *Homo Ludens: A Study of the Play Element in Culture* (Boston: Beacon Press, 1955); and Roland Barthès, *Mythologies* (Paris: Éditions du Seuil, 1957). Although Barthès tries to view mass culture from a Marxist point of view, many of his insights are very valuable.

The entire issue of *Esprit*, Vol. XXVII, No. 6 (July, 1959) was devoted to "Le Loisir." The following articles from this issue were especially suggestive: Joffre Dumazedier, "Réalités du loisir et idéologies"; Alain Touraine, "Travail, loisirs et société" (Dumazedier's and Touraine's articles cover the whole range of mass culture and its social consequences); Georges Rottier, "Loisirs et vacances dans les budgets familiaux"; Michel Crozier, "Employés et petits fonctionnaires parisiens"; Janine Larrue and Bruno Chevrant-Bruno, "Loisirs ouvriers"; and Henri Raymond, "Hommes et dieux à Palinuro" (a sociological study of the behavior of French vacationists at a popular resort).

The following are analyses and surveys that gave me information on specific points: *Institut National de la Statistique des Études Économiques: Bulletin mensuel de statistique*, Supplement, March and July, 1954 —which published the results of a survey of radio-listening habits; "La presse, le public, et l'opinion," a special issue of *Sondages*, No. 3 (1955) on newspaper reading habits and readers' attitudes; and *Cahiers d'études de radio-télévision* (quarterly since 1955)—which publishes articles by social scientists on the social and psychological functions of radio and television broadcasting.

The following works all refer to American mass culture, but some of their analytical concepts can be used (with caution) for France: David Riesman, *Individualism Reconsidered* (Glencoe, Ill.: Free Press, 1955); Bernard Rosenberg and David Manning White (eds.), *Mass Culture: The Popular Arts in America* (Glencoe, Ill.: Free Press, 1957); Reuel

Denney, *The Astonished Muse* (Chicago: University of Chicago Press, 1957); the spring, 1960, issue of *Daedalus* (Journal of the American Academy of Arts and Sciences)—which is devoted to "Mass Culture and Mass Media"; and *The Sunday Comics*, a privately printed (1956) sociopsychological study of what the comics meant to a selected sample of readers—made by the survey division of Science Research Associates in Chicago.

CHAPTER 10. A NATION IN SEARCH OF A MISSION

Of the numerous attempts to examine Frenchmen's conception of their national mission those in the following books were particularly suggestive to me: Karl Epting, *Das französische Sendungsbewusstsein im 19. und 20. Jahrhundert* (Heidelberg: Kurt Vorwinckel Verlag, 1952); Friedrich Sieburg, *Gott in Frankreich?* (Frankfurt-am-Main: Societäts-Verlag, 1929); Ernst Curtius, *The Civilization of France* (see notes to chap. 2); and Guillaume de Bertier de Sauvigny's *Some Historical Clues to French Politics* (Yellow Springs, Ohio: Antioch Press, 1958).

On the racial argument see Jacques Barzun's *The French Race* (New York: Columbia University Press, 1932) for the eighteenth century, the writings of the Count de Gobineau (who stresses the Germanic inheritance) for the nineteenth century, and Fustel de Coulanges (who stresses the Roman inheritance) for the early twentieth century. On the popular verbal level the argument has continued down to the present, with the Gauls as the favorite ancestors of most Frenchmen. In his *France* (Ann Arbor, Mich.: University of Michigan Press, 1959) Albert Guérard debunks much of the Gallic inheritance.

In his *Géographie économique et humaine de la France* (2 vols.; Paris: A. Colin, 1946–48—these two volumes are called, collectively, Volume VI of the series "Géographie universelle," edited by P. Vidal de la Blache and L. Gallois) Albert Demangeon explains how France has had a world influence disproportionate to her size because of the painstaking adaptation of her civilization to geographical conditions—with special emphasis on avoidance of overcrowding, on high standards of craftsmanship, and on the early formation of a class of free peasants. Jean Gottmann's *La Politiques des états et leur géographie* (Paris: A. Colin, 1952) shows how a nation's geography can influence its government's policies. Charles Morazé's *Les Français et la République* (Paris: A. Colin, 1956) reasserts the view that France is the crossroads of the Continental, Mediterranean, and Atlantic worlds. The following textbooks in geography and history give millions of French schoolchildren some of their notions about their country's mission: Ernest Granger, *La France* (Paris: Fayard, 1947), and Étienne Baron, *Histoire de la France* (Paris: Librairie l'École, 1948)—in the upper grades; Albert Troux,

242

Suzanne Vidal de la Blache, and Robert Mangeot, *Histoire de la France* (Paris: Hachette, 1950)—in the lower grades.

On the influence of the French Revolution in other countries see: Jacques Godechot, *La Grande Nation: L'expansion de la France dans le monde de 1789 à 1799* (2 vols.; Paris: Aubier, 1956); Leo Gershoy, *The Era of the French Revolution, 1789–1799: Ten Years That Shook the World* (Princeton, N.J.: Van Nostrand, 1957); and Robert R. Palmer, *The Age of Democratic Revolution* (see notes to chap. 3).

The following works are merely a sample of those in which French intellectuals stated their conceptions of France's mission between 1815 and 1940 (for a full bibliography on this subject see the work by Karl Epting cited above): Joseph de Maistre, *Soirées de Saint-Pétersbourg, ou entretiens sur le gouvernement temporel,* in *Oeuvres Complètes* (14 vols.; Lyon: Vitte et Perrussel, 1884–86), Vol. IV; François Pierre Guillaume Guizot, *Histoire de la civilisation en France depuis la chute de l'Empire Romain* (Paris: Didier, 1846); Napoléon-Louis Bonaparte, *Napoleonic Ideas* (New York: Appleton & Co., 1859—the original French edition: *Des idées Napoléoniennes,* was published in Brussels in 1839); Alexis de Tocqueville, *Nouvelles Correspondences entièrement inédites* (Paris: Lévy, 1866); Ernest Renan, *La Réforme intellectuelle et morale* (Paris: Michel-Lévy, frères, 1871); Hippolyte Taine, *Notes on England* (London: Isbitser & Co., 1874)—in which the author compares France and England; Maurice Barrès, *Scènes et doctrines du nationalisme* (Paris: F. Juven, 1902); Jean Jaurès, *Pages choisies* (Paris: Rieder, 1922; Jacques Bainville, *Histoire de France* (Paris: A. Fayard, 1924); Charles Seignobos, *Histoire sincère de la nation française* (Paris: Rieder, 1933); Georges Duhamel, *Scènes de la vie future* (Paris: Mercure de France, 1930); Henri Massis, *Défense de l'occident* (Paris: Plon, 1927); Pierre Drieu La Rochelle, *Genève ou Moscou* (Paris: Gallimard, 1928) and *Gilles* (Paris: Gallimard, 1939); Jean Giraudoux, *Pleins pouvoirs* (Paris: Gallimard, 1939). Raymond Aron gives a good recent view of France's mission in a book he wrote with August Heckscher, *Diversity of Worlds* (New York: Reynal & Co., 1957).

The following books on France's recent foreign and colonial policies were helpful: Ernest B. Haas, *The Uniting of Europe* (Stanford, Calif.: Stanford University Press, 1958); Edgar S. Furniss, Jr., *France, Troubled Ally* (New York: Harper, 1960); Herbert Ingram Priestley, *France Overseas: A Study of Modern Imperialism* (New York: D. Appleton-Century Co., 1938); Georges Hardy, *Histoire sociale de la colonisation française* (Paris: Larose, 1953); P.-F. Gonidec, *L'Évolution des territoires d'outre-mer depuis 1946* (Paris: Pichon, 1958); Ellen Hammer, *The Struggle for Indo-China* (Stanford, Calif.: Stanford University Press, 1954); Charles-André Julien, *L'Afrique du Nord en marche* (Paris: Juillard, 1952);

Germaine Tillon, *Algérie en 1957* (Paris: Éditions de Minuit, 1957); Jacques Soustelle, *Aimée et souffrante Algérie* (Paris: Plon, 1956); Richard and Joan Brace, *Ordeal in Algeria* (Princeton, N.J.: Van Nostrand, 1960); Pierre Moussa, *Les Chances économiques de la communauté franco-africaine* (Paris: A. Colin, 1957); Jean-Marc Léger, *Afrique française, Afrique nouvelle* (Ottawa: Le Cercle du Livre Français, 1958); Pierre and Renée Gosset, *L'Afrique, les africains* (Paris: Juillard, 1958)— these were the two travelers who were asked about Little Rock by a Senegalese student.

The survey on French youth was made by the French Institute for Motivation Study among French men and women between the ages of eighteen and twenty-five and published in an issue of *Réalités*, No. 111 (February, 1960), entitled "What Are They Thinking?" Although this plush magazine represents a conservative, upper-middle-class point of view, the survey itself seems to have been conducted objectively.

Index

Becquerel, Henri, 74
Bell, Marie, in *Un Carnet de bal*, 175
Benda, Julien, *La Trahison des clercs*, 106–7
Bergson, Henri, 69, 74, 106
Berlioz, Hector, 162
Bernanos, Georges, 103; *Le Journal d'un curé de campagne*, 105; opposes technology, 79
Bernard, Claude, *Introduction à l'étude de la médicine expérimentale*, 70, 71
Bidault, Georges, becomes a Rightist, 128
Birth control, 65–66
Birth rate. *See* Population growth
Bloch, Marc, 75
Blondel, Maurice, 79
Blum, Léon, 114, 115, 120–21, 123, 213
Bonapartism, 111–12, 131
Bonheur, Rosa, 165
Books, paperbound, wide dissemination before World War II, 169
Boulanger, General Georges, threat to Third Republic, 111–12
Boulez, Pierre, 153–54, 155
Bourgeois "dynasties," conservative influence of, 59, 61, 64
Braque, Georges, 84, 151
Bresson, Robert, 196
Breton, André, and Surrealists, 83, 104
Briand, Aristide, 112; suppresses 1910 strike, 118
Broglie, Louis-Victor de, prince, 71, 74
Brunschvicg, Léon, 71
Budget. *See* Fiscal policy
Buffet, Bernard, 151–52
Bureaucracy: functioning of under Vichy, 6; increased power since early 1950's, 10; and parliament, 7; and pressure groups, 9
Business trusts as pressure groups, 9. *See also* Monopolistic organizations
Butor, Michel, 148; *La Modification*, 149–50
Buying habits: example of women's clothing, 16; objection to standardization, 15, 16–17

Camelots du Roi and February 6 (1934) riots, 113–14
Camus, Albert: *L'Étranger* (*The Stranger*), *La Peste* (*The Plague*), 137–39; *La Chute* (*The Fall*), *L'Homme révolté*

(*The Rebel*), *Le Mythe de Sisyphe*, 143–45
Capital investments: effect of, on agriculture questionable, 50; improved productivity of industry, 50, 54; private, 13, 51–55; public, 13
Carné, Marcel, directs *Le Jour se lève* (*Daybreak*), 174
Carnival, traditional character of, 158–59
Carpentier, Georges, 168
Cartels. *See* Monopolistic organizations
Catholic church: and mass culture, 163–64, 195, 199–200; and Revolution (1789), 36
Catholicism: history and description of practice of, 37–45; and politics, 40–41; and population growth, 41; recent revival of, 37; and social classes, 40–41
Catholics: geographical distribution of, 37–38, 41; lay associations as pressure groups, 9
Céline, Louis-Ferdinand, 106
Chansonniers, 178
Chaplin, Charlie, 193; popularity in France, 171–72
Charles X, 110
Charon, Jean, 75
Chautemps, Camille, attacked by Rightists, 116
Chevalier, Maurice, 179
Child-training, 24–30; French and American compared, 23, 27–28
Christian Democrats, 126, 131
Civic spirit: family influence on, 62; history of decline in, 5; revival of, 19
Civil servants: and modernization, 9; as pressure group, 9
Clair, René, 172, 174
Claude, Georges, 180
Clemenceau, Georges, 112, 118
Clouzot, H. G., 190, 196
Cocteau, Jean, 98, 166
Colette, Sidonie Gabrielle, 98
Colonial lobbies as pressure groups, 9
Colonial policy, 218–25
Comic strips, 172, 190–91
Communist party: in Liberation period, 125–27 *passim;* and literature, 101–5 *passim;* and mass culture, 182; and Popular Front, 114, 115, 116, 119–20; and workers, 2, 4, 40, 44
Compagnons de la Tour de France, 160

Index

Lévy-Bruhl, Lucien, 75
Liberation period, 64; ideologies of, 124–26
Literature: and Catholics, 104–6; and Marxism, 89, 101–5 *passim;* nineteenth century, 72, 73; 1920's and 1930's, chap. 5; 1940's and 1950's, 135–51
Living standards, 20–21; and new marketing techniques, 15; reasons for rise in 1950's, 11; urban and rural compared, 18. *See also* chap. 9 *passim*
Lloyd George, David, 118
Lorjou, Bernard, 151–52
Louis XIV, influence of French culture beginning with, 207
Louis XVI, 110; pressure groups under, 5
Louis Philippe, 110, 210
Lumière, Louis, 180
Lyautey, Marshal Louis-Hubert-Gonsalve, colonial policy of, 219
Lycée, 30, 32–33; curriculum, 32; methods of instruction, 32. *See also* Secondary schools

Magazines, 186–87 *passim,* 192; ownership and control of, 200–201; wide dissemination of before World War II, 169
Maistre, Joseph de, on France's mission, 210
Mallarmé, Stephan, 72
Malraux, André: on Algerian War, 222; *La Condition humaine (Man's Fate), L'Espoir (Man's Hope),* 101–4; on France's mission, 209
Malthus, Thomas Robert, 46, 56
Malthusianism: and birth control, 65–66; of businessmen, 46–55 *passim,* 57; of self-employed Frenchmen, 56–58; and struggle for status, 58–66; of workers, 55–57
Manessier, Alfred, 151
Marcel, Gabriel, 79–80, 140
Mardi Gras. *See* Carnival
Maritain, Jacques, 79
Marketing techniques: backwardness of, 52; recent innovations, 14–15, 57
Marriage contracts, 23, 60
Marshall Plan, 131
Martin du Gard, Roger, 45, 97
Marx, Karl, 56; and French intellectuals, 134, 144

Mass culture, nineteenth-century, 161–64
Massenet, Jules, 165
Masson, André, 83
Massu, General Jacques, 133
Matignon agreements, 121
Matisse, Henri, 81–82, 85, 87, 151, 166
Mauriac, François, 43, 45, 130; on Algerian War, 222
Maurois, André, 135
Maurras, Charles, 211; supports Vichy regime, 123
Meissonier, Ernest, 162
Mendès-France, Pierre, premier 1954–55, 132; and European Defense Community, 216–17; and *Front Républicain* (1956), 129–30; tries to discourage drinking, 167
Messiaen, Olivier, 154
Michaux, Henri, 147
Middle Ages, French leadership in, 206–7
Milhaud, Darius, 84, 85–86
Minaux, André, 151–52, 154, 155
Mission civilisatrice and French Empire, 218–20
Mondrian, Piet, 82, 166
Monnet Plan, 9; uniqueness of, 13
Monopolistic organizations: desire to preserve small and middle-sized business units, 48; France compared with other industrial countries, 47–48; keep prices high, 51; reluctance to expand production, 47, 48, 53
Montaigne, Jean de, 68
Montand, Yves, 189–90
Montherlant, Henri de, 103, 106
Morocco, 219, 221
Moslems: numbers in France, 37; in Algeria, 222–23
Mounier, Emmanuel, 80
Mouvement Républicain Populaire (MRP). *See* Christian Democrats
Movies: *The 400 Blows,* 202–3; *The Lovers,* 185; "New Wave," 190, 196; 1920's and 1930's, 171–78; 1940's, 195–96; 1950's, 185, 188, 189, 196–97
Music: electronic, 153; 1920's and 1930's, 84–88; 1940's and 1950's, 152–54; popular, used by serious composers, 85
Musique concrète, 152–54

249

Napoleon I, Bonaparte, 218; killed civic spirit, 5; reforms, 157
Napoleon III, 131, 210
National character, 24–27, 204; theories of, 230–31
NATO, 215
Neoprimitivism: in art, 80; in music, 85
"New novel" (nouveau roman), 148–51
Newspapers, 188, 192; ownership and control, 200–201; wide dissemination of before World War II, 169
"New Wave" movies, 190, 196, 202–3
Nohain, Jean, 196

Occupational distribution, France compared to other countries, 19
Offenbach, Jacques, 162

Pagnol, Marcel, Marius-Cesar-Fanny series, Topaze, 176–77
Paris: architecture, 4; art and fashion center, 206, 211; inhabitants, 4; practicing Catholics in, 38
Paris-Match, 200–201, 202
Parliament, importance of standing committees in, 8
Parochial schools and the state, 36
Pascal, Blaise, 79
Patachou, 190
Perrault, Charles: Cinderella, 194; Mother Goose stories, 160, 188
Perrin, Jean, 75
Pétain, Henri Philippe, and Vichy regime, 6, 123, 125, 215
Philosophy, religious, 79–80
Philosophy of science. See Science, philosophy of
Piaf, Edith, 178
Picasso, Pablo Ruiz, 73, 81, 82, 151, 165
Pinay, Antoine, 50
Planck, Max, 74
Poincaré, Henri, 71, 75
Poincaré, Raymond, 112
Political system, Third and Fourth Republics, 4–10
Politicians, behavior of, 6, 111, 112, 116, 128–30, 133, 227–28
Popular Front, 114–17, 119–22; raised workers' hopes, 17; spirit of in films, 173
Popular songs, 178–80, 189, 197
Population growth: and abortion rate, 22, 66, 235; and Catholicism, 41; fac-

tors in, 21–22; halted by mid-nineteenth century, 65
Population movement: effects on artisans, 18; effects on farmers, 18. See also Urbanization
Positivism: Bergson attacks, 69; influence in late nineteenth century, 69–70
Poujade, Pierre, 131–33
Poujadism, 114, 130–31, 239
Poulenc, Francis, 84, 85, 86
Presse du Coeur, 188–89, 195
Pressure groups: description and history, 8–9; French and American contrasted, 5; and Mendès-France, 129
Primary schools, 35–39, 44–45; curriculum of, 29; discipline in, 29; methods of instruction in, 29; postgraduate courses in, 31
Professional schools: enrolment, 33. See also Grandes écoles
Protestants, numbers of in France, 37
Proust, Marcel, À la recherche du temps perdu, 93–95
Psychoanalysis, changing attitudes toward, 78
Public opinion research, 229
Puppet shows, 188

Rabelais, François, 35
Racine, Jean, 33
Radical Socialist Party, 113–14, 118, 131; antifeminism of, 62; and Popular Front, 115–16, 122
Radio, 188, 196; caters to variety of tastes, 195; conservatism of, 200–202; influence of before World War II, 170–71; ownership and control, 200–201; state and commercial compared, 194
Rainier, Prince, 188; popularity of, 186–87
Rassemblement du Peuple Français (RPF). See Gaullism
Ravel, Maurice, 86–88
Renan, Ernest, 211
Renoir, Jean, 173
Resistance movements, 64, 123–26
Revolt of the Masses: contradicts traditional class solidarity, 20; and rising levels of aspiration, 16, 17. See also chap. 9 passim
Revolution (1789), 36; and bourgeoisie, 60; and Catholic church, 36; gener-

ated civic spirit, 5; influence of in other countries, 208–9; and laicism, 36; and mass culture, 156–57; and religious practice, 38; and "Revolt of the Masses," 16
Ricardo, David, 56
Rimbaud, Arthur, 72
Robbe-Grillet, Alain, *La Jalousie*, 148–49
Romain, Jules, 45
Rosay, Françoise, 193
Rossi, Tino, 179
Rostand, Jean, 45
Rouault, Georges, 83
Roussel, Albert, 88

Sablon, Jean, 179
Sagan, Françoise, 147, 187
Saint-Exupéry, Antoine de: on Munich agreement, 214; *Terre des hommes* (*Wind, Sand, and Stars*), *Vol de nuit* (*Night Flight*), 99–101, 103
Saint-Saëns, Camille, 162
Saint-Simon, Claude-Henri, Comte de, and technocracy, 10
Sarraute, Nathalie, 148, 155; *Tropismes, Martereau*, 150–51
Sartre, Jean-Paul: *Les Chemins de la liberté* (*The Roads to Freedom*), 139; *Huis clos* (*No Exit*), *Les Mains Sales, Le Diable et le Bon Dieu, Les Séquestrés d'Altona*, 141–43
Satie, Erik, 84, 85
Schaeffer, Pierre, and *musique concrète*, 152–53
Schönberg, Arnold, 85, 154
Science: French contributions in, 74–76; government support of, 225; philosophy of, 69–71, 74–77; reasons for decline of in France, 76–79
Scientific management: and economic growth, 13; and incentives to workers, 13–14
"Scientism," opposition to, 77–80
Secondary schools: enrolment, 33; examinations, 30; parochial, 30. See also *Lycée*
Ségur, Comtesse de, 190; expressed reactionary Catholic views, 42–44
Sieyès, Abbé, 60
Simenon, Georges, 190
Simon, Claude, 148
Singier, Gustave, 151

"*Les Six*," 84–86 *passim*
Small business: decreasing importance of, 14; and taxation, 48; weaknesses of, 49–50
Social barriers, 3, 21, 30–35 *passim;* changing interpretations of, 233–34; early twentieth century, 58; hinder industrial growth, 55–56; since 1945, 64. See also chap. 9 *passim*
Social security system: comparison with rest of Western Europe, 2; and economic growth, 49; family allowances supplement wages, 20; and public debt, 51
Social structure, nineteenth-century, 157–58
Socialist Party, 118; and Popular Front, 115–16, 122
Soulages, Pierre, 151, 154
Soustelle, Jacques, staffs radio and television stations with Gaullists in 1958, 201
Sports: attitudes toward, before World War II, 167–68, 170; current participation in, 198; spectator, 192, 202, 203
State, French attitudes toward, 6–7
Stavisky affair, 112–13
Stendhal (Henri Beyle), *Le Rouge et le Noir*, 65
Stravinsky, Igor, 73, 84, 85–86, 165
Sue, Eugène, 162
Suez crisis (1956), 130, 217
Surrealists, 83
Syndicalism. *See* Trade-union movement

Tal Coat, Pierre, 151
Tanguy, Yves, 83
Tati, Jacques, *Mon Oncle*, 196–97
Taxation: and economic growth, 48; France compared with Germany and Great Britain, 54; and small business, 48, 49
Teachers: current shortage of, 35; French and American salaries compared, 35; laic bias of, 31–32; training, 31–32
Technical schools: enrolment in, 33; new, 34–35
Technocracy, political limitations of, 10
Technology: and agriculture, 18; destroys traditional culture, 164

Television: caters to different tastes, 195; conservatism of, 200–202; influence on popular attitudes, 198–99; interviews and quiz shows, 192–94; news broadcasts, 188, 201–2; ownership and control, 200–201; state and commercial compared, 194; variety shows, 196

Theaters: amateur, 198; government subsidized, 170

Third Republic, political crises, 111–23 *passim*

Tour de France bicycle race, popularity of, 192, 203

Trade associations, as pressure groups, 9

Trade-union movement: history and description of, 117–19, and Popular Front, 119–22

Trade unions: as pressure groups, 9, reasons for weakness, 2

Traditional culture, functions of, 158–61

Trenet, Charles, 179

Tunisia, 219, 221

Universities, enrolment in, 33, 35

Urbanization: compared with Great Britain and Germany, 12; and mass culture, chap. 9 *passim;* and religious practice, 38; and segregation of classes, 161

Utrillo, Maurice, 84

Valéry, Paul: *La Crise de l'esprit, Le Cimetière marin*, 90–93; opposes technology, 79

Varèse, Edgar, 153–54

Verne, Jules, 162; *Michael Strogoff*, 44

Veterans' leagues: and Algerian War, 133; and February 6 (1934) riots, 113; as pressure groups, 9

Vichy: bureaucracy, 6; policies, 123

Villon, Jacques, 151

Voltaire (François-Marie Arouet): and enlightened despotism, 207; and laicism, 35; *Candide*, 26

Voluntary organizations: agricultural training groups, 18–19; for building apartments, 19; current growth of, 198; paucity of until late 1940's, 5

Wages and salaries, 198; current examples, 20; leveling trend since 1900, 19–20

Wilm, Pierre-Richard, 175–76

Women: changing roles and status, 22–23; current attitudes toward marriage, 184–87 *passim;* influence of *Elle* on, 184–87; modern mindedness, 23; religious practice of, 38, 39; right to vote in 1945, 64. See also *Presse du coeur*

World War I: effect of casualties on social structure, 61; effect on humanist values, 90; effect on traditional culture, 164; France's role in, 211–13; and technology, 12, 212

World War II, economic regression caused by, 12

Wrestling, popularity of, 192

Zay, Jean, quoted, 86–87

Date Due